D1196298

KING JOHN
New Perspectives

KING JOHN
New Perspectives

EDITED BY

Deborah T. Curren-Aquino

DELAWARE
Newark: University of Delaware Press
London and Toronto: Associated University Presses

Associated University Presses
440 Forsgate Drive
Cranbury, NJ 08512

Associated University Presses
25 Sicilian Avenue
London WC1A 2QH, England

Associated University Presses
P.O. Box 488, Port Credit
Mississauga, Ontario
Canada L5G 4M2

Library of Congress Cataloging-in-Publication Data

King John : new perspectives.

Bibliography: p.
Includes index.
1. Shakespeare, William, 1564–1616.   King John.
2. John, King of England, 1167–1216, in fiction, drama, poetry, etc.   I. Curren-Aquino, Deborah T., 1949–   .
PR2818.K56   1988   822.3'3   87-40529
ISBN 0-87413-337-8 (alk. paper)

The paper used in this publication meets the requirements of the American National Standard for Permanence of Paper for Printed Library Materials Z39.48-1984.

Printed in the United States of America

To the
Shakespeare Association of America

Mad world, mad kings, mad composition!

War, war, no peace! Peace is to me a war.

The Lady Constance speaks not from her faith,
But from her need.

I am amaz'd, methinks, and lose my way
Among the thorns and dangers of this world.

What surety of the world, what hope, what stay,
When this was now a king, and now is clay?

Shakespeare, *King John*

Contents

Preface

THE TWELVE ESSAYS IN THIS VOLUME ARE THE RESULT OF TWO SEMINARS on *King John* which I chaired at the annual conference of the Shakespeare Association of America in Montreal on 28 and 29 March 1986. Eight of the essays are revised versions of papers originally presented in Montreal; the remaining four are new contributions by several of those who served in the capacity of respondent.

I wish to thank the entire group of seminar participants (twenty-three in all) for their generous giving of intellect, energy, and tactful cooperation, all of which made for two days of intense and spirited discussion. I would also like to thank *Theatre Journal* for permission to reprint sections of Phyllis Rackin's essay which appeared in volume 37 of that publication. The dedication of the present anthology provides a way of thanking the Shakespeare Association of America for approving the original seminar proposal on *King John,* without which this volume would never have been realized. I would be remiss if I did not specifically acknowledge Ann Jennalie Cook, the former executive secretary of the association, whose advice and never-flagging patience and gracious manner were an answer to a prayer in the course of planning and running the seminars. Special thanks must be given to Eileen Soria for the meticulous attention she gave to the typing of the manuscript. All writers and editors should be so fortunate as to have one of her caliber by their side. I am equally indebted to Beth Gianfagna and Ann Harvey of Associated University Presses for their editorial expertise in seeing the manuscript through publication. The support and encouragement of Barbara Mowat, Chairman of the Folger Institute, and my mentors, E. Catherine Dunn and Rev. William J. Rooney, will always be appreciated. I am also grateful to the Richard N. Foley Faculty Research Fund at The Catholic University of America, which was of enormous help during the seminar stage of this project. I would like to remember my father, Robert, who was with me when this volume was first envisioned, and my mother, Adelaide, who has been with me to see it to completion. The greatest but least adequate "thank you" goes to my husband John for his sharp eye, good ear, relentless questions, thoughtful observations, and good humor in making *King John* part of our daily marital concord. His many ways of assistance could never be trivialized by a number.

Introduction

King John Resurgent

DEBORAH T. CURREN-AQUINO

> Yet Fame, nor Favour ever deign'd to say
> *King John* was station'd as a first-rate play.

IN THE FIRST FOLIO, HEMINGE AND CONDELL PLACED *THE LIFE AND Death of King John* first among the history plays, presumably because of the chronological ordering of the kingly reigns being dramatized. It has not been first since, either in the study or on the stage. The lines from Cibber's prologue to his adaptation *Papal Tyranny* (first performed in 1744) that are quoted above have over the centuries proved to be the general opinion. In fact, as one of Shakespeare's most neglected works, *King John* could well be labeled "the forgotten history play." Called a "curst" piece by an anonymous writer to Cibber,[1] it was for Edward Dowden a drama with little to strengthen or gladden the heart.[2] Described as "comparatively tentative" and "strangely faltering,"[3] *King John* has been criticized for lack of unity and telic design,[4] episodic and faulty plot structure,[5] absence of both a clearly defined protagonist and a governing central theme,[6] inconsistency of style,[7] rejection of "cosmic lore,"[8] flat characterization and "ethical muddles,"[9] and egregious failure to allude to Magna Charta.[10] Often its "defects" have been justified by focusing on *The Troublesome Raigne*, the anonymous play generally regarded as Shakespeare's major source. *King John,* so the argument goes, is not top-drawer Shakespeare because he was only doctoring someone else's play at the request of his acting company. M. M. Reese and Robert Ornstein attribute its failings—what E. K. Chambers calls "hack work"— to Shakespeare's boredom with the assignment.[11] When not dismissed or given short shrift,[12] the play is either reluctantly tolerated as an experimental "bridge" connecting the two tetralogies or damningly

11

praised with the excessive qualification of one who "doth protest too much."[13]

As late as 1960, James Calderwood, in his influential thematic study of the play's preoccupation with honor and commodity, observed that the attention paid to *King John* was limited, for the most part, to questions of source, with little attempt to study the play for its own artistic merit.[14] Seventeen years later, Emrys Jones echoed Calderwood's concern when he wrote:

> *King John* is still misunderstood and absurdly underrated. Criticism has failed to clarify its real character, its tone, its vision. Indeed, of all Shakespeare's early plays this is the one that has receded furthest from us, so that a special effort is needed to recover it. We need to see it afresh, facing its oddities in the hope that, rightly understood in the context of the plays as a whole, they will assume an expressive value.[15]

Year after year the Modern Language Association and *Shakespeare Quarterly* annual bibliographies have shown little if any research being done on the play, and professional productions have been far and few between in our century.[16] To adapt Pope's comment in the *Dunciad* on Cibber's *Papal Tyranny*, it seemed as though *King John* "in silence" would "modestly expire."

Time, however, may have finally caught up with Shakespeare's *King John*. The present volume is intended as a contribution to the recovery effort called for by Jones in a context that bodes well for a resurgent *John*. The last few years have witnessed a number of penetrating critical essays dealing with questions of genre, structure, dramatic technique, language, historical process, and performance history (see the Select Bibliography). The annual *Shakespeare Quarterly Bibliography* for 1984 represented a banner year for *King John* scholarship, listing ten entries under criticism alone—admittedly not much if one's standard is *Hamlet* or *King Lear*, but definitely a far cry from the years not so long ago when the average number of critical essays ranged between one and three. Recently Frances Shirley edited a collection of influential criticism on the play, and A. R. Braunmuller has completed his Oxford *King John*; waiting in the wings are the editions of L. A. Beaurline (Cambridge) and Joseph Candido and Charles Forker (MLA Variorum), along with the forthcoming Garland annotated bibliography—all of which should provide the necessary scholarly, critical, and textual apparatus needed for a vital recovery. The 1985 Ashland production marked the fourth time the Oregon Shakespearean Festival (founded in 1935) staged the play; there was also a production in the same year in Berlin at the Theater im Palast; and the BBC version that aired in the United States in 1985 (a production that for better or worse will be with us forever given its availability on videotape) brought *King John* to the general populace. Finally, when the seminar that gave rise to this volume was first proposed to the Shakespeare Association of America, it proved so popular that two sessions were needed.

If for no other reason than the way in which its characters, situations, and speeches provide a virtual mother lode for Shakespeare's major tragedies,[17] *King John* merits critical attention. A far more compelling reason, however, lies in its profoundly prophetic affinity with the temper and theater of our time. Adrien Bonjour's 1951 essay on the structure of the play may well have been the catalyst in getting *King John* scholarship on the right track—the literary study of the play itself—but the essay that has proved seminal in temperament for this anthology, contextualizing it in ways both tacit and overt, is "*King John:* The Ordering of This Present Time," in which Sigurd Burckhardt makes the stirring claim that "when he wrote *King John,* or quite possibly in writing it, Shakespeare was or became a 'modern.' "[18] (The frequency with which this essay is cited by the contributors to the volume is noteworthy in itself.)

With its "savage irony" and "continual trampling of objective meaning in a stampede of paradox and oxymoron,"[19] *King John* is a most fitting play for a century that has suffered through two world wars; witnessed a holocaust that raised disturbing questions about the human creation supposedly only a "little lower than the angels"; seen the heroic, the absolute, and the certain give way to the pragmatic, the relative, and the contingent; and come to the grim realization after Korea, Vietnam, Watergate, and the Iran-Contra affair that national leaders are not superhuman but plagued with human frailty and all too capable of error, whether moral, political, or military. The vacillation of the English lords and political figures like John and Philip of France is no enigma to modern man; neither is the lack of "cosmic lore" which points to a world that pays homage to the immanent rather than the transcendent; nor is the Bastard's "Commodity" speech, articulating an age marked by "indifferency, / From all direction, purpose, course, intent" (2.1.579–80). Remarkably familiar are the isolation and alienation experienced by Faulconbridge who, through his bastardy, is alone and cut off from legitimate family bonds; the casuistry and Orwellian "double-speak" of Pandulph in his encounters with King Philip and the Dolphin; and the Bastard's public relations campaign in the final scene. Faulconbridge's abrupt shifting of gears from a moral response upon the discovery of Arthur's body to the pragmatic "I'll to the King" (4.3.157) is chilling but not shocking to a world grown accustomed to the separation of ethics and politics. A play that "probes rather than pronounces,"[20] with characters who feel lost, confused, "whirl[ed] asunder and dismember[ed]" (3.1.330), speaks cogently to a time in which the traditional commonplace of nurturing mother earth has given way to the cold, mechanical image of spaceship earth, an image that captures with frightening precision the flux and aimless drifting of modern man. The auditioning of the kings before the citizens of Angiers to determine the legitimate King of England, the absurd strategy (agreed upon by warring factions) to sack the city before deciding who will be its king, the human ineffectuality of Hubert who can neither kill nor, judging from the lords' verdict, not kill Arthur, and the death of John who shrivels up and dies with a whimper and not a bang—all make the play very much at home in a century that has known existentialism and the absurd, and moved from the order of new criticism to the indeterminacy of deconstruction.

The two most striking registers of the play's "modernness" are found in the iteration of incredulity and the dizzying, chaotic speed with which events occur and reversals take place. Where the interrogative governs *Hamlet*, the imperative *King Lear*, and the hyperbolic *Antony and Cleopatra*,[21] a sense of disbelief and amazement reverberates throughout the world of *King John*.[22] John's reaction to the "madcap" Faulconbridge and Lady Faulconbridge's dismay at her son's behavior in the first scene present amazement in relatively lighthearted fashion. But as the action moves along, the incredulity becomes decidedly darker: e.g., Constance's "It is not so. . . . It cannot be. . . . I do not believe" (3.1.4, 6, 9) when she hears of the wedding of Lewis and Blanch, King Philip's "I am perplex'd, and know not what to say" (3.1.221) when Pandulph spins his web of rhetorical equivocation, Hubert's troubled "My lord?" (3.3.66) when John gives his cryptic order for Arthur's death, John's "Bear with me, cousin, for I was amaz'd" (4.2.137) and his questioning of the prophetic five moons (4.2.185), the Bastard's litany of "ifs" (4.3.59, 96, 118, 124, 125, 127) when he discovers Arthur's body, his exclamation "O inglorious league!" (5.1.65) when he learns of John's submission to Rome, and Salisbury's response "May this be possible? May this be true?" (5.4.21) upon hearing of Lewis's intended treachery. The most poignant cry of disbelief needs no gloss for modern audiences who live with daily incredulity in the face of international terrorism and the threat of nuclear annihilation; it is, of course, the Bastard's "I am amaz'd, methinks, and lose my way / Among the thorns and dangers of this world" (4.3.140–41).

The second index to the play's modern temper, one often bordering on the nightmarish, is the amazing speed with which Shakespeare's "muse travels lightning-winged, being here, there, and everywhere in the space of a few minutes."[23] As the anonymous writer to Cibber noted in 1745:

> One feels before one knows one is to feel! The effect almost precedes the act, at least keeps pace with it. . . . Constance plagues us in this manner, at every entrance. John does the same. He no sooner takes Arthur prisoner, and sends his cousin to England upon business of moment, but, in the very Field of Battle, on the spot, attacks Hubert at once, gives him no time to pause, works him to his bloody purpose, and speeds for England for fresh business.[24]

Inauspicious occurrences come in pairs—John's learning of the invasion of England and his mother's death (4.2.110–24)—or in triplicate—Lewis's hearing that

> The Count Melune is slain; the English lords
> By his persuasion are again fall'n off,
> And your supply, which you have wish'd so long,
> Are cast away, and sunk on Goodwin sands.
>
> (5.5.10–13)

In act 2, Chatillion suddenly appears in answer to Constance's wish, and no sooner has he told of John's promised arrival than John himself is on the scene. The French will later take a lesson from John's temporal feat; in act 4, scene 2, when the messenger delivers the news of the invasion, he says to John:

> The copy of your speed is learn'd by them;
> For when you should be told they do prepare,
> The tidings comes that they are all arriv'd.
>
> (113–15)

Constance in act 3 curses the nuptials of Blanch and Lewis, and immediately, in answer to her curse, Pandulph enters to excommunicate the English king. It is no wonder that John finally cries "Withhold thy speed, dreadful occasion!" (4.2.125), but to no avail for this is a play in which "the spirit of the time . . . teach[es] . . . speed" (4.2.176). "What's done is done" is not a possibility in the world of *King John* where what is done is undone only to be done again. Arthur living when supposed dead and dead when thought living is paradigmatic of the broken vows, the vacillating political figures, the king who gives up his crown only to be recrowned, and the odds that rapidly shift in and out of one's military favor as they do for both the Bastard and Lewis in the final scenes.

Plans misfire, action is canceled, and "purposes [are] mistook" in an atmosphere of flux, motion, and uncertain process. The dislocation of time, something well known to modern sensibilities and realized in the expressionist, symbolist, and absurdist plays of the twentieth century, creates "a shaping pattern" of "repeated reversals of expectations."[25]

There are, of course, other affinities with modern drama, affinities presumably recognized by Dürrenmatt in his adaptation of *King John*, by John Arden in his powerful treatment of the same historical period, *Left-Handed Liberty*, and by John Barton in his avant-garde RSC production at Stratford in 1974.[26] Certainly the emphasis on talk and discussion (what Douglas Wixson labels the debate-like structure of the play)[27] calls to mind the works of Shaw—perhaps nowhere more strikingly than in the scene between Lewis and Pandulph, anticipating as it does, the Cauchon-Warwick exchange in *St. Joan*. The pregnant pauses of Pinter do not seem centuries removed from the dialogue between John and Hubert in act 3:

> *King John.* Good Hubert, Hubert, Hubert, throw thine eye
>   On yon young boy. I'll tell thee what, my friend,
>   He is a very serpent in my way,
>
>   .   .   .   .
>
>   He lies before me. Dost thou understand me?
>   Thou art his keeper.
> *Hubert.*   And I'll keep him so,
>   That he shall not offend your Majesty.
> *King John.*   Death.
> *Hubert.* My lord?
> *King John.*   A grave.
> *Hubert*   He shall not live.
> *King John.*   Enough.
>   (3.3.59–66)

Undoubtedly, the scene that hauntingly stays with an audience weaned on the haptic and barren world of Beckett's *Waiting for Godot* is the night encounter between Hubert and the Bastard on a vague and seemingly timeless plain. As if they are emerging from a nightmare world at best and hell at worst, these two characters, filled with anxiety and uncertainty, haltingly search each other out:

> *Hubert.* Who's there? Speak ho! speak quickly, or I shoot.
> *Bastard.* A friend. What art thou?
> *Hubert.*   Of the part of England.
> *Bastard.* Whither dost thou go?
> *Hubert.* What's that to thee? Why may not I demand
>   Of thine affairs, as well as thou of mine?

Bastard. Hubert, I think?
Hubert.   Thou hast a perfect thought.
    I will upon all hazards well believe
    Thou art my friend that know'st my tongue so well.
    Who art thou?
Bastard.   Who thou wilt. . . .

(5.6.1–9)

Other modern trappings include the lack of a clearly defined hero and the almost endless shifting of perspective, which provokes an ambivalence of response highlighted in Blanch's lament:[28]

> Which is the side that I must go withal?
> I am with both, each army hath a hand,
> And in their rage, I having hold of both,
> They whirl asunder and dismember me.
> Husband, I cannot pray that thou mayst win;
> Uncle, I needs must pray that thou mayst lose;
> Father, I may not wish the fortune thine;
> Grandam, I will not wish thy wishes thrive:
> Whoever wins, on that side shall I lose;
> Assured loss before the match be play'd.

(3.1.327–36)

Culturally and theatrically then, *King John* is a kindred spirit. It is the history play closest in temper and structure to the two Shakespearean tragedies which more than any other have been possessively adopted by the twentieth century. As Emrys Jones reminds us, Hamlet's "view of human behaviour and, by implication, of human history" could easily find a place in *King John:*

> Purpose is but the slave to memory,
> Of violent birth, but poor validity,
>
> . . . .
> This world is not for aye, nor 'tis not strange
> That even our loves should with our fortunes change:
>
> . . . .
> But orderly to end where I begun,
> Our wills and fates do so contrary run
> That our devices still are overthrown,
> Our thoughts are ours, their ends none of our own. . . .

(*Ham.,* 3.2.188–213)

And certainly the "positioning and repositioning" so distinctive of *King Lear* is likewise intrinsic to the shaping of *John.*[29] In the flux that fashions a "mad world, mad kings, mad composition!" (2.1.561), characters speak more from their need than from their faith. Anticipating the "tremulous cadence" of modernity and envisioning a world where "the centre cannot hold," Shakespeare creates in *King John* a play provocatively charged with the urgency, anguish, and relevance of "now."

The essays that follow span a variety of approaches from the time-honored ones of source study, genre, imagery, theme, and character to the current interests in historiography, feminism, pragmatics, performance history, and perspectivism. Taken as a group they show that "the strength of contemporary *King John* criticism . . . lies in its demonstration that the play's questions are grounded in reassessments of historical process and inquiry, of genre, of character, of dramaturgy, and of coherence that help to energize Renaissance thought itself."[30] A review of the volume's "core vocabulary" reveals such iterative entries as "ambivalence," "ambiguity," "confusion," "division," "*Realpolitik*," "deconstruction," "demystification," "vacillation," "cynicism," "satire," "parody," "irony," "inconclusion," "subversion," "reduction," and "dialectic."

In the first essay Marsha Robinson explores the historiographic methodology of *King John*. Disagreeing with those who would evaluate the play in terms of the stylistic and generic expectations created by the two tetralogies, Robinson argues that in writing *John* "Shakespeare experimented with a fresh approach to history." Instead of using conventional strategies of recall and prognostication to recreate a historical process that links the past, present, and future—as he does in his other history plays—Shakespeare ironically invokes those same strategies to sever the present from the events of both the past and the future, thus satirizing the historiographical process itself. "Parodying conventional historiographic statement and ironically juxtaposing actual events and the meanings assigned to them, Shakespeare exposes the disparity between the events of history and their conventional representations." In her discussion of *John's* generic subversiveness, Robinson's essay looks ahead to Virginia Vaughan's treatment of the play's subversion of the medieval chivalric ideal, Phyllis Rackin's study of the subversive powers of women, and Larry Champion's focus on an ending that subverts closure.

While a number of essays refer in passing to *The Troublesome Raigne of Iohn King of England*, the generally accepted source for Shakespeare's *John*, Guy Hamel provides a detailed and fresh look at the play in his comparative study of the two works. For Hamel, Shakespeare's "assault on formulas—on commonplaces and conventionalities, on presentation and representation, on ceremony and rite . . . reveals itself in almost every departure from" the earlier play.

In the defense offered in recent Shakespearean criticism of "the separate-but-equal" versions of multiple text plays, Hamel finds a climate conducive to "an unprejudiced view of the maligned *Troublesome Raigne* that by extension will give us a better understanding of those features most radically altered by Shakespeare as he went about the creative shaping, adapting, and transforming of his major source.[31]

Drawing upon the recent work of "new historicist" criticism, Virginia Vaughan discusses the ideological subversiveness of *King John*, a play that radically rejects the sixteenth-century treatment of John as a proto-Protestant martyr and "deconstructs" the propagandistic *Troublesome Raigne*. Vaughan locates Shakespeare's subversion of the medieval chivalric ideal in the character of the Bastard who chooses to be a "new man" and advance without the traditional means of patrimony and land. The tripartite feudal system of king, church, and nobles, which undergoes a complete breakdown, is ultimately reimposed only after the death or disappearance of the play's dissidents. In Shakespeare's deliberate interjection of "anachronistic elements that manipulate the temporal relationship between present and past," Vaughan sees the play's confrontation of "two time frames, medieval and Renaissance . . . as mirroring England in the 1590s at a crucial transition from the last vestiges of a medieval/feudal system to the modern age of individualism."

The final section of Vaughan's essay, where she discusses the disappearance of the women from the play's action, leads directly into Phyllis Rackin's feminist study of patriarchal history and female subversion. Rackin examines the paradoxical role of women in *King John* who ostensibly have no voice or place within the tradition of masculine historiography but who, nevertheless, manage, by their very presence as "the keepers of the unspoken . . . reality" of legitimacy, to subvert the patriarchal historical record. More insistent in this play than in the first tetralogy, the women "imply that before the masculine voice of history can be accepted as valid, it must come to terms with women and the subversive forces they represent" as they counter the dictates of primogeniture, succession, and dynastic genealogy, the ideological triumvirate at the very core of Tudor orthodoxy. The episode crucial to Rackin's thesis and one which she deals with at some length is the encounter between Lady Faulconbridge and the Bastard in act 1.

Directly addressing the matter of generic classification, Barbara Traister finds *King John* to be a different kind of history play largely because of its reductive treatment of cast size, spectacle, ritual and ceremony, and, most important, kingship. Her thesis is that possession without majesty leads to royal failure, and John is a king who lacks the so-called "second body" of "sacred majesty." His personal, informal, and "unceremonial" style of kingship proves inadequate because the world of *King John* is one of international politics and not the holiday world of the comical history of Tudor dramatists like Greene and Dekker who depict kings mingling with their subjects on more or less equal terms. Traister's discussion of the quality of John's kingship provides a larger context for Joseph Porter's study of the "nakedness" of John's speech acts in chapter 9.

Moving away from issues of source, historiography, and genre, Dorothea Kehler and Joseph Candido address the philosophical tenor of the play. Kehler, seeking an answer to the question of whether or not God has withdrawn from the world of *King John*, examines how religious imagery and rhetoric (oaths and invocations) are deployed throughout the play in a way that reinforces the ambivalence and division often noted in the scholarship. She finds a secular, hypocritical jesting with heaven dominating the first three acts and a contrapuntal tension between secularism and providentialism—hypocrisy and piety—developing in the last two. In the final moments, however, the question of "God's presence or absence is displaced," for the Bastard's "rousing clarion call," devoid of all spiritual reference (whether jesting or pious), marks the new faith of "bellicose nationalism."

Where Kehler approaches the play's meaning through religious rhetoric, Joseph Candido focuses the tension and ambivalence of *King John* through a thematic analysis of the characters' psychological longing for "purity" in a corrupt and decadent setting. This longing, be it political, moral, or behavioral, is so pervasive that the atmosphere of "moral pollution" distinguishes *King John* from Shakespeare's other histories. While the central duality of purity versus adulteration surfaces in the actions and speeches of many of the characters, it is the Bastard, a product of adultery, who forges in "the trenchantly emblematic scene" where he discovers Arthur's body a meaningful and dynamic relationship between the two opposites. He becomes a "moral oxymoron"—the embodiment of "wholesome impurity, 'good' adulteration," and "his ideological bastardy becomes the touchstone of his political superiority."

Although a number of essays ultimately come around to the character of the Bastard, Michael Manheim's makes this figure central. In contrast to Candido's interpretation with its ethical component, Manheim's view of the Bastard's "coming of age" is essentially rooted in politics. He accepts the critical consensus that the Bastard of the first act is different from that of the last, but he argues for a development that reconciles the divisions and contradictions often noted by scholars. This integration of character manifests itself in what Manheim describes as the four voices of the Bastard: (1) the voice of a young, untried political opportunist; (2) the voice of one rudely awakened to the true nature of political reality and "That smooth-fac'd gentleman, tickling commodity" (2.1.573); (3) the voice of deepening awareness of the realities of this world and of intensifying loyalty to the crown; and (4) the final voice of the attractive Machiavel. For Manheim, there is a natural progression from one voice to the next.

Joseph Porter continues the examination of character but from the perspective of pragmatics or speech act theory. His focus is John and the Bastard. For Porter, John's speech "may make him the least illocutionarily explicit" of any Shakespearean monarch. His propensity for the laconic, reserved, and inexplicit imparts a "nakedness" to his verbal action. Where most critics accentuate the differences between the king and his "madcap" illegitimate relation, Porter (while acknowledging that they "stand in notable contrast as verbal actors, each with his own significantly characteristic range of speech acts") emphasizes certain verbal similarities that "manifest a deep and troubled fraternality between them."He thus takes Manheim's conclusion that the Bastard becomes John's spokesman a step further by pointing to the Bastard's internalization of John's interrogative verbal action and his tendency to change subject and direction of address abruptly. A fusion of psyches is the result.

Turning from a literary focus to a theatrical one, the essays of Carol Carlisle and Edward Brubaker explore the play through the lens of performance history. Stopford Brooke once commented that "the actress who should undertake the part of Constance is scarcely born in a century."[32] Carlisle's analysis of the interpretation of Constance, "the jewel of *King John*,"[33] by three leading actresses of their respective periods—Sarah Siddons, Helen Faucit, and Claire Bloom—shows that Brooke's statement needs qualification, probably in the cases of Faucit and Bloom and definitely in the case of Siddons. While each differed markedly in her representation of Constance's personality and manner, given her own individual qualities and the prevailing acting style and tastes of the time (and in the case of Bloom, the nature of the medium itself), all three were "constant" in making "maternal love, not selfish ambition, the mainspring of the character." In suggesting that Bloom's Constance was influenced by recent study of the political realities and the subversive powers of women in a patriarchal society, Carlisle's essay points back to Phyllis Rackin's.

Where most Shakespearean festival companies shun *King John*, Ashland seems to have taken it very much to its box office heart, having staged it several times in this century and chosen it as one of the productions to celebrate the fiftieth anniversary of the Oregon Shakespearean Festival. Edward Brubaker stage-managed *John* (1959) and directed it (1969) for the festival and thus brings an engagingly personal dimension to our understanding of this play in his essay "Staging *King John:* A Director's Observations." Where Eugene Waith contends that *King John* might fare better with modern audiences if directors allowed it to work its affective charms by focusing on emotionally charged scenes and the passionate intensity of characters like Constance instead of looking "first for a pattern of ideas,"[34] Brubaker favors an approach that emphasizes cerebral activity rather than visual splendor and emotional release. Finding the theatrical tradition of lavish *King John* productions that project "the pageantry of celebratory history"—a tradition to which audiences have become conditioned since the eighteenth century—"simply wrongheaded," Brubaker challenges directors, actors, audiences, and, by extension, scholars to see *King John* "as a play for thinking people," one that may even be comic in the Brechtian manner of keeping "the audience thinking rather than stirred up by the issues it raises."

The final essay by Larry Champion, appropriately enough, takes up the issue of closure by directing our attention to the play's almost rhythmic principle of dramatizing different perspectives and evoking shifting responses. Critical dissatisfaction with the ending of *King John* has been longstanding and is perhaps best summed up in Burckhardt's speculation that Shakespeare "saw no way to put Humpty Dumpty together again."[35] Running throughout the present volume is a sensitivity to the tenuous, contingent, ironic, and inconclusive nature of the final moments. But even more important, what seems to culminate in Champion's essay is an acceptance of the questions raised by the ending as being of a "formal" piece with all that has gone before, "a key to Shakespeare's larger pattern." The point of departure for Champion is John's comment in act 4, scene 2: "I have a way to win their loves again. / Bring them before me" (168–69). These lines, for which Champion provides five possible meanings, seem "to set in motion a series of actions which methodically cancel out any presumed moral or political virtue in the historical process, reducing government and society to the chaos of individual machination at worst and an unstable nexus of conflicting self-interest at best." Adding to the spectator's increasing "dislocat[ion] during the play's closure" is the enigmatic character of the Bastard. In his refutation of critics who see the Bastard as a positive force in the play, Champion completes what the earlier contributors began, namely, the movement toward a less-than-heroic, "non-idealized" Bastard: The character "who does the best he can" (Hamel), who (like many good men) finds himself in a position of "falsify[ing] the past" (Robinson), who enters into a "troubled fraternality" with one of Shakespeare's least likable kings (Porter), and who, whether as the voice of "bellicose nationalism" (Kehler) or as the new attractive Machiavel (Manheim), "is the best we can expect from political man . . . in the unweeded garden" (Candido), becomes in the end, if a hero at all, one by "default" (Champion).

What can be found in the essays taken collectively is a deepening awareness of Shakespeare's complex experimentation with the history play. This experimentation is apparent in his undercutting the staples of such drama: for example, memory, prophecy, primogeniture, dynastic genealogy, ceremony, and ritual. It is there in the divided legacy of Coeur de Lion among John, Arthur, and the Bastard, [36] a division that prompts the citizens of Angiers to offer the city up to the king once they know who the king is. The prominence given to an unhistorical character and the depiction of a king who is not killed in battle but who dies at the hand of a fanatical monk—"a clod / and module of confounded royalty" (5.7.57–58)—further illustrate Shakespeare's ironic and satiric shaping of history. *King John,* then, is a history play with a twist, one written in a different vein from the others, one more indeterminate and open than fixed and closed. To embellish a point made by Larry Champion, Shakespeare may have "deconstructed" the history play.

Joseph Candido is correct to invoke Norman Rabkin, whose theory of "complementarity" offers the best means for grappling with the "energy and turbulence" resonating throughout *King John.*[37] Rabkin defines "complementarity" as "the basis of a mimesis which appeals to the common understanding because it recalls the unresolvable tensions that are the fundamental conditions of human experience."[38] What we find in the system of dualities operating with centrifugal force in the play—dualities like medieval/Renaissance, subversion/containment, male/female, history/antihistory, formality/informality, secularism/providentialism, and purity/adulteration—is a dynamic and fluid tension that permits a commingling of opposites without abandoning the individual makeup of the elements so commingled. In Shakespeare, more often than not, it is a case of "both/and" rather than "either/or," and *King John* is no exception, as contradictions and antinomies go beyond the level of rigid polarization to that of fluid interpenetration. Complementarity may allow us to explore without explaining away the "centers of energy and turbulence" radiating from the play.

The recent resurgence of *King John* may derive from a growing recognition of the play as one for our time. It was not, after all, a play for the nineteenth century; productions then had to add people, horses, and pageantry to make it acceptable, thus transforming it into something other than what it was. But today, after the events of this century, a play in which the unthinkable happens—the English nobles abandon their country to fight for France—and the nightmare materializes—the impregnable "sceptred isle" is actually invaded (the only time this happens in Shakespeare's histories)—has special meaning for us. Where *Henry V* is one side of the picture, *King John* is the other, the nether side. Like a satyr play it stands in opposition to the ideals of kingship expressed in the two Henriads. Played with sharps and flats and the lower keys, *King John* mocks and inverts the themes, conventions, and strategies generically associated with the history play. Dramatically, Shakespeare seems to have anticipated the fall of Alice down the rabbit hole, the topsy-turvydom of Gilbert and Sullivan, the disquisitory nature of Shavian drama, the barren landscape of Beckett, the alienation and cerebral quality of Brechtian theater, and the angry young men of Osborne.[39] Among Shakespeare's dramatic "offspring," *King John*, lacking the comfort of a surrounding tetralogy, is a "loner," and, like its most popular character, has become "a bastard to the time" (1.1.207), either ignored, tolerated, or forced to assume a theatrical image untrue to its real self. If it is not to expire modestly in silence, perhaps we should echo the words of another Shakespearean bastard who vigorously invokes the gods to "stand up for bastards!"

A Note on Documentation for This Volume

Full bibliographical information is not included in any of the notes to this volume for those works that also appear in the Select Bibliography. Throughout, unless otherwise noted, all quotations from Shakespeare's plays are taken from *The Riverside Shakespeare*, ed. G. Blakemore Evans et al. (Boston: Houghton Mifflin, 1974).

Notes

1. From "A Letter to Colley Cibber," quoted in the New Variorum *The Life and Death of King John*, ed. Horace H. Furness, 553.
2. Edward Dowden, *Shakespeare: A Critical Study of His Mind and Art* (London: Routledge and K. Paul, 1875), 172.
3. See Derek A. Traversi, *An Approach to Shakespeare* 1:179; and Emrys Jones, *The Origins of Shakespeare*, 233, respectively.
4. See Charles Gildon, cited in Furness, *The Life and Death of King John*, 596; and E. M. W. Tillyard, *Shakespeare's History Plays*, 232.
5. William Oxberry, cited in Furness, *The Life and Death of King John*, 599–600;

Robert Ornstein, *A Kingdom for a Stage*, 86; E. Jones, *Origins*, 233; and Tillyard, *Shakespeare's History Plays*, 215.

6. E. Jones, *Origins*, 233; M. M. Reese, *The Cease of Majesty*, 261; M. Guizot, cited in Furness, *The Life and Death of King John*, 606; and Robert B. Pierce, *Shakespeare's History Plays*, 144.

7. E. Jones, *Origins*, 234.

8. Tillyard, *Shakespeare's History Plays*, 218, 226, 232.

9. Ornstein, *Kingdom*, 85, 96.

10. Thomas Campbell, cited in Furness, *The Life and Death of King John*, 605.

11. Reese, *Cease of Majesty*, 261; Ornstein, *Kingdom*, 86; and E. K. Chambers, *Shakespeare: A Survey* (London: Sidgwick and Jackson, 1925), 99–100.

12. Moody Prior, *The Drama of Power: Studies in Shakespeare's History Plays* (Evanston, Ill.: Northwestern University Press, 1973); John Wilders, *The Lost Garden: A View of Shakespeare's English and Roman History Plays* (Totowa, N. J.: Rowan and Littlefield, 1978); and Sally Beauman, *The Royal Shakespeare Company: A History of Ten Decades* (London: Oxford University Press, 1982). Prior reduces the play to a parenthetical reference (336) and a footnote (355 n. 9); Wilders, to a single clause (135); and Beauman refers to the play by way of a single photo caption for the 1948 Stratford-upon-Avon production. It was not until the third edition of *An Approach to Shakespeare* that Derek Traversi got around to *King John*, and Peter Alexander, in his *Shakespeare's Life and Art* (London: Nisbet, 1939), gives it one and a quarter pages (85–86), the only play to receive such limited treatment in the volume.

13. Among those who tolerate it are Reese and Ornstein, the latter barely hiding his disdain. Those who praise the play with qualification include the following: Dr. Johnson, who says that "*The Tragedy of King John*, though not written with the utmost power of Shakespeare, is varied with a very pleasing interchange of incident" (cited in Furness, *The Life and Death of King John*, 596); Nathan Drake, who finds that "if *King John*, as a whole, be not entitled to class among the very first-rate compositions of our author, it can yet exhibit some scenes of superlative beauty and effect," (cited in Furness, *The Life and Death of King John*, 598); Tillyard, who finds "the play . . . a wonderful affair, full of promise and of new life, [but] as a whole . . . uncertain of itself" (*Shakespeare's History Plays*, 233); and Pierce, who calls it "rich but untidy" (*Shakespeare's History Plays*, 144). Among the few who have felt no need to apologize for *King John* are John Masefield ("a truly noble play" [*William Shakespeare*, 85]), H. von Friesen ("*King John* may be considered a thoroughly well-shaped and modulated work exhibiting superior application and great care" [cited in Furness, *The Life and Death of King John*, 615]), and J. A. Heraud ("The tragedy of *King John* is admirable in structure, and capable of being placed on the stage without alteration. It is, indeed, almost a classic for its regularity, as it is for the genius displayed in it" [cited in Furness, *The Life and Death of King John*, 610]).

14. James L. Calderwood, "Commodity and Honour in *King John*" in *Shakespeare The Histories*, ed. Eugene M. Waith, 85.

15. E. Jones, *Origins*, 235.

16. Gone are the days when there were rival productions in the same city, in the same years (Drury Lane and Covent Garden in 1760 and 1766). The closest approximation in recent memory occurred in 1974 when two major Stratford productions were staged on opposite sides of the Atlantic. For brief accounts of major productions of the play since World War II, see Tice Miller's "*King John*" in Samuel Leiter, ed., *Shakespeare Around the Globe*, 283–95.

17. E. Jones, *Scenic Form in Shakespeare*, 89,112.

18. Adrien Bonjour, "The Road to Swinstead Abbey," 253–74; Sigurd Burck-

hardt, *"King John:* The Ordering of This Present Time," *ELH* 33 (1966): 133–53, reprinted in Burckhardt, *Shakespearean Meanings,* 116–43; see particularly 117. All subsequent references to Burckhardt's essay in the present volume are to his book.

19. Eamon Grennan, "Shakespeare's Satirical History," 26, 32.

20. Virginia Mason Vaughan, "Between Tetralogies," 412.

21. See Madeleine Doran's study of these plays in *Shakespeare's Dramatic Language* (Madison: University of Wisconsin Press, 1976).

22. See Ralph Berry, *The Shakespearean Metaphor,* 26–36, particularly 30–33.

23. Francis Gentlemen, cited in Furness, *The Life and Death of King John,* 596.

24. "Letter to Colley Cibber," in Furness, ed., 553–54.

25. Vaughan, "Between Tetralogies," 415.

26. For descriptions of the Barton production, see Peter Thomson, "The Smallest Season: The Royal Shakespeare Company at Stratford in 1974," *Shakespeare Survey* 28 (1975), 138–41; Richard David, *Shakespeare in the Theatre* (Cambridge: Cambridge University Press, 1978), 174–81; and Tice Miller's "King John" in *Shakespeare Around the Globe,* ed. Leiter, 291–92. To cite but one example of Barton's different (some might say bizarre) conception of the play, the John/Hubert persuasion scene (3.3) was staged with Hubert giving the King a massage.

27. Douglas C. Wixson, "'Calm Words Folded Up in Smoke,'" 111–27.

28. Critics interested in perspective and response include Wixson, Alexander Leggatt ("Dramatic Perspective in *King John,*" *1–17*), Larry S. Champion ("'Confound Their Skill in Covetousness,'" 36–55), and Jonathan Reeve Price ("*King John* and Problematic Art," 25–28).

29. E. Jones draws these analogies in *Origins,* 246, and *Scenic Form,* 169, respectively.

30. Carol Duane, "*King John* Criticism: 1960–1985," paper presented at the first session of the *King John* seminar of the Shakespeare Association of America Conference on 28 March 1986, 12.

31. In the present volume as well as at the two seminar sessions in Montreal, there was total agreement regarding *The Troublesome Raigne* as Shakespeare's major source and not, as E. A. J. Honigmann argues in the introduction to the New Arden edition, a work that follows *King John,* thus being derivative in nature (xix, liii–lviii).

One textual matter that does not share the same consensus, at least in the essays that follow, is the Hubert/Citizen question. Hamel sees the two characters as distinct, whereas Manheim and Kehler, in keeping with the views of J. Dover Wilson and Honigmann, find Hubert and the Citizen of Angiers to be one and the same.

32. Stopford A. Brooke, cited in Furness, *The Life and Death of King John,* 585.

33. A. C. Swinburne, cited in Furness, *The Life and Death of King John,* 619.

34. Eugene M. Waith, "*King John* and the Drama of History," 211.

35. Burckhardt, *Shakespearean Meanings,* 134.

36. See William Matchett, "Richard's Divided Heritage in *King John*" in *Essays in Shakespearean Criticism,* ed. J. L. Calderwood and H. E. Toliver, 152–70.

37. Norman Rabkin, *Shakespeare and the Problem of Meaning* (Chicago, Ill.: University of Chicago Press, 1981). Candido in his essay refers to pp. 25 and 61 in Rabkin's text.

38. Norman Rabkin, *Shakespeare and the Common Understanding* (New York: Free Press, 1967), 27.

39. It may be of quixotic interest that two actors who played the Bastard in this century, Richard Burton in the 1953 Old Vic production and Kenneth Haigh for the Caedmon recording, also played the role of Jimmy Porter in John Osborne's *Look Back in Anger,* one doing so on the stage (Haigh) and the other in the film version (Burton).

KING JOHN
New Perspectives

1

The Historiographic Methodology of *King John*

MARSHA ROBINSON

ONE OF THE DISTINCTIVE STYLISTIC FEATURES OF THE SHAKESPEAREAN history play is the artful recreation of history as past, present, and future. Calling attention to the "network of references" to both the past and the future in these plays, Wolfgang Clemen observes that "Shakespeare not only handled episodes from the historical past, but he translated into drama elements inherent in history itself. For history demonstrates how the past grows into the present and leads on to the future."[1] In the history plays these retrospective and prospective passages not only reflect Shakespeare's consciousness of the historical process but serve as a commentary on the historiographic process. While recall imitates the way by which historical events are retrospectively reframed and emplotted by the historian (whose rhetorical and generic fashioning of the past informs it with meaning),[2] prognostication often dramatizes the self-conscious shaping of historiographic meaning by the makers of history.

For many readers *King John* proves disappointing precisely because it does not manifest the stylistic qualities which Clemen identifies as the definitive marks of the Shakespearean history play. Evaluating *King John* in terms of stylistic expectations created by the first tetralogy, Robert Ornstein, for example, observes that "Even as the opening scene lacks prophetic overtones, it creates no historical perspective, no sense of the past such as exists in the plays of the first tetralogy." For Ornstein, the play's failure to evoke a sense of the historical process is evidence of a " 'falling off' of Shakespeare's artistry."[3]

Rather than conclude that *King John* is an artistic failure because it does not measure up to the stylistic expectations created by the two tetralogies, I wish to argue that the play reveals Shakespeare's experiment with a fresh approach to history. As David Scott Kastan argues, Shakespeare discovers in the writing of *King John* that history is itself an "artifact" and that its "fictions of stability" are the cultural counterparts of the dramatist's fictional ordering of the past.[4] More than just acknowledging these artifacts as myths, Shakespeare reexamines the rhetorical structures by which historical knowledge is communicated. His aim in this play is not merely to recreate the past but to dramatize the process by which historical experience is translated into historiographic meaning. Parodying conventional historiographic statement and ironically juxtaposing actual events and the meanings assigned to them, Shakespeare exposes the disparity between the events of history and their conventional representations. The distinctive historiographic methodology of *King John* supports this satiric depiction of the past. First of all, rather than framing the dramatic present, the "now" of history, in retrospective and prospective passages that so often impose historiographic interpretations on that present, *King John* parodies such strategies. In addition, interpretive patterns ascribed to events are ironically discredited by the testimony of the facts. As a result, the locus of the play is neither the past (historical retrospection) nor the future (speculation). Approaching historical experience inductively through his presenter the Bastard, Shakespeare places the auditor in the historical present as an eyewitness to events. Through the Bastard's naïve and unbiased eyes, we observe the historical process unfold firsthand, assessing the motives that actually direct historical choices and drawing conclusions about the patterns that govern historical change. This empirical examination of the past is implicitly set against those retrospective and prospective emplotments that impose generic form upon the past.

In the history plays of the first and second tetralogies, recall is often used to invoke an ideal past against which the present can be measured, to articulate historiographic patterns that legitimate or condemn a present course of action, or to interpret present events in terms of historiographic patterns invested with teleological meaning. Thus, for example, Richard II's deviance from the historiographic models embodied by his noble grandfather and father is articulated in York's idealized recall of Edward III and the Black Prince (*Richard II* 2.1.171–83). Unlike his own son, the Black Prince reenacts the chivalric feats of his father, renewing in his own person his father's historiographic fame. Richard's failures to renew a glorious past are characterized in terms of conventional formulas for national and monarchical success—domestic peace and foreign conquest. Similarly, in *Henry V*,

Henry's achievements are consciously reframed in terms of historiographic expectations and models. Passages of recall repeatedly invoke the past, and we are to perceive Henry's exploits as not only a reenactment of the past—a renewal of the "feats" of his "mighty ancestors," Edward III and the Black Prince (*Henry V* 1.2.102,116)—but a re-creation of the conventional accounts in which the conquest of France is emplotted as epic or romance. Shakespeare thus demonstrates the way in which the historical present embodied by sons as successors is comprehended in terms of the historiographic interpretations of a more distant past.

In *King John*, however, the present is consciously divorced from the past. The device of recall is parodied, and historiographic models of the past are challenged. In the very opening moments of the play the legitimation of the present in terms of past models is immediately countered by the Bastard's acknowledgment of his illegitimacy as well as Elinor's admission that John's authority is legitimized not by inherited titles bequeathed from the past but by his *de facto* power (1.1.40). The Bastard's celebration of his illegitimacy—"Legitimation, name, and all is gone" (1.1.248)—might in fact serve as a clue to the historiographic strategy of the entire play in which historical experience is inductively studied apart from the presuppositions or arrangements provided by conventional historiography. The official past is not used to impose meaning upon the present; names and titles—suggestive of historic reputation often falsely perpetuated by the historian—are discredited, and the process of legitimation by which the status quo is invested with moral and teleological significance is exposed. Rejecting inheritance, a symbol of the influence of the past on the present—"I am I, howe'er I was begot" (1.1.175)—the Bastard not only contravenes the retrospective glance of historiography but establishes the experiential present as the focus of the play.[5]

The pattern continues in act 2 when Philip ironically invokes the past and the glorious chivalric reputation of Arthur's "great forerunner" (2.1.2), Coeur de Lion, for an inglorious end, winning the helpless Arthur's submission to an ignoble alliance with Richard's murderer, Austria:

> Arthur, that great forerunner of thy blood,
> Richard, that robb'd the lion of his heart,
> And fought the holy wars in Palestine,
> By this brave duke came early to his grave;
> And for amends to his posterity,
> At our importance hither is he come
> To spread his colors, boy, in thy behalf,

And to rebuke the usurpation
Of thy unnatural uncle, English John.
Embrace him, love him, give him welcome hither.

                                              (2.1.2–11)

Shakespeare thus satirizes the self-serving invocation of the past to legitimize choices which are solely a response to occasion.

While Shakespeare's use of recall challenges conventional notions of historical continuity, his treatment of Richard Coeur de Lion's heroic reputation parodies historiography's aggrandizement of the past. Austria's recounting of the chivalric deeds of this idealized figure is reductively juxtaposed with a less flattering account of his exploits. Recalling Richard's sexual conquest of Lady Faulconbridge as a mock-heroic version of his fabulous conquest of the lion, the Bastard exposes Coeur de Lion's famed valor—his "fury and unmatched force" (1.1.265)—as the expression of an amoral aggression, thus tarnishing the reputation perpetuated by the historian's idealized treatment of the past as epic or romance. The Bastard thus removes his father from the realm of historic fictions into the brazen world of history. While exemplars dignify and unify the record, historical experience suggests that the amorphous self cannot be represented by such patterns, nor can any single incident supply an accurate portrait of character when behavior so often reflects the shaping of circumstances.[6] The Bastard's cynicism about historical reputation and the good-natured tolerance with which he accepts a picture of the past more dissonant and disturbing than the official version establish a disinterested and realistic perspective that prepares the auditor for the task of distinguishing historical fact from the fictions created to refashion the past.

Like recall, prognostication in *King John* also serves to satirize historiographic interpretations. Instead of creating a historical perspective which foreshadows the historiographic meanings that will be assigned to the events being dramatized (as is the case in Shakespeare's other histories),[7] prognostication in *King John* calls into question the very process of ascribing patterns to events, thereby severing history as event from historical contemplation. Rather than connecting past and future into a coherent story, prophetic passages, by proving false and disconfirming the historical models they project, deny such coherence and suggest the arbitrary and subjective character of historical interpretation.

It is important to note that prognostications do more than predict events; they often set forth models of history which appear to describe a metaphysical or teleological order inherent in events themselves. In *King John* this mythologizing of history is recognized as a politic stratagem. Pandulph, its chief practitioner, describes the methodology involved when he assures the Dolphin that the English nobles will seize upon Arthur's death as an opportunity to "check" John's reign, justifying their rebellion by translating "natural" events into historical signs and patterns:

> No natural exhalation in the sky,
> No scope of nature, no distemper'd day,
> No common wind, no customed event,
> But they will pluck away his natural cause
> And call them meteors, prodigies, and signs,
> Abortives, presages, and tongues of heaven,
> Plainly denouncing vengeance upon John.
>
> (3.4.153–59)

By portraying such mythologizing of the past as a tactic of those who would usurp history and shape it to their wills, Shakespeare ridicules historical interpretations and questions the processes by which historical explanation is generated.

Philip of France provides another example of the way in which anticipation is used satirically to expose the distance between events and the historiographic meanings assigned to them. Anticipating the rebirth of Geoffrey's royal prerogative in his son Arthur, Philip identifies the "sequence of posterity" as the inherent model or pattern for historical and legal succession. Thus he metaphorically conflates historical change or succession with biological regeneration:

> This little abstract doth contain that large
> Which died in Geffrey; and the hand of time
> Shall draw this brief into as huge a volume.
>
> (2.1.101–3)

The representation of Arthur as an abstract of his father—a renewal of the past in the present—and as a volume yet to be written—a symbol of the historiographic future—links biological inheritance with the chronicle record, which ironically does not confirm the "sequence of posterity." Not only does Geoffrey's record die in Arthur, whose projected place in history is not borne out, but the record of John's succession belies the inviolability of the pattern of primogeniture that Philip describes as natural and inevitable.

Once again pronouncing on the historical record, Philip anticipates the historiographic significance of the alliance he has forged with England. Predicting that "this blessed day / Ever in France shall be kept festival" (3.1.75–76), Philip anticipates the yearly commemoration of the wedding of Lewis and Blanch as a "holy day" (82). Like an "alchymist" (78), the sun, an emblem of Providence, seems to Philip

to confirm his expectations, transforming the prosaic world of history
into a golden one, and disconfirming Constance's anticipation of a day
of infamy (83–95). This alchemic transformation proves to be but an
illusion as the "holy legate" (3.1.135),Pandulph, God's official representative, immediately appears to divest the alliance and the day of the
sanctification and the historical significance ascribed to it. By juxtaposing affirmations of transcendent meaning with interpretation and
an outcome that belie the ceremonial significance of the wedding day,
Shakespeare calls attention to historical patterns as the product of
human fashioning. His dramatization of the reversal of ceremonial
expectations elicits in the auditor the very response which the nobles,
warning John, identify as the effect of his arbitrary invocation of
ceremony:

> It makes the course of thoughts to fetch about,
> Startles and frights consideration,
> Makes sound opinion sick, and truth suspected. . . .
>
> (4.2.24–26)

Arousing our suspicion of historical interpretations that invoke ceremonial patterns, Shakespeare exposes the falsehood of those who
invest historical events with teleological meaning in order to legitimate
partisan choices and perpetuate their own biases, identifying them
with divine purpose or natural law.

By confronting the auditor with the arbitrary and subjective nature
of those patterns which seem indigenous to events and by introducing
prognostications which never materialize, Shakespeare undermines
the very patterns that would unify events and create a coherent con-
tinuum, thereby rendering the present and the future discrete. Thus
neither the projected reign of Arthur nor the alliance of England and
France becomes part of the record. Moreover, the historiographic
patterns these nonevents are said to support are themselves revealed as
the fictions of men who would control history. Even Pandulph's prediction about the politic behavior of the nobles (3.4.145–59), a pattern
based on actual observation of political behavior, does not totally
account for the historic process, for although he correctly anticipates
the opportunism of the nobles, he does not anticipate that Lewis's
purpose will be finally thwarted by the responses of men like Melun
and the Bastard. Only the mysterious prophecy of Peter of Pomfret
(4.2.147–54), an empirical statement predicting nothing more than the
date and time of John's demise and offered as fact (154), is borne out.
Significantly, this datum is associated with the interpretations and
speculations of those who would attempt to invest time with a meaning
that favors their own covert purposes. While for Pandulph Ascension-

day commemorates John's oath of allegiance to the Pope (5.1.22–23), for John himself, privy to the prophecy, it takes on quite a different meaning as one speculation is temporarily supplanted by another:

> Is this Ascension-day? Did not the prophet
> Say that before Ascension-day at noon
> My crown I should give off? Even so I have.
> I did suppose it should be on constraint,
> But (heav'n be thank'd!) it is but voluntary.
>
> (5.1.25–29)

The schism between event and meaning or fact and interpretation is indicative of the historiographic perspective of *King John*. The focus of the play is the "now" of history. By literally cutting himself off from the past and rejecting the political manipulation of history represented by recall and prognostication, the Bastard becomes the spokesman for this perspective. Rather than viewing the past through an historiographic lens, he inductively examines the present from the point of view of an outsider who has no legitimate relationship to the past. The Bastard has neither a bias to support nor a historiographic model to uphold. In the person of the Bastard, Shakespeare observes events as they transpire and translates the rhetoric in which they are framed as historic deeds into a language that penetrates the pretensions of kings and princes.

The Bastard's role as the experiential observer of political events echoes the new approach to the past that characterizes the thinking of Jean Bodin, Machiavelli, and others. Campaigning for a more objective historiography, Bodin decries the power of emotion, which prevents men from honestly examining the past, and expresses serious reservations about an historiography that supplies moral judgments rather than presenting the facts and allowing the reader to make his own assessments.[8] Because history is a record of the emotional biases of engaged minds—its patterns a reflection of the relationship of the historian to his material—Bodin warns the reader of history to consider "whether the historian has written a treatise about his own concerns or those of others; whether his work deals with compatriots or foreigners; enemies or friends; military discipline or civil; finally, whether it is of his own age or of an earlier period, for his contemporaries or for posterity."[9] Bodin thus draws a distinction between the events of history and the arbitrary and selective nature of the historic record which imperfectly reflects the past and therefore cannot be wholeheartedly embraced. For Bodin the "truth of the matter" can only be discerned if one approaches history with a disengaged mind and a cautious skepticism: "We must remember what Aristotle sagely said, that in reading history it is necessary not to believe too much or to disbelieve flatly."[10] Likewise concerned with objectivity, Machiavelli points to the proliferation of idealized histories describing states that never existed "in the real world" as evidence of the habit of "neglect[ing] the real to study the ideal."[11] Machiavelli views the capacity for empirically observing experience from a realistic perspective—"an intelligence that sees things as they are"—as a prerequisite for the successful prince.[12]

Gifted with such an intelligence, the Bastard inductively examines specific events and independently forms his own assessment of their significance, which is at variance with official historiographic interpretation. For example, before Angiers he stands apart from a conventional scenario in which sovereignty is disputed and the question of rightful allegiance demands that participants make a moral or legal choice. Dispelling the illusion, created by each king's assertion of his rights, that historical choices are moral ones, the Bastard observes the cynical posture of the citizens of Angiers and likens them to spectators in a theater who merely gape at the horrors and injustices of history as a kind of spectacle. Not only does the Bastard call attention to the pragmatism of the citizens of Angiers and the moral pretenses of John and Philip, he counters the historiographer's conventional (moral or romantic) plotting of historical experience with his own satiric model of events. A *reductio ad absurdum*, this cynical model takes the form of a modest proposal.[13] The Bastard humorously urges the two kings to join hands against the stubborn citizens of Angiers—"Turn thou the mouth of thy artillery, / As we will ours, against these saucy walls" (2.1.403–4)—and having ravaged the city, to then "Turn face to face and bloody point to point" (390), defying each other (406) in deadly combat. The Bastard's proposal creates a metaphorical picture of the political and historical process that the play dramatizes. The battlefield becomes an image of history's stage. The physical movement and deployment of armies, strategically shifting positions on the field, reiterated in the term "turn," imitate the amoral indirection or bias operative in historical choices. Such choices, the Bastard inductively concludes, are pragmatic responses to occasion and not expressions of moral purpose or intent (2.1.580). Ridiculing history's absurd dramas, the Bastard's politic scenario echoes in its very language—"turn"—the mental flexibility that Machiavelli recommends to the successful prince: "It is good to appear merciful, truthful, humane, sincere, and religious; it is good to be so in reality. But you must keep your mind so disposed that, in case of need, you can turn to the exact contrary." The Bastard shows us that the historical process is the working out of opportunistic thought, a reflection of minds "ready to shift as the winds of fortune and the varying circumstance of life may dictate."[14]

The Bastard thus prepares us to experience history as realistic or ironic drama. From France's betrayal of Arthur to the final frenzied scenes of the play in which King John and the nobles shift positions in relation to each other and to France in response to the grotesque assault of "occasion" (4.2.125), the moral and psychological patterns that we expect will unite the past with the present are belied by the experience of history itself. Although isolated and unexpected expressions of human integrity—Hubert's defiance of John and Melun's confession—momentarily reaffirm these expectations, circumstance, not principle, ultimately appears to determine the outcome of events.

Rather than look for continuity between the past, present, and future, we come to acknowledge that change is often governed by the unpredictable responses of opportunistic men to the shifting winds of circumstance. Our bewildered response to history as experienced is articulated in the Bastard's troubled reaction to the enigmatic death of Arthur:

> I am amaz'd, methinks, and lose my way
> Among the thorns and dangers of this world.
> How easy dost thou take all England up
> From forth this morsel of dead royalty!
> The life, the right, and truth of all this realm
> Is fled to heaven; and England now is left
> To tug and scramble, and to part by th' teeth
> The unowed interest of proud swelling state.
>
> (4.3.140–47)

We sense the peril evoked in the implicit image of history as a moral wilderness, and also, overwhelmed by what Shakespeare elsewhere calls the "revolution of the times" (2 *Henry IV* 3.1.46), we, with the Bastard, confess our inability to find our way. Events themselves prove unamenable to the patterns that would lend them significance or coherence.

In light, then, of the Bastard's role as an observer of events as they happen, along with his skepticism about historical interpretation and his realistic estimation of the historic process itself, how do we explain his final identification with the voice of the biased historian? Is he a demythologizer turned mythologizer? Certainly his prognostication of England's invincibility (5.7.110–18) cannot be unequivocally embraced by an audience that has shared the Bastard's present-oriented skepticism and witnessed the disparity between actual events and the meanings prospectively ascribed to them.

One might suggest that in juxtaposing a detached and engaged perspective, Shakespeare reiterates a tension that Bodin recognizes as an obstacle to a more objective historiography. Not only do bad men appropriate history for their own ends, but good men, in their moral zeal, often falsify the past: "The first attempts to embroider history occurred when it was thought fine to use an honorable lie for the praise of virtuous characters and the vituperation of evil."[15] Capable of skepticism and detachment, the Bastard is at once a man of integrity with a vision of what ought to be, an attachment to right, and a loyalty to his own country.[16] It is these commitments (or biases if you will) that emerge as the Bastard shifts roles. His statements about the past and future imitate the retrospective and prospective discourse we have come to identify with historicizing, and his passionate tones echo the emotional engagement of a partisan observer or court historian. Read as the words of a compatriot, his pronouncements, as Bodin would have recognized, describe not what is but what might be or should be. The prediction of English success is conditional—"If England to itself do rest but true" (118)—and represents that element of historicizing which cannot be regarded as fact.

The historiographic methodology of *King John* might well be summarized by briefly comparing it with the methodology of *Henry V.* In the final play of the second tetralogy Shakespeare creates an idealized perspective, retrospectively evoking the past through the lens of a partisan narrator who emplots that past as epic or romance. In *King John,* however, our perspective is that of a disengaged presenter who inductively examines the historical moment apart from the retrospective interpretations of the historiographer and who responds with a satiric emplotment that mocks both the historical process and the historiographic one. While the Chorus in *Henry V* allows us to transform historical deeds into the ceremonial history of the court historian,[17] instructing the auditor to "see" and "behold" the past through the selective eye of an idealizing imagination, the Bastard, witnessing events as immediate experience, comments on what he actually sees. In the light of this predominantly realistic perspective, the audience views with detachment any effort to impose a moral or teleological pattern on events, conscious that such patterns represent the efforts of participants (be they benign or self-serving) to control or refashion history. One might conclude, then, that in *King John* the parody of historiographic strategies like recall and prognostication, coupled with the play's focus on the immediate experience of the political world, reflects Shakespeare's consciousness of the disparity between history as objective fact and history as subjective reenactment of the past. In the politic world of *King John,* historiography becomes the handmaiden of commodity, supplying the legitimation that lends dignity and authority to political decisions dictated by the "tug and scramble" of expediency.

Notes

1. Wolfgang Clemen, "Past and Future in Shakespeare's Drama," *Proceedings of the British Academy* 52 (1966): 233.
2. Hayden White, "The Historical Text as Literary Artifact" in *The Writing of History: Literary Form and Historical Understanding*, ed. Robert H. Canary and Henry Kozicki (Madison: University of Wisconsin Press, 1978), 43–47. White argues that the historian perceives the past generically, "emplotting" it as tragedy, comedy, romance, or satire. In this essay I use White's term "emplotment" and its variants to refer to both this process and the historical artifact itself.
3. Robert Ornstein, *A Kingdom for a Stage*, 88.
4. David Scott Kastan, " 'To Set a Form Upon That Indigest,' " 4–5, 14–15.
5. In "Truth in *King John*," 401–2, 409, Robert C. Jones, discussing the Bastard's role as a fictional character who speaks for truth as fact as well as truth as right, notes that it is he who pursues the heroic role of avenging his father's death. Jones identifies the Bastard himself with the ideal historiographic icons of the first and second tetralogies. One might add, however, that while in the other plays the ideal is presented as chronicle history and associated with the historical past, in *King John* the fictions of history are recognized for what they are. Supplanting the conventional romantic emplotment of the past with a realistic one, Shakespeare demythologizes history. As Jones argues, the heroism dramatized by the avenging Bastard is a fictive event that not only has no counterpart in the record, but is contrary in its spirit and motivation to the actual events of history.
6. James R. Siemon, *Shakespearean Iconoclasm* (Berkeley and Los Angeles: University of California Press, 1985), 71–74. Siemon discusses the contrast between Sidney's iconic view of character as idea or exemplar and Montaigne's iconoclastic conception rooted in historical experience. Siemon argues that Montaigne, challenging poetic pattern, contends that the self is "shapeless and diverse" and defends this position by demonstrating that individual incidents in a man's life will support contradictory notions of his character. Circumstances, Montaigne concludes, shape behavior, and no single incident can be translated into a pattern or even be comprehended apart from its specific context.
7. For example, in *Henry VIII* Shakespeare juxtaposes the realistic and treacherous political milieu that gave birth to Elizabeth with Cranmer's famous prognostication. Invoking what Paul Hernadi has described as the "revisions of history by historiography" ("Re-presenting the Past: A Note on Narrative Historiography and Historical Drama," *History and Theory* 15 [1976]: 50), Shakespeare rehearses in the rhetoric of Biblical eschatology and pastoral nostalgia the idealization of Elizabeth's reign, interpreting the often tragic present of the play as the prologue to a golden age.
8. Jean Bodin, *Method for the Easy Comprehension of History*, tr. Beatrice Reynolds (New York: Columbia University Press, 1945), 51–54.
9. Bodin, *Method*, 43.
10. Bodin, *Method*, 42.
11. Niccolo Machiavelli, *The Prince*, trans. Robert M. Adams (New York: Norton, 1977), 44.

12. J. W. Allen, *A History of Political Thought in the Sixteenth Century* (London: Methuen, 1928), 469.

13. H. M. Richmond, *Shakespeare's Political Plays*, 106–7. Richmond notes the "Swiftian irony" of the Bastard's "proposal."

14. Machiavelli, *The Prince*, 50–51.

15. Bodin, *Method*, 43.

16. See R. Jones, "Truth in *King John*," 402. Jones observes that the Bastard becomes less the representative of the actual and more the spokesman for "what *ought* to be" as "the actual and the right . . . drift more hopelessly apart." One might suggest then that the closing commentary, moving beyond the realm of historical discourse into the realm of poetry, reiterates the tension between fiction and history personified by the Bastard. As Bacon argues in *The Advancement of Learning (The Advancement of Learning and New Atlantis*, ed. Arthur Johnston [Oxford: Clarendon Press, 1974], 81), poetry inspires by "submitting the show of things to the desires of the mind" rather than the testimony of reason which "doth buckle and bow the mind unto the nature of things."

17. Eamon Grennan, " 'This Story Shall the Good Man Teach His Son': *Henry V* and the Art of History," *Papers on Language and Literature* 15 (1979): 371–72.

2
King John and *The Troublesome Raigne*
A Reexamination

GUY HAMEL

THE COMPARISON OF SHAKESPEARE'S *KING JOHN* TO THE ANONYMOUS *The Troublesome Raigne of Iohn King of England* has been done so often that one should offer some justification for doing it again.[1] My reasons are both specific and general. The immediate cause is a recent note by Sidney Thomas supporting the "orthodox" opinion that *The Troublesome Raigne* precedes *King John*.[2] That claim now seems to me so strong as to need no further elaboration or support. One need no longer hedge or leave an escape route in assuming that *King John* derives ultimately from *The Troublesome Raigne*.

The larger justification for this study is the defense offered in Shakespearean criticism of the past few years for the independent authority of the separate versions represented by multiple-text plays.[3] I do not suggest that this essay is to be considered as a contribution to the debate (or paper war) between those who adhere to the notion of a definitive text and those who support the separate-but-equal status of differing versions. I do, however, trust that the new willingness to entertain the merit of inferior or even "bad" texts provides a climate of tolerance permitting an unprejudiced view of the maligned *The Troublesome Raigne*.[4]

Certainly, *The Troublesome Raigne* has been generally misprized. E. K. Chambers calls it a "terrible" play.[5] The bias introduced by the Shakespearean alternative has, one must feel, influenced the contempt for it expressed in the bardolotrous past: Edward Rose describes the play as "rude," as descending at its worst to "mere schoolboy doggerel"; in its anti-Romish spirit it is "violent and vulgar," in dialogue "rather dull, and lacking in variety and finish," and in construction

wanting "neatness and clearness."[6] Most recent opinion has hardly
been more generous. M. M. Reese, for example, is as strongly expressive as Rose: *The Troublesome Raigne's* "pasteboard characterization," its "meaningless iteration of defiance and lament" must have
struck Shakespeare, the prospective reviser, as "wearisomely unsubtle
and familiar."[7] But, if one sets it against the surviving historical plays
of the period, *The Troublesome Raigne* is a remarkably advanced work.
One need only read the chronicle accounts of the times of King John
and contemplate assembling the vicissitudes of his victories and de-
feats overseas and the confusing alternations of his wavering fortunes
at home into a sequence of dramatic events bearing some sense of
coherence to appreciate the craftsmanship of the playwright. As Simmons remarks, "Of the known contemporary dramatists, only Shakespeare and Marlowe show the structural powers for handling such
sprawling events from the chronicles."[8]

The striking novelty of *The Troublesome Raigne*, however, is the
invention of the Bastard, a character who, so far as it is possible to
determine, is created from slight and scattered hints in the chronicles.[9] As a parodistic figure the Bastard brilliantly mocks the dynastic
confusions attending the state of John Lackland. The appositeness of
the cases is, if anything, more strongly urged in *The Troublesome
Raigne* than in *King John*. The younger Faulconbridge insists on the
inviolate sanctity of the laws of succession:

> let *Fauconbridge* enioy
> The liuing that belongs to *Fauconbridge*,
> And let not him possess anothers right.[10]

The legal principle involved is different in each play. In *The Troublesome Raigne*, John states clearly that legitimacy is the issue. If
Philip, though the elder, is illegitimate, then "by *Englands* law" his
patrimony devolves upon his rightly born younger brother. In *King
John*, John cites a quite different rule. Marriage is the guarantor of
legitimacy. If a cow is impregnated by a neighbor's bull, the resulting
calf belongs to the farmer who owns the cow. In each play the issue is
settled by the same act of volition. Philip declares his bastardy. Doing
so in *The Troublesome Raigne* he conforms to a law that disinherits him.
The Bastard's repudiation of his estate in *King John* is more quixotic
and made in circumstances that weaken the precise parallelism between the Bastard and John. The principle that the cow-owner keeps
the calf makes the semblance of legitimacy—born in wedlock—a
consideration superior to the fact of illegitimacy—sired by a neighbor.
The shift seems related to a hardening of moral tone in *King John* and
to a reconsideration of the place of the Bastard that gives him more

independence as well as more prominence than he has in the earlier play. The point to make now, however, is the remarkable inventiveness that underlies the creation of such a character. A way to appreciate the achievement of the author of *The Troublesome Raigne* is to recognize that he fixes in the person of the Bastard the thematic elaboration, the dramatic expansion, and the energy conventionally provided by the comically reflective underplot of Tudor drama.

What is even more significant about the Bastard, however, is that he is contained within a context that is generically foreign. He belongs in historical romance. His place is in works like the Earl of Huntingdon plays. He is in his fictional kind the counterpart of Robin Hood; and the King John of his acquaintance should properly be the wicked fabular-figure of the Robin Hood tales. A principal consequence of the presence of "historical" characters in such plays—the Prince of Wales in *Friar Bacon and Friar Bungay*, King James and King Edward in *George a Greene*, and the like—is to authenticate the stuff of legend. By reversing the relation of figure and ground, the author of *The Troublesome Raigne* qualifies the formulaic security of romance. *King John*, as I shall argue later, exploits the possibilities of the generic doubleness, but the crucial accomplishment is achieved by *The Troublesome Raigne*. Indeed, the originality of *The Troublesome Raigne* is such that, despite the banalities and gross inadequacies of the play, it is difficult not to suspect that Shakespeare had a hand in it, at least in the plotting. No other of the possible candidates seems nearly so likely.[11]

As a revision of *The Troublesome Raigne, King John* shows "improvements" that are often enough direct and modest. Infelicities are removed. Hardly has Chatillion claimed in *The Troublesome Raigne* that John has no right to "the Kingdom of *England*" than he addresses him as "King of *England*" (1.1.45). The Chatillion of *King John* is guilty of no such imbecility. He speaks to "the borrowed Maiesty of England" (TLN 9; 1.1.4) and gives his addressee no title. One may also observe in *King John* a sort of dramatic common sense not always present in the earlier play. In *The Troublesome Raigne* Constance and Arthur are present throughout the negotiations that lead to the marriage of Lewis and Blanch. For the last forty-four lines of the scene, while the deal is effected, Constance is forced to keep an uncharacteristic and inexplicable silence. In the equivalent scene in *King John* she is absent, and the king of France remarks that it is a very good thing she is, "for this match made vp, / Her presence would haue interrupted much" (TLN 861–62; 2.1.541–42). Yet, concern for explicitness or mundane clarity seems to have been of no regard during revision. John in the opening scene of *The Troublesome Raigne* decides to meet the challenge of Philip by reinforcing his strongholds on the continent before the

French are prepared for him. To that end he privately advises Pembroke to conduct Chatillion to the coast, "But not in hast; for as we are aduisde, / We meane to be in *Fraunce* as soone as he" (1.1.62–63). In *King John* the king simply avers that, however quickly Chatillion returns to France, "ere thou canst report, I will be there" (TLN 30; 1.1.25). The explanation of ways and means is not the strong suit of *King John*.

The attempt to characterize the changes made to *The Troublesome Raigne* has led to judgments that are rather question-begging and critically suspect. May Mattsson speaks for many commentators when she describes Shakespeare's editorial function as "removing unessential, undramatic material."[12] Bullough emphasizes how much by his alterations Shakespeare "gained in economy" over his original.[13] As descriptive terms these are problematic. Even to demonstrate dramatic economy—presumably the achievement of an effect with a lesser expenditure of words and theatrical time—proves difficult. A claim might be made for Shakespeare's handling of a speech in which Pandulph denounces John. The condemnation is made in terms that evoke Counter-Reformation campaigns against Elizabeth. After the battle in which Lymoges is killed and Arthur captured, Pandulph promises "free pardon" to those who will undertake "holy warres" against the "English heretiques" (1.10.8, 15). In the altered version, Pandulph, who has exercised his antischismatic vocabulary earlier in the play, substitutes for the obligations of the faith in the assault against John a cynical assurance to Lewis that the expectations of *Realpolitik* favor his ambitions. John will find himself forced to murder Arthur and will by the deed lose the support of his countrymen. The echo of Elizabethan circumstances, however, is introduced by Philip's complaint, without parallel in *The Troublesome Raigne*, that "a whole Armado" of his forces has been "scattered" (TLN 1384–85; 3.4.2–3). Though the reference in *King John* is brief and oblique, its import is much the same as that of the long speech by Pandulph in *The Troublesome Raigne*.

A different sort of economy is gained by substituting for three messengers bearing one message each to the Dolphin in *The Troublesome Raigne* one messenger with three items of information to give. The results, however, represent something other than the saving of time and manpower. The circumstances are not quite identical. The messengers enter in *The Troublesome Raigne* to inform Lewis, respectively, that the English lords have abandoned him, that his fleet has been lost on Goodwin Sands, and that the English forces have been "ouerwhelmed" attempting to cross the Lincoln Washes. The messenger in *King John* has a somewhat different report:

> The Count *Meloone* is slaine: The English Lords
> By his perswasion, are againe falne off,
> And your supply, which you haue wish'd so long,
> Are cast away, and sunke on *Goodwin* sands.
>
> (TLN 2536–39; 5.5.10–13)

In one case Lewis is given a final item of welcome news to offset the first two reports. In *King John* all the news is bad. The audience's perception of Lewis's success is quite different in each play.

It seems to me altogether evident that these last examples represent the substitution of one dramatic effect for another and cannot be adequately judged according to such a criterion of "improvement" as "economy." One striking factor in these two accounts is the extent to which details are shuffled. The same information is given to the audience and the same things happen in both plays; but the terms and placing of presentation are crucially different. One more example—slight though it may be—is sufficient further illustration. The death of Queen Elinor is a datum in each play. We are told of the event in *The Troublesome Raigne* after the death of Arthur and the rebellious intentions of the English lords have been confirmed. The "distraught" king in a despairing catalog of his woes informs the Bastard that his mother, his "onely hope and comfort in distresse, / Is dead" (2.2.117–19). In *King John* the information is provided much earlier in the play. A messenger enters after the lords leave because they think Arthur is dead (although we know him to be still alive) and informs John that a French fleet is underway and that Elinor is dead. In the first case the information is given secondhand and corroborates a process of deteriorating fortune. In *King John* the news is news indeed to all, and it helps to initiate the train of events that brings about the king's downfall. The result of such alterations, petty in themselves though many may be, is to bring about a transformation of the original play.

The scene between Arthur and Hubert provides an especially telling illustration of the consequences of Shakespeare's adjustments to his original. The presentation in *The Troublesome Raigne* centers on the moral status of Hubert's commission. The debate between the two is formal, proceeding for some time in rhyming couplets shared between the two speakers. The matter is resolved by a decision of "conscience":

> My King commaunds, that warrant sets me free:
> But God forbids, and he commaundeth Kings.
>
> (1.12.122–23)

In *King John* the appeal is purely one of pity. Indeed, the pathos of Arthur's innocent words so moves Hubert that he decides to "be

sodaine, and dispatch" lest the boy "with his innocent prate . . .
awake my mercie" (TLN 1598–1600; 4.1.25–27). When Arthur reads
the warrant commanding that he be blinded, he asks simply, "Haue
you the heart?" Hubert, at the end of the debate, surrenders to the
appeal for mercy. There is a sharp, almost total, distinction between
the matter of "conscience" in *The Troublesome Raigne* and the matter
of the "heart" in *King John;* and each episode is shaped to emphasize
its central concern.[14] The opening of the scene in *The Troublesome
Raigne* is marked by irony. Hubert, in order to lure the prince within
reach of the accomplices who are to help in the blinding of Arthur,
invites the boy to leave the room in which he has been imprisoned and
"take the benefice of the faire euening" (1.12.13–14). Arthur expresses his gratitude: as one "to whom restraint is newly knowen" the
chance to get out is welcome, and he "would not loose the pleasure of
the eye" (16–19). By contrast, the opening section in *King John*
stresses the bonds of friendship that exist between prisoner and war-
der, bonds that render Hubert's task especially heinous. Shakespeare
sacrifices the irony that in *The Troublesome Raigne* produces an effect
of detachment: we are aware that Arthur's words have a sardonic other
meaning. The irony in the revised version is generated by Arthur's
innocent expression of affection for his prospective executioner: the
doubleness of those words is deeply sensed by Hubert, and our
attention is on the emotional tension of the exchange between the
speakers.

Shakespeare also adapts the imagery of the original to his new
treatment of the episode. Once he has decided to spare the prince,
Hubert in *The Troublesome Raigne* sets aside the instruments of blinding, saying, "Goe cursed tooles, your office is exempt" (125). Arthur
notes in *King John* that the coal and the hot iron have cooled as if they
"would not harme" him:

> All things that you should vse to do me wrong
> Deny their office: onely you do lacke
> That mercie, which fierce fire, and Iron extends.
> (TLN 1697–99; 4.1.117–19)

In *The Troublesome Raigne* the "office" of the instruments of torture
"is exempt" as a result of Hubert's moral decision to discard them.
There is little sense of the innate impropriety of the use to which they
were to be put. The emphasis is upon volition. In *King John* the denial
of "office" is treated as a sympathetic reaction of matter itself rebelling
against the misuse intended by Hubert; it precedes and justifies
Hubert's decision. Even iron has feeling. And one other very small

touch may suggest Shakespeare's concern for the separate integrity of his new version. Arthur's first line in the scene in *The Troublesome Raigne* is "Gramercie *Hubert* for thy care of me." Despite the stronger emphasis in *King John* on the prince's gratitude to his keeper, "gramercie" disappears. In the Shakespearean canon "gramercie" is used eight times, always in address to an inferior, usually a servant, or with condescension. It is removed from *King John* presumably because the implications of servility are inappropriate.

One cannot, however, build very far on the excision of one word. Shakespeare shows himself in general indifferent to the language of *The Troublesome Raigne.* Verbal echoes are very few; and they are represented mostly by the appearance of words in places altogether detached from the original context. In the first scene of *The Troublesome Raigne* the Bastard frightens his mother into admitting his true paternity by swearing to do to her "As cursed *Nero* with his mother did" (1.1.370). Very near the end of *King John* the Bastard addresses the rebel lords as "bloudy Nero's ripping vp the wombe / Of your deere Mother-England" (TLN 2406–07; 5.2.152–53). This occurrence, of course, need not be a remembrance from *The Troublesome Raigne;* but there are only four other references to Nero in Shakespeare's plays, and this sort of recollection of vocabulary does seem to happen elsewhere.[15]

Those terms that are picked up from *The Troublesome Raigne* may be guides to the informing concerns of *King John.* Early in *King John* Chatillion speaks of Arthur's claims to "this faire Island, and the Territories" (TLN 14; 1.1.10). The curious "Territories" is glossed by its use in *The Troublesome Raigne,* where it clearly means an adjunct or subordinate possession.[16] The distinction between England and the rest of the inheritance initially claimed by John proves to be crucial—to my mind, central to the "historical" character of the play—as John comes to be presented less as a Plantagenet claimant to part of his father's empire and more simply as King of England. The separateness—and the greater significance—of England is indistinct in *The Troublesome Raigne,* despite the references to the "Territories," but prominent in *King John,* where it is supported by such references, all unique, as that to "English *Iohn*" (TLN 303; 2.1.10) and by the Gaunt-like picture of England as a "Water-walled Bulwarke" (TLN 320; 2.1.27).

A second noteworthy extension of the language in *The Troublesome Raigne* is the reapplication of its images—though *King John* ignores the imagistic expression of its predecessor almost completely. When the adaptation is made, the consequences may be striking. Salisbury in *The Troublesome Raigne* greets the invading Lewis with these words:

Welcome the balme that closeth by [?up] our wounds,
The soueraigne medcine for our quick recure,
The anchor of our hope, the onely prop,
Whereon depends our liues, our lands, our weale,
Without the which, as sheepe without their heard,
(Except a shepheard winking at the wolfe)
We stray, we pine, we run to thousand harmes.

(2.3.188–94)

In *King John*, Salisbury has recourse to the same body of imagery:

I am not glad that such a sore of Time,
Should seeke a plaster by contemn'd reuolt
And heale the inueterate Canker of one wound,
By making many.

.   .   .   .

But such is the infection of the time,
That for the health and Physicke of our right,
We cannot deale but with the very hand
Of sterne Iniustice, and confused wrong.

(TLN 2263–66; 2271–74; 5.2.12–15; 20–23)

The speech in *The Troublesome Raigne* is puzzling because the extent of
the irony is uncertain. Salisbury seems honest in his respect for the
Dolphin of France as a balmy shepherd; but the notion that a foreign—especially French—prince may be the savior of the English
realm violates the deepest convictions of Elizabethan political doctrine. Salisbury is completely deluded. Yet the absolute nature of his
conviction and his naïve faith that a disease must have a remedy are
characteristic of the play. The Salisbury of *King John* knows very well
that the physic is wrong. The more he extends the imagery of disease,
the more clearly he betrays the error of his action in supporting the
invader. He bespeaks a world of confused moral direction.

Michael Manheim writes of the "unrelenting alteration of language"
that marks Shakespeare's adaptation of the earlier play. So thor-
oughgoing is the revision of *The Troublesome Raigne* that Shakespeare,
says Manheim, "not only improved *TR*; he nearly obliterated it."[17]
Amid the general obliteration there is, however, one major feature of
the original so thoroughly curtailed as to represent very nearly the
repudiation of a literary practice, a rejection that goes beyond a
preference for different words and images or an alternative style. *The
Troublesome Raigne* is in all sorts of ways devoted to ritualistic expression. Formulism is endemic. Messengers, ambassadors, and heralds, all such people, deliver themselves with a full reliance upon the
high terms of their office. Here, for example, is the Sheriff of North-
amptonshire (in part):

Please it your Maiestie these two brethren unnaturally falling at odds about their Fathers liuing haue broken your highnes peace, in seeking to right their own wrŏgs without cause of Law, or order of Iustice, and unlawfully assembled themselues in mutinous manner, hauing committed a riot, appealing from triall in their Countrey to your Highnes. (1.1.75–81)

The *King John* equivalent is the following from Essex (in full):

> My Liege, here is the strangest controuersie
> Come from the Country to be iudg'd by you
> That ere I heard: shall I produce the men?
>
> (TLN 51–53; 1.1.44–46)

A posturing and self-conscious rhetoric is almost the norm of expression in *The Troublesome Raigne*. The lines below represent Constance in rather moderate, though still representative, form:

> I trouble now the fountaine of thy youth,
> And make it moodie with my soles discourse,
> Goe in with me, reply not louely boy,
> We must obscure this mone with melodie,
> Least worser wrack ensue our malecontent.
>
> (1.4.230–34)

Granted, the occasion is emotional—the words are spoken to Arthur on the wedding day of Lewis and Blanch, a day that confirms the alliance that destroys her hopes to advance her own son—and the speaker is by nature excessive. Yet, the nearest equivalent in *King John* evinces a different poetic character:

> . . . thou art faire, and at thy birth (deere boy)
> Nature and Fortune ioyn'd to make thee great.
> Of Natures guifts, thou mayst with Lillies boast,
> And with the halfe-blowne Rose. But Fortune, oh,
> She is corrupted, chang'd, and wonne from thee,
> Sh'adulterates hourely with thine Vnkle *Iohn*,
> And with her golden hand hath pluckt on France
> To tread down faire respect of Soueraigntie,
> And made his Maiestie the bawd to theirs.
>
> (TLN 971–79; 3.1.51–59)

The difference is not only one of improved poetic and dramatic skill. The alliterative patterns of *The Troublesome Raigne* represent a dependence upon schemes that are less indexes of meaning and emotion than substitutes for them. The device signifies the effect; therefore the device is the effect. The complaint by the second Constance that Fortune capriciously mars what Nature has made good hardly represents novelty of thought. But her utterance is not doctrinal, it is personal. Moreover, it is linked to claims elsewhere in the play about the workings of Fortune, and it finds echoes in other instances that relate desert to personal appearance: the Bastard looks like Coeur de Lion; Hubert's "abhorr'd aspect" invites his employment as a villain; Arthur wishes to keep his eyes only to "look on" Hubert. Constance has more to say in *King John* than in *The Troublesome Raigne* and very little of it is restrained; but her passion escapes the confines of rhetorical models and therefore represents the singularity of her feeling, not the universality of the mode.

The repudiation of verbal formulas is brought explicitly into *King John* by the Bastard. Given to "a good blunt" directness himself, he is contemptuous of verbal excess. When the Citizen of Angiers defies the besieging armies with words of warlike bombast, the Bastard mocks his presumption.[18] Lewis's unprincipled declaration of love for Blanch in words reflecting the worst kind of courtly posturing receives a like condemnation. *The Troublesome Raigne* gives the Bastard no such lines.

The original versions of the two speeches ridiculed by the Bastard are not nearly so effusive as the parodies that replace them for the obvious reason that the conventions of expression in *The Troublesome Raigne* allow neither self-reflection nor much departure from a norm already rhetorically excessive. The introduction of the parody and the explicit repudiation of the style that the Bastard derides have two important implications. The first is that words are represented as both effective and deceptive. (The characters in *The Troublesome Raigne* realize that people lie, but their play provides no access through language to the identification of at least some of the liars. In *King John* we know that Lewis the wooer is lying.) The second development pointed to by the Bastard's literary criticism is that, simply by drawing stylistic distinctions, the play acknowledges its variety. With occasional exceptions the persons in *The Troublesome Raigne* adhere to the house style. *King John*—this is its most immediately evident literary advantage over its source—has fluent access to a range of modes. The consequences are not confined to the obvious merits that make *King John* a livelier, richer, and more interesting play. We have shifted from a fundamentally homogeneous context to one marked by variability. There is scope for a variety of voices and, consequently and eventually, for a variety of points of view.[19]

The theatrical equivalent of the purging of verbal forms is the rejection of ceremony. Even without comparing *King John* to *The Troublesome Raigne* one might notice that *King John* is unusually lacking in formal action for a history play. When one compares the work to *TheTroublesome Raigne* the difference is extremely telling, in part because the earlier work is highly ritualistic. *The Troublesome Raigne* begins with a solemnity absent from *King John*. The impression created by the first speeches of Elinor and John is that the king has just ascended the throne and is giving his first audience. Chatillion and the Sheriff express their business with a generous resort to the terms of their office. At almost every possible opportunity *The Troublesome Raigne* exhibits formality. In *King John*, when he appears in England for the first time, Lewis simply walks on stage with his allies. The matching scene in *The Troublesome Raigne* has the following:

> Messenger enter.
> *Penbrooke.* What newes Harrold.
> The right Christian Prince my Maister, *Lewes* of *Fraunce*, is at hand,
>   comming to visit your Honors, directed hetherby the right
>   honorable *Richard* Earle of *Bigot*, to conferre with your Honors.
> *Penbrooke.* How neere is his Highnesse,
> *Messenger.* Ready to enter your presence.
> Enter *Lewes*, Earle *Bigot*, with his troupe.
>
> (2.3.146–55)

This sort of thing goes on all the time. One reason that there are, as noted earlier, three messengers in *The Troublesome Raigne* where one serves in *King John* is likely the greater scope for formal business afforded by the separate entries and representations. Seldom does anyone get on stage in *The Troublesome Raigne* without being announced. Incidents of tableau-like solemnity abound. The English lords swear formally on the altar to serve Lewis; the French lords swear formally, placing their hands on the same altar, to kill the English traitors once John is overcome; the rebels kneel before the dying John with daggers in their hands to signal their devotion to him and to Prince Henry. *King John* is much more offhand in each of these instances: the first two, in fact, are merely reported.

The most important ceremony missing is, of course, the coronation. Comparing Shakespeare's treatment of the "long chaotic" scene in which John is crowned in *The Troublesome Raigne* to the companion piece in *King John*, Manheim remarks that "the coherence of the scene is of course greatly enhanced by its beginning after the crowning rather than before it." The events are, he says, "honed, compressed, tightened, unified, and poetically enriched."[20] Manheim's judgments of *The Troublesome Raigne* depend, properly enough, on the perspective afforded by *King John*. Yet, the coronation should not be so easily dismissed. One cannot know how elaborate the business on stage may have been, but it obviously involved more than clapping a coronet on

John's head. The fault of the ceremony is that it is too decisive. The king becomes, however suspect his motives for the second coronation, a consecrated being. How much stronger must be our reaction to seeing John surrender his crown and humbly sue to get it back from Pandulph when we have witnessed his assumption of regal dignity. Ritualistic events—and this one above all—tend to resolve the possibility of ambiguities. The coronation is not an event challenging the coherence of the scene in *The Troublesome Raigne;* it is the point of reference for all the other events.

The assault on ceremony is of a piece with the removal of verbal formulas because both represent in the earlier play an acceptance of reductive formulas. The king finds himself in *The Troublesome Raigne* perfectly comfortable with the design of romantic history. When he comes to adjudicate the Faulconbridge quarrel he resorts to a contrivance from folk stories: he devises an *ad hoc* ceremony requiring the mother and the older brother to swear thrice to Philip's legitimacy. Robert is understandably upset. It does seem unlikely that his mother will proclaim herself an adulteress or his brother declare himself a bastard. The scheme, of course, works. The play does not remain at this naïve level. Romance is circumscribed by the true happenings of history. Nevertheless, the folk element represents a factor from which *The Troublesome Raigne* never escapes and that *King John,* in its much more sophisticated understanding of its historical genre, must suppress. The devices of romance like the other formal presences of *The Troublesome Raigne* imply the controlling influence of convention. The difficult moral and historical issues of the play are given simplistic solutions that the formulaic structure of the presentation appears to validate:

> My King commaunds, that warrant sets me free:
> But God forbids, and he commaundeth Kings.
>
> (1.12.122–23)

> The Pope of Rome, tis he that is the cause.
>
> (2.2.158)

> Let *England* liue but true within it selfe,
> And all the world can never wrong her State.
>
> (2.9.45–46)

Such statements seem to have as much an ontological as a dramatic reference.

A third class of cancellation evident in *King John* concerns the details of exposition. The changes are especially prominent in the second part of the play—the scenes after John's return to England. Almost every detail in the narration is amended from the original. *The Troublesome Raigne*, especially in its account of the lords' rebellion and of John's dealings with Peter of Pomfret, is explicit and patiently reasonable about the order and timing of events and about the motives of the participants. Shakespeare's treatment of such details is cavalier. The version in *King John* manifests an impressive sense of "economy." The details suppressed may represent "unessential material," but not in terms of the ordinary laws of evidence. The reader who places the two plays side by side must conclude, I think, that for the author the elements obliterated were not merely expendable but inimical to the informing principles of the new play. It is probably true that the causality so carefully articulated in *The Troublesome Raigne*, satisfying as it may be to our affection for intelligible order, is unnecessary to dramatic presentation and may, in fact, obscure more important values. In *King John*, however, Shakespeare undermines rational explanation to such a degree as to call into question our ordinary faith in narrative exposition and our trust that events are knowable.[21]

Certainly, there is no reason to believe that the relative indifference to causality in *King John* means that Shakespeare is careless about the integrity of his play. The treatment of Hubert in these last episodes reveals, again, consistent differences in the issues that concern him. In both plays Hubert insists when the king blames him for Arthur's death that he had a "warrant" for his action. In *The Troublesome Raigne*, John replies in words that echo Arthur's successful argument against Hubert that the "seal," because it establishes their deliberate commitment to an evil intention, damns them both. The speech appears to confirm the validity of Arthur's position. After the king's seven-line comment in *The Troublesome Raigne*, Hubert reveals that he has not killed Arthur. The issue remains one of moral legality. Although the king in *King John* also avers that the seal will "witnesse against vs to damnation" (TLN 1943; 4.2.218), he accuses his accomplice of the ultimate guilt because Hubert's "abhorr'd aspect" invited villainy and because when the king "spake darkly" of his intentions Hubert did not interrupt but did "let [his] heart consent." The question is shifted, as it is in the scene with Arthur, to center on human relations and the promptings of the heart.

The added dimension of personal involvement is also extended in Hubert's next appearance. Hubert's attempt to persuade the lords that he is innocent of Arthur's death is both poignant and ironic in *The Troublesome Raigne*, but the episode is essentially self-contained. Hubert interrupts the lords as they mourn Arthur's death to assure them that he has spared the prince and that, if they rejoin the king, he will "conduct young Arthur streight" to them. They reject his claims of innocence, and he departs. In *King John*, Hubert's protestations that he is guiltless of the death of Arthur offer an important test of the Bastard's powers of judgment. His cynicism has been well enough instructed that he realizes Hubert may be lying, but he reserves a decision. The episode becomes for the Bastard emblematic of the "vast confusion" that permits at best qualified moral responses. Hubert, permitted to mourn the loss of "sweet breath" from the "beauteous clay" that was Arthur and to bear away the body, is allowed to express his last offices of affection and pity. The love that Arthur both invokes and prompts when he convinces Hubert to spare him is allowed a fitting extension.

Shakespeare's unwillingness to restrict himself to the narrow and almost legalistic conclusion given Hubert's dilemma in *The Troublesome Raigne* reflects his systematic suppression in *King John* of the comfort created by expressions that carry their own innate impetus towards resolution. His assault on formulas—on commonplaces and conventionalities, on presentation and representation, on ceremony and rite, on phrases and acts that breed their own termination, result, and pieties—reveals itself in almost every departure from *The Troublesome Raigne*. The coronation scene begins in *The Troublesome Raigne*, and only in *The Troublesome Raigne*, with John's boast of his security and success. (Indeed, a major reason for his second coronation is that the ceremony is to represent a "confirmation" of his triumph and to offer an outward "witnes" of the loyalty demonstrated by the lords towards their king and of the "Kingly care" of his subjects that John is consequently bound to express. Shakespeare, characteristically, neglects such explanations.) The dramatic presentation in *The Troublesome Raigne* intimates a medieval scheme of fall from prosperity. The author of the address "To the Gentlmen Readers" that prefaces the *Second part of the troublesome Raigne of King Iohn* appears to have such a view of matters. He reminds his readers that they last saw "Iohn repleate with blisse," but that none can withstand "the changeles purpose of determinde Fate." Such hints of limitation Shakespeare avoids. The suppression of the anti-Catholic business seems to me to answer to similar considerations. Certainly, a Bale-like John would be too simple for the play. Even in *The Troublesome Raigne* John's status as a prefigurement of Henry VIII is occasional and qualified. The objection to the antimonastic material is that it is in its way also restrictive. A number of suggestions have been made to explain why Shakespeare discarded the episodes with the monks and friars altogether: that they were too crude and antiquated; that he was of the old faith himself; that he could not afford to offend his patron, the Catholic Earl of Southampton. Such factors may, indeed, have had some force. But, certainly, one fault in material of this kind by the time of *King John* is its inflexibility. It is the stuff of burlesque, the matter of *fabliaux*. Even the scene in which the monk decides upon and plans the murder of the king cannot be presented seriously. The abbot, who overhears the monk, believes with farcical consequences that it is his own murder that is being contemplated. The antimonastic matter is generically confining in a play that as part of its strategy in establishing its own form appears to avoid even the incidentally schematic.[22]

The clearest entry into Shakespeare's altered concept of the play is to be made through the Bastard. He has his genesis in fable; and in *The Troublesome Raigne* as a *character* he never fully escapes the limiting conditions of his fictional context. The lines of the story are very clear, consistent, and satisfying. He discards the humdrum security of a yearly two thousand marks (raised in *King John* to "a faire fiue hundred pound a yeere") in favor of adventure and honor. He serves the lady Blanch in courtly fashion. He redeems Coeur de Lion's lion's skin from the craven Lymoges and offers his trophy to Blanch as a "Ladies fauour" and souvenir of his "first aduenture." Though Lymoges evades the Bastard's challenge to a duel, as John tells his kinsman, the "honors thine" from the exchange. Later, the Bastard slays his adversary, thus revenging the death of Coeur de Lion. In the last scenes he is John's faithful captain and the proper spokesman for the patriotic declaration that ends the play. In his second coming in *King John* the Bastard is not so romantic a figure. His chivalric identity, his courtly service, even his heroic actions are curtailed. Instead of actually fighting with Lymoges on stage and defeating him, the Bastard walks on stage carrying a property head and complaining that he needs to catch his breath. Freed from the restrictions of type, he is allowed to become a commentator on events and a guide for our judgments of them. He nevertheless remains, as Robert C. Jones emphasizes in his helpful essay on *King John*, a "fictive presence."[23] One result of that status is that he is limited in his scope of action. He cannot alter events that he was not actually able to influence in the first place. He cannot prevent the English forces from drowning in the Lincoln Washes. History governs fiction. The Bastard of *King John* has moved further into history than is the case with his romantic counterpart, and consequently in his double identity as "historical" and as fictional character he witnesses to the interchange of history and fable. On the one hand, fiction gives way to history. On the other, fiction provides what history lacks: form.

The Bastard in *King John* diverges steadily from his prototype until, near the end of the play, the two figures surprisingly coalesce. The rousing nationalistic appeal with which he closes the play is more eloquent than its matching piece in *The Troublesome Raigne*, but the import is the same. In *The Troublesome Raigne* the closing address is perfectly sufficient because there has been nothing in the play to challenge its simple affirmations. Indeed, the authority of declarative formality has been steadfastly advanced throughout the work. However, the adequacy of the Bastard's speech in ordering the closure of the more complex presentation of *King John* has been a central issue in the criticism of the play.

Some dislike the message and some the messenger. Burckhardt thinks that Shakespeare "saw no way to put Humpty Dumpty together again" and that "the orthodox sentiments at the end are *faute de mieux*."[24] Virginia Mason Vaughan expresses a similar judgment: "In the attempt to reach some sort of closure, Shakespeare withdraws from the tensions and reversals which animate the play and reimposes the standard formula of chronicle history."[25] Julia C. Van de Water finds the role assumed by the Bastard in the last part of *King John* incompatible with his character as it is initially established. The reason the Bastard has the last word is "simply that among the unprepossessing characters in this play there was no one else to whom Shakespeare could give his fine patriotic lines."[26]

More responsive to the play are those accounts of its conclusion that describe a link between the insufficiency of the Bastard and the limits of what it is possible to say. Alexander Leggatt concentrates on Shakespeare's use of the Bastard as "an unstable amalgam of participant and commentator" who at the close of the play becomes, as he is in the earlier scenes, "a point of reference" whose "primitive, amoral virtues" offer "the only way of living in a violent, chaotic world."[27] For Leggatt the limitation of the Bastard's judgment corresponds to the narrow scale of possibilities offered by the world depicted in the play. For Eamon Grennan the Bastard in his last speech paradoxically undermines the official patriotism he advances. Throughout, the Bastard has been the agent of Shakespeare's mocking of the assumptions of *historia*. By surrendering his position "in so blatant and inevitably problematic a way," the Bastard "sustains the critique he appears to have abandoned."[28] Jones connects the need to make sense of time with the conscious attempts of the character, once he is forced to abandon his role of "angry observer," to create right by asserting the only "fiction" that is serviceable.[29]

The study of what Shakespeare has done to *The Troublesome Raigne* corroborates the sense expressed by those quoted earlier of a conflict between the formal expectations of poesy (or of *historia*) and the disorderly confusions of experience. By undermining the steadfast causality of *The Troublesome Raigne,* Shakespeare so qualifies the principles to which the Bastard's last appeal makes implicit reference as to affirm nothing much more than our need for closure.

There is nothing to be observed about *King John* that cannot be known without recourse to *The Troublesome Raigne.* The comparison of the two plays does, however, give a greater prominence to those features that are most radically altered from the original. It is easy to see how much Shakespeare added. It is surprising to discover how much he was willing to sacrifice. Dropped are scenes that must have had popular appeal: "faire *Alice* the Nun" discovered in the abbot's treasure chest, for example, and the Bastard chasing the cowardly Lymoges around the stage and stripping him of his lion's skin. The first might be discarded without much care, but why the second? Such elements, presumably, could not be accommodated within the design of *this* history, though the Gadshill escapade and scenes of low-life clownage are acceptable in *1 Henry IV.* The indifference to motives and narrative detail that the source declares with considerable emphasis seems willfully negligent: it is one thing to inherit muddle and another to create it.

And yet the somberness that closes over the play precludes the larks with the comic monks and the buffoonery of the chase after Lymoges. *King John* opens with a marvelous display of energy and high spirits. The defiant John promises Chatillion that should he be "as lightning" in his return to France, the King of England will (by means unspecified) be there before him. The madcap Bastard throws away his inheritance preferring the "spirit of Plantagenet" to the worldly security of the Faulconbridge estate. But the adventures very soon turn sour for reasons all the more disturbing in that they are unclear and not easily avoided. What should John have done? Uncertainty becomes the prevailing condition of the play. Events assume the character they have when they are experienced within time—alms to entropy: confusing, discontinuous, arbitrary, and marked by an irony merely incidental. Arthur kills himself in a desperate attempt to escape the king's rancor when there is no longer any danger; John gets blamed for killing his nephew after he decides not to harm him. Conventional appeals to agencies outside time are pointless. The Providence that wrecks the French navy on the Goodwin Sands and drowns the English army in the Lincoln Washes seems to have difficulty deciding what side it is on. There are "historical" gains accomplished by John's reign. Prince Henry inherits an English crown free of the uncertainties of imperial ambitions and the impediments of doubtful right that marked his father's ascent to the throne. Only the very large perspective of all the histories is capable of recognizing the importance of that accomplishment. Lacking such vision, the Bastard does the best he can.

Notes

1. Writing in 1960, James L. Calderwood complains that critics have been so preoccupied with "the source problem of the play, especially . . . the relationship between *King John* and *The Troublesome Raigne*," that the character of the play "as a work of art in its own right has been largely ignored" ("Commodity and Honour in *King John*" in *Shakespeare: The Histories*, ed. Eugene M. Waith, 85). For extensive discussion of the relation between the two plays (hereafter in the notes generally referred to as *KJ* and *TR*), see especially the introductory matter in the Cambridge edition, ed. J. Dover Wilson, the New Arden edition, ed. E. A. J. Honigmann, and the New Penguin edition, ed. Robert Smallwood. See also Edward Rose, "Shakespeare as an Adapter," reprinted in the *TR* facsimile prepared by Charles Praetorius, v–xvii; Geoffrey Bullough, ed., *Narrative and Dramatic Sources of Shakespeare* 4:4–24; Virginia M. Carr, *The Drama As Propaganda*, 1–20; and J. L. Simmons, "Shakespeare's *King John* and Its Source," 53–72.

2. Sidney Thomas, " 'Enter a Sheriffe': Shakespeare's *King John* and *The Troublesome Raigne*," 98–100. Professor Thomas's note concerns the stage direction in the folio at line 50. The character introduced has no lines and no one is indicated as speaking to him. Thomas points out that the "Shrive" who enters at the corresponding place in *TR* is "an active speaker and participant in the action" of the play and that he identifies himself by name. Moreover, his presence is explained: the sheriff has quelled the "riot" caused by the quarreling brothers and has escorted them to court at their own request to be judged by the king rather than by "triall in their countrey." It is possible, as Thomas recognizes, that Shakespeare provided the nonspeaking sheriff as a means of bringing the fighting Faulconbridges on stage and that the author of *TR* expanded on the business. It is, however, very much likelier that the stage direction is vestigial and owes its presence to the *TR* original. Thomas's conclusion remains the most convincing explanation of the crux despite recent reconsiderations of his argument. See E. A. J. Honigmann, "*King John, The Troublsome Reign*, and 'documentary links,' " 124–26; Paul Werstine, " 'Enter a Sheriffe' and the Conjuring up of Ghosts," 126–30; and Thomas, " 'Enter a Sheriffe': A Shakespearean Ghost," 130.

3. The (battle?) ground of the newest bibliography has been *King Lear*. As early as 1976, Michael J. Warren concluded from his study of Q and F that these are "separate versions of *King Lear*, and that eclecticism cannot be a valid principle in deciding readings." (See "Quarto and Folio *King Lear* and the Interpretation of Albany and Edgar," in David Bevington and Jay L. Halio, eds., *Shakespeare Pattern of Excelling Nature* [Newark: University of Delaware Press, 1978], 105.) The consequences of the anticonflation movement are exploited at large in Gary Taylor and Michael J. Warren, eds., *The Division of the Kingdom: Shakespeare's Two Versions of "King Lear"* (Oxford: Clarendon Press, 1983). See also Steven Urkowitz, *Shakespeare's Revision of "King Lear"* (Princeton: Princeton University Press, 1980). It would be inappropriate to try to provide here a readers' guide to all the documents in a substantial and controversial field of study. My purpose in invoking the approach represented in the texts I have named is to gain the advantage of treating the *TR* as if it were a quarto antecedent to the folio *KJ*.

4. Two of the most influential defenders of the opinion that *TR* must be derivative rather than original show themselves influenced by their low regard for the play. For Peter Alexander it is "difficult to understand" that, if *TR* is the source of *KJ*, it should be artful enough in its structure to be copied by Shakespeare and "yet show so little corresponding modesty or cunning in its writing" (*Shakespeare's Life and Art* [London: James Nisbet, 1939], 85). It is easier to believe that the author of *TR* duplicated the events, which were easy enough to follow, but lacked the wit to match the language. Honigmann argues that the *TR* "features some recognized 'bad quarto' characteristics, being (i) a tissue of stolen phrases; (ii) a text much more untidy than 'foul paper plays' usually are, which, moreover, contains summarizing and descriptive directions" (New Arden *KJ*, lvii). The mere existence of "bad quartos" as a category has had an influence on the assessment of *TR* according to that law by which a hypothesis creates evidence. Dover Wilson admits that his own claim for the "priority of the inferior text" is challenged by Pollard's recognition of "bad quartos" as "a special class by themselves" (Cambridge *KJ*, xix–xx). The opinion that *TR* is a "bad quarto" version of a play by Shakespeare of which *KJ* is the good version is advanced by E. M. W. Tillyard, *Shakespeare's History Plays*, 217.

5. E. K. Chambers, *William Shakespeare*, Vol. 1 (Oxford: Clarendon Press, 1930), 367.

6. Rose, "Shakespeare as an Adapter" in Praetorius, vi–viii.

7. M. M. Reese, *The Cease of Majesty*, 262. The author of *TR* is, however, praised by Simmons ("Shakespeare's *King John*") and by John Elson, who remarks upon his "skill as a plotter" and his "creative power" in the "depiction of the Bastard's magnetic personality" ("Studies in the King John Plays," 185).

8. Simmons, "Shakespeare's *King John*," 54.

9. A list of the possible antecedents for the Bastard is provided by Dover Wilson, Cambridge *KJ*, xxxix–xli. The character, Wilson concludes, "appears to be compounded of most of the valiant bastards in English history" (xli). See also Honigmann, New Arden *KJ*, xxii–xxv.

10. *TR* 1.1.127–29. Quotations are taken from the Praetorius facsimile edition of *The Troublsome Raigne*. For the quotations from *King John* I have provided both the through-line number (TLN) assigned in Charlton Hinman's *Norton Facsimile of the First Folio* (New York: Norton, 1968) as well as a reference to the *Riverside Shakespeare*.

11. None of the attributions that have been made carries much conviction. See the summaries of the candidates in Dover Wilson, Cambridge *KJ*, xviii–xx and Bullough, ed., *Sources* 4:4. Sigurd Burckhardt notes incidentally that he is drawn to the possibility, advanced by Courthope in 1916, that Shakespeare is the author of *TR*. Burckhardt is reluctant, as I am, to insist upon a claim so open to dispute and, anyway, ancillary to the argument of his essay as to mine (*Shakespearean Meanings*, 118 n. 1). I raise the unprofitable question of authorship because one's willingness to entertain the possibility of a Shakespearean influence on *TR* is related to the estimation one has of its quality. Burckhardt finds in *TR* the "decisive question" concerning the doctrine of degree that becomes the center of the reworked version (125). For Wilson, Courthope's bizarre suggestion of Shakespeare's authorship of *TR* is "one of the curiosities of criticism" (xix).

12. May Mattsson, *Five Plays about King John*, 8.

13. Bullough, *Sources* 4:20.

14. The scene is discussed at length by Burckhardt. He emphasizes that Arthur in *KJ* "never once employs the argument of higher authority and more terrible sanc-

tions" (*Shakespearean Meanings*, 121). For Burckhardt the switch to an appeal based on compassion signals Shakespeare's desire to make *KJ* a critique rather than a confirmation of Tudor doctrines of authority.

15. Another possibly reshuffled word is the epithet "dunghill" which Bigot addresses to Hubert. Reese takes the term to indicate that the lords "are plainly influenced by aristocratic dislike of the low-born Hubert" (*Cease of Majesty*, 276). However, in *TR* the Bastard addresses Lymoges as a "dunghill swad" (1.2.140), and the Duke of Austria, however base his conduct, is hardly baseborn.

16. At 1.2.2 Philip refers to Arthur's title to the "*Albion* Territories," an expression which seems in the context to mean the continental parts of the Angevin inheritance. Much later in the play the rebellious nobles are asked to swear allegiance to Lewis "as true and rightfull King to *England, Cornwall* and *Wales,* & to their Territories" (2.3.221–23).

17. Michael Manheim, *The Weak King Dilemma in the Shakespearean History Play,* 130.

18. TLN 761–70; 2.1.446–55. I find no sufficient reason for believing that the spokesman for the people of Angiers is Hubert. That the use of his name was brought about by confusion over doubled parts seems likelier than that the one character who becomes the active Hubert of the second half of the play begins his career as the Citizen of Angiers. Manheim's construction of a duplicitous Hubert whose mask of neutrality as representative of Angiers conceals a Machiavellian design to trick the French into accepting John's right to rule in England asks a lot of the evidence. See Manheim, *The Weak King Dilemma,* 147–50.

19. The old style of *TR* is not so thoroughly "obliterated" that no trace remains in *KJ*. It is a testament to the stylistic breadth of *KJ* that the old-fashioned formulaic writing can be resurrected—and to good effect. After Philip of France at Pandulph's entreaty abandons John, there is the following exchange:

> *Constance.* O faire returne of banish'd Maiestie.
> *Elinor.* O foule reuolt of French inconstancy.
>
> (TLN 1254–55; 3.1.321–22)

So the two might have expressed themselves in *TR* (although they do not). These are the last words that they speak in each other's presence, whereas in *TR* they have rather extended "brawles," as Arthur calls them, later. The couplet of *KJ* links the two women, the most bitter and perhaps the ultimate antagonists of the play. Shakespeare brings the two together again when the Messenger reports that they have died within three days of each other. *TR* gives us no last word on Constance. Shakespeare's scheme is satisfyingly neat; and his modest couplet in an old style has its satisfying place in the scheme.

20. Manheim, *The Weak King Dilemma,* 137.

21. Robert Ornstein comments at some length on the loss of clarity in *King John.* He writes: "Although one cannot anticipate from one scene to the next which way the action of *The Troublesome Reign* will turn, the plot is lucid at every moment. One understands precisely why John does what he does, because his motives and intentions are always made explicit. . . . We cannot say that for reasons of dramatic economy Shakespeare was compelled to omit essential information about John's motives, because not many additional passages would have been needed to elucidate John's behavior and anticipate his plans. Two or three dozen lines added at the proper places in the dialogue would have dissolved the opacity of crucial scenes and lent fluidity to the plot" (*A Kingdom for a Stage,* 90). There is, for Ornstein, who regards *King John* as a deeply flawed work affected by Shakespeare's "boredom with the

assignment" of revising an old play, no particular purpose in the changes: "My impression is that Shakespeare was careless rather than obtuse" (99). Carelessness and obtuseness are not, of course, the only possibilities. The narrative system of *TR*, which stresses the intelligibility of plot and motive, seems to me replaced by a dramatic system, which implies the limitation of full understanding that characterizes real experience.

22. Simmons takes the view that the "Protestant cause" as it is presented in *TR* is "extraneous and jarring" because it has little bearing on the "genuine moral conflicts—the one between the king's and the rebel forces and the one within John himself" ("Shakespeare's *King John*," 57). It was a mistake "to let John's defiance of the Pope represent an absolute spiritual value. . . . The structure and moral effect of *TR* clearly became incoherent as a result of the author's use of the Protestant cause as an absolute appeal, and Shakespeare carefully avoided it" (58).

23. Robert C. Jones, "Truth in *King John*," 397.
24. Burckhardt, *Shakespearean Meanings*, 134, 140–41.
25. Virginia Mason Vaughan, "Between Tetralogies," 419.
26. Julia C. Van de Water, "The Bastard in *King John*," 146.
27. Alexander Leggatt, "Dramatic Perspective in *King John*," 15–16.
28. Eamon Grennan, "Shakespeare's Satirical History," 31.
29. R. C. Jones, "Truth in *King John*," 417.

3

King John

A Study in Subversion and Containment

VIRGINIA M. VAUGHAN

ALONE AMONG SHAKESPEARE'S ENGLISH HISTORIES, KING JOHN portrays the early Plantagenet rule when England was feudal, its governors and culture Anglo-Norman rather than distinctively English. If, as Graham Holderness has recently argued, the Henriad depicts Shakespeare's sophisticated understanding of the fourteenth/fifteenth-century decline of feudal society,[1] surely *King John* is even more remarkable, for it reveals the dramatist's awareness of conflict between collective identities and the individual, between centralized royal authority and independent nobles, and between Church and State—conflicts that were inherent in the feudal system from its inception. Like Shakespeare's other history plays, *King John* depicts what Alessandro Serpieri describes as "the great structural and epistemological crisis that occurred between the sixteenth and seventeenth centuries, a crisis that can be summarized as the conflict between a *symbolic model* of the world (a classical-medieval-Renaissance heritage) and a *syntagmatic model* of the world, inaugurating the relativism of the modern age."[2]

King John demonstrates, perhaps even more than the Henriad, Shakespeare's understanding of English history. Close examination of the written text shows that Shakespeare knew the distinction between the feudal law of the early thirteenth century and the Tudor statutes of his own day. From the beginning he takes pains to set the play in the context of John's reign. At the same time, he deliberately interjects anachronistic elements that manipulate the temporal relationship between present and past, confronting the audience with both at the same time. The result is Brecht's "alienation effect";[3] these anachronisms remind the audience that it is watching a reenactment of history, an awareness that is reinforced by references to "playing" in the text. The result is dual perspective. Moreover, as John R. Elliott has shown, Shakespeare exploited both the villainous medieval John and the sixteenth-century proto-Protestant John to craft a complex and ambiguous hero.[4]

King John is not the mirror of Elizabethan policy that Lily B. Campbell described in 1947;[5] it is not a strict didactic representation of Tudor ideology. Its confrontation of two time frames, medieval and Renaissance, however, does mirror England in the 1590s—at a crucial transition from the last vestiges of a medieval/feudal system to the modern age of individualism.

Shakespeare's *King John* is notable in its rejection of received tradition. The audience who came to see it in the 1590s had its own sense of a mythical King John, a text inherited from sixteenth-century polemical writers. In drafting *John,* the playwright explored materials from Holinshed and various chroniclers. But he also played against this inherited text. From Tyndale forward, John's reign had been seized as an exemplum of what papal intervention would do to England. Throughout the sixteenth century, Tudor ideology transformed John into a Protestant martyr who defied the pope and was assassinated by a priest but whose struggle forecast England's independent Protestant identity. Elliott summarized the received sixteenth-century image of John:

> John became firmly identified with a set of religious-political doctrines that were at the heart of official Tudor policy: hatred of the Pope, obedience to the King, resistance to foreign intervention, and intolerance of all forms of civil dissension. Indeed, John became the standard symbol for English Protestant writers of the patriot-martyr.[6]

Tyndale's *Obedience of a Christen Man,* first printed in 1528, cited John as an example of how papists are "all wayes both rebellious and disobediente to the Kynges." In John's reign, argued Tyndale, the legate of Rome absolved all the lords of the realm from their obedience to the king. "Wolde he not have cursed the kynge with his solemne pompe, because he wolde have done that office which God commaundeth every kynge to doo and wherfore God hath put the swerde in every kynges hande?"[7] Tyndale saw John's reign as proof of the incompatible demands of Church and State, especially when the Church sought universal hegemony. Tyndale, like other Tudor apologists, saw the solution to this conflict in royal supremacy. If the king were head of the Church, there could be no conflict between Church and State.

John Bale also used King John as a vehicle for Protestant propa-

ganda in 1538–39. Bale's *Kyng Johan* is the hero of a homiletic
morality play and a forerunner of Henry VIII: John fails to wrest his
kingdom from papal intervention, where Henry would prevail. Less
well known is Foxe's inclusion of John in his *Boke of Martyrs*. In an
account reprinted verbatim in Grafton's *Chronicles,* Foxe praised John
for his defiance of Pope Innocent III and graphically described John's
death by poisoning at Swinstead Abbey.

John also served as a textbook example of the evils of civil disorder
in the *Homilie Against Disobedience and Wylful Rebellion* (1571), propaganda issued by the State to be read in parish churches. The sixth
homily describes the events of John's reign as a warning of what might
happen to Elizabeth if Catholic conspiracies were not suppressed.
Then, as in 1571, the pope had discharged citizens of their oath of
obedience if they would proceed against the rebellious monarch. The
Homilie exhorts:

> Nowe had Englishmen at that tyme knowen their duetie to their prince set
> foorth in Gods worde, would a great manye of the nobles and other
> Englishmen, naturall subjectes, for this forraigne and unnaturall usurper
> his vayne curse of the kyng, and for his fayned discharging of them of their
> othe of fidelitie to their naturall Lorde, uppon so sclender or no grounde at
> al, have rebelled against their soveraine Lorde the King . . . woulde they
> being Englishmen have procured so great shedding of English blood, and
> other infinite mischeefes and miseries unto Englande their naturall coun-
> trey, as dyd folowe those cruell warres and trayterous rebellion, the fruites
> of the Bishop of Romes blessinges?[8]

In the official Tudor reconstruction of history, it is clear who was at
fault. If the nobles had known their duty, they would have obeyed
their king, just as Elizabeth's subjects should resist the pope and obey
her. Tudor ideology chooses royal authority over the English lords: it
appropriates the entirely different circumstances of John's reign and
reinterprets them to support the Tudor doctrine of royal supremacy.
Magna Charta is ignored.

Anthony Munday continued to use John as an exemplum in his
frantic pre-Armada diatribe, *A Watch-woord to England* (London,
1584). For John, as for Elizabeth, the pope was the enemy who
attempted to deprive Englishmen of their rights. Papal abuses included

> the accursing of king *John;* the receiving him vassaill: the making his
> Realme subject and feudatorie to the Pope: the arming his Subjectes
> against him: the poysoning of him at length: the giving the Land to the
> French Kinges sonne; the invading thereof by the *Dolphin* of *Fraunce:* his
> so long possessing a great part of it; the rebellion of the Barons to take the

French mens part: all the mischeefes that fell in all this while, were they not the good workes of Popes and Papistes.[9]

John had seen the Church for what it was. His failure to separate from it had cost England her rights; failure to support Elizabeth's government could cost Tudor Englishmen their rights.

Munday's anti-Spanish, anti-papal polemic catered to fears of a Catholic uprising in favor of Mary, Queen of Scots, then prisoner in England. By the time the anonymous *The Troublesome Raigne of Iohn King of England* was written, however, she was no longer a threat.[10] Her death made it easier for *The Troublesome Raigne's* author to capitalize on the similarities with John's reign and emphasize Arthur's (implying Mary's) competing claim to the throne and subsequent death. *The Troublesome Raigne's* author also continued the tradition of Tyndale, Foxe, and the *Homilie* by making John's reign a vehicle for Tudor/Protestant ideology. *The Troublesome Raigne* is virulently anti-Catholic and anti-Spain. If we assume that this polemical play was Shakespeare's chief source for his own version of *King John*, the result is a fascinating study in intertextuality. For in deconstructing *The Troublesome Raigne* and reconstructing the events of John's reign into a new drama, Shakespeare subverted much of the Tudor ideology embedded in the original. What had been unified and didactic in *The Troublesome Raigne* became fragmented. In 1944 Tillyard criticized *King John* for its lack of unity; the play could not be read as a reflection of Elizabethan doctrine.[11] In the play's major episodes, subversive threads unbalance the precarious order of John's rule and contradict maxims of Tudor ideology—particularly royal supremacy, the legitimacy bestowed by patrilineal inheritance, and the validity of religious authority. No wonder Tillyard found Shakespeare's play to be thematically inconsistent.

Regardless of what they think of the priority issue, most critics agree that *King John* makes much more of John's illegitimacy than does *The Troublesome Raigne*.[12] Chatillion's opening speeches that question John's "borrowed majesty" are echoed in Elinor's disclaimer, "Your strong possession much more than your right" (1.1.40). If John's mother's conscience doubts his claim, then his legitimacy is also doubtful to the spectator. Moreover, Elinor's remark raises the central issue of kingship from the reign of William the Conqueror down to Elizabeth: what is the distinction between right and possession? After he had won England by conquest, William made a feeble hereditary claim. Elizabeth's grandfather, Henry Tudor, spent a prodigious amount on chroniclers to prove—even fabricate—his own genealogy.

Once one had safe possession, one could then worry about lineal inheritance. Elinor clearly knows what the future Elizabeth would likewise come to believe.

Once patriarchal inheritance is subverted in the macrocosm, it falls apart in the private sphere. We see this when a country gentleman comes to court to receive royal judgment. As we know and Shakespeare may have known, John was the last king able to make such judgments, for Magna Charta reserved this right to the Court of Common Pleas. The Faulconbridge episode, in other words, is clearly historical, placed in the past by Shakespeare. It shows John as feudal king, intimately involved in the lives of his subjects. But as feudal king and judge, John can only make a judgment that subverts his own claim to inherit. By strict feudal law, the eldest son inherits: wills are irrelevant. (This would make Arthur true king of England.) Who, however, can attest to the legitimacy of the eldest son? As Phyllis Rackin wisely observes, the quarrel between Philip and Robert Faulconbridge, "like the quarrel between Arthur and John over the English throne, hinges on ambiguities and ruptures in the relationship between legal and biological inheritance."[13] The quarrel shows inconsistencies in feudal law that existed from the Norman conquest. In arbitrating this dispute, John admits that the relationship between father and son, which can only be validated by the mother's fidelity, must be a legal fiction. Whether Philip is a bastard or not—only his mother knows for sure—is irrelevant. He is the legal heir. Thus women, who otherwise have no power in the patriarchal scheme of things, can by infidelity subvert the entire process.

In lines not derived from *The Troublesome Raigne*, Robert asks a legalistic question:

> Shall then my father's will be of no force
> To dispossess that child which is not his?
>
> (1.1.130–31)

Akin to the disputed will of Richard Coeur de Lion, the elder Faulconbridge's will has no force of law. Here Shakespeare reproduces, as Arden editor E. A. J. Honigmann notes, feudal law as it existed in John's reign. Only with legal statutes passed under Henry VIII could a will disinherit a lineal heir. (A most intriguing fact, given the nature of Henry VIII's will and his decision to leave the throne to his two bastardized daughters if Edward VI died without issue.) Under feudal law, Robert's cause is lost.

Whatever the legal complications of this dispute, biological reality wins out. Philip, who looks more like Coeur de Lion than a Faulconbridge, is given the right to choose. He can select patrilineal inheritance, maintain his land, and receive £500 a year. Or, he can become a soldier of fortune, disclaim his inheritance, and follow Elinor. In *King John* there is no trance that forces Philip into accepting the truth as there is in *The Troublesome Raigne.* Instead, the Bastard freely chooses between two carefully delineated options. He rejects his feudal inheritance and the land that was the ultimate source of feudal power to become a "landless man." He is motivated by more than Elinor's blandishments—he wants to determine his own identity. In risking his future, he resembles the Elizabethan adventurers who sought fortunes through profiteering and royal largesse. When he changes his name to Sir Richard Plantagenet, he is henceforth indebted to the crown for status and material wealth and therefore less able to resist royal authority. (The nobles who have their own land and, thereby, power, can more freely go their own way.) Moreover, the Bastard associates himself with a court that, like Elizabeth's, imposes a facade of chivalry on Renaissance *Realpolitik.*

When the Bastard chooses to be a Renaissance individualist, he becomes by definition a marginal figure, outside the collective identities of church, court, and family. His bastardy marks him as an outsider who can comment on courtly society but never feel completely at home in it. He sees the court as fertile territory for his "mounting spirit," a place where he can rise in power, wealth, and status and exercise "his unfailing ear for pretense and pomposity."[14] His comments to his mother are a final inversion of medieval expectations; he substitutes what had been deemed a sin, her infidelity, for the sin of refusing Richard the Lion-hearted. He absolves her, and himself, of any blame.

The public and private halves of act 1, scene 1 establish the central conflict of the play: who has the right of inheritance? If patrilineality is at best a convenient legal fiction designed to ensure continuity, how can we determine who is the rightful king? And if mothers are the particular keepers of legitimacy, what can we do when two mothers— Elinor and Constance—each maintains that her son is the legitimate heir?

These questions are emblematically portrayed in the frustrating impasse before Angiers where "rights" are modified according to the changing winds of political expediency. The guarantors of lineal right—the women who attest to male legitimacy—are powerless without armies behind them. Without Philip on her side, Constance has only rhetoric to support her cause. The women have identity only in their relationships to men, as wives or mothers. The one woman who has a hereditary claim (once Arthur is dead) does not pursue it for herself. Rather, Blanch's claim becomes a pretext for Lewis to seize power in her name. Or, as Elizabeth knew and Mary Stuart did not, to exercise power in her own right a medieval/Renaissance woman must have no husband and no son. Nonetheless, women have strong voices in the middle sections of *King John*. Their subversive plaints raise nagging doubts as to whether we can ever discern the "rightful" ruler. Hereditary "right" becomes an even more absurd legal fiction, for it inspires the deaths of thousands.

Angiers also muddies the distinctions between spectator and performer, between Shakespeare's Elizabethan audience and the roles of medieval kings played by his actors. Though John mentions his anachronistic cannons in act 1, here they are repeatedly mentioned by both armies.[15] Is this just an accident, or is Shakespeare reminding us that the setting isn't really medieval France? The English troops are not a medieval army. They are described in terms that can only apply to Elizabeth's own soldiers of fortune:

> all th' unsettled humors of the land,
> Rash, inconsiderate, fiery voluntaries,
> With ladies' faces and fierce dragons' spleens,
> Have sold their fortunes at their native homes,
> Bearing their birthrights proudly on their backs,
> To make a hazard of new fortunes here.
>
> (2.1.66–71)

The confusion of actor and audience is underlined before the gates of Angiers, where scaffolding on the battlements is really scaffolding in the theater, and citizens in the audience stand as citizens of Angiers:

> As in a theatre, whence they gape and point
> At your industrious scenes and acts of death.
>
> (2.1.375–76)

History itself is a pageant enacting industrious scenes of death.

The citizens of Angiers are asked, as is Shakespeare's audience, to choose the rightful king: Arthur, represented by the French, or John, represented by the English. In Elizabethan England they would have no doubt. But in the Angevin period distinctions between French and English were not so simple. The citizens' fealty is owed to the rightful monarch; in return for fealty they are to receive protection—the *quid pro quo* of feudal law.

The stalemate ends with the Bastard's *Realpolitik* proposal that French and English forces combine to blow the town apart. Fealty no longer matters. Angiers responds by using the discourse of courtly love to ritualize and thereby resolve the power struggle. As often occurred in Elizabeth's court, art transforms a tug-of-war into a mating dance. The Citizen of Angiers describes Blanch in the perfect rhetorical blazon:

> If lusty love should go in quest of beauty,
> Where should he find it fairer than in Blanch?
> If zealous love should go in search of virtue,
> Where should he find it purer than in Blanch?
> If love ambitious sought a match of birth,
> Whose veins bound richer blood than Lady Blanch?
> Such as she is, in beauty, virtue, birth,
> Is the young Dolphin every way complete:
> If not complete of, say he is not she,
> And she again wants nothing, to name want,
> If want it be not that she is not he.
> He is the half part of a blessed man,
> Left to be finished by such as she,
> And she a fair divided excellence,
> Whose fullness of perfection lies in him.
>
> (2.1.426–40)

He urges the Renaissance, Neoplatonic ideal of perfect sexual union, in which opposites complete each other. Thus the discourse of Renaissance love poetry patches up a convenient political alliance, just as the Neoplatonic ideal of Gloriana kept a court and country united.

As the Bastard observes, this citizen "gives the bastinado with his tongue." John and Philip are won not by words but by political expedience. Blanch is bargained off for five French provinces and 30,000 marks. Arthur is to be pacified with a Dukedom.

This cynical arrangement cannot contain the unruly emotions expressed in Constance's stylized grief. Her unbound tresses visually emphasize her passionate struggle against the restraints of patriarchy.[16] She is the reverse of Lady Faulconbridge in that she knows her son's legitimacy. Yet like Lady Faulconbridge, she has no legal power to establish that legitimacy. Her political strength is in Philip's army.

The Bastard remarks this shift "From a resolv'd and honorable war / To a most base and vile-concluded peace" (2.1.585–86) but chalks it up to "Commodity." This peace, though expedient for both sides, is doomed. Pandulph's entrance introduces, then subverts, the other major collective source of power in feudal Europe: the Church.

Shakespeare's treatment of the third estate is far less specific than *The Troublesome Raigne's.* The earlier play portrays John as the warlike Christian fighting against the financial and sexual abuses of a hopelessly corrupt Roman Catholic hegemony. Shakespeare's discourse is far less inflammatory. John does declare himself "supreme head" and charges that "no Italian priest / Shall tithe or toll in our dominions" (3.1.153–54). But Shakespeare's text includes no abbey-looting scene; John's death by poison is mentioned only in passing; and he has no dying prophecy beatifying Henry VIII. *King John* is politics, not polemics.

John's resolve reflects Renaissance individualism. He asserts, "Yet I alone, alone do me oppose / Against the Pope, and count his friends my foes" (3.1.170–71). Pandulph, in turn, takes a medieval view of the Church's wholeness. Even so, his cynical use of excommunication for political purposes undercuts the Church's collective ideal. The Crusades, for example, were partly inspired by a vision of gaining the Holy Sepulchre for Christendom, but inspired also by the need for a common enemy for Europe's newly Christianized warrior bands.[17] The crusades were to be a collective enterprise. Pandulph's use of excommunication to make France fight when and where he wants shows the pitfalls of such policy. Lewis refuses to be a puppet to the Church and desists only when he loses English support.

Pandulph is the only representative of the Church in the play. (*The Troublesome Raigne* contains fornicating priests and nuns, a monk who poisons John, and an abbot who absolves the murderer.) His main concern is political power. When John submits to the pope, Pandulph gladly cancels the excommunication and becomes a peacemaker. The conflict between Pandulph and John in *King John* is thus not a conflict between Catholic and Protestant. It is a struggle between Church and State for control—the same struggle that led to civil war in the seventeenth century. By lessening the anti-papal discourse of his predecessors, Shakespeare stresses the venality of the established church, whether Catholic or Protestant. It is the power to delegitimize John's rule and just as suddenly relegitimize it rather than particular religious doctrine that signifies.

A tendency to ignore specific doctrine is equally apparent in the blinding of Arthur. In *The Troublesome Raigne* this scene is straightforward exposition of the Tudor doctrine of nonresistance. Hubert begins with the key assumption of the homilies:

> a subject dwelling in the Land
> Is tyed to execute the Kings commaund.
>
> (1391–92)

Arthur's response is the Protestants' during Mary's rule, the Catholics' under Elizabeth's: God's commands are superior to the king's. Hubert and Arthur debate the issue in legalistic stichomythic couplets until Hubert finally capitulates:

> My King commaunds, that warrant sets me free:
> But God forbids, and he commaundeth Kings.
>
> (1435–36)[18]

This is the official Anglican position, as explained in Bishop Thomas Bilson's *The True Difference Betweene Christian Subjection and Unchristian Rebellion* (1586). The loyal subject must never rebel, but he may passively disobey any commands he believes are immoral. He must never lift a hand against the king.[19] *King John*'s version of this scene eschews doctrine. Arthur, like Shakespeare's Henry VI, is trapped by lineage into a role he is unsuited to play and does not want. He, like Henry, longs for pastoral escape from the march of genealogy that imprisons male heirs even as it privileges them. Arthur sighs, "So I were out of prison and kept sheep, / I should be as merry as the day is long" (4.1.17–18). When Hubert shows him the royal warrant, Arthur's appeal is not to ideology but to Hubert's emotions and to their friendship. Stressing his innocence of any crime, Arthur begs for mercy. When Hubert finally relents (4.1.121), he offers no reason. He only admits that John's offer of "treasure" was what bought him in the first place. For Hubert, neither obeying nor disobeying John has anything to do with doctrine. In Shakespeare's drama, it is not ideology that changes people; it is individual affective needs.

The conflict between nobles and monarch begins in act 4 with John's recrowning. Pembroke reacts negatively, arguing that the ceremony is unnecesssary because

> The faiths of men ne'er stained with revolt;
> Fresh expectation troubled not the land
> With any long'd-for change or better state.
>
> (4.2.6–8)

John has undermined his own position, casting doubt on "the antique and well-noted face of plain old form." John mistakenly believes (as did Shakespeare's Richard II) that a ceremony can ensure reality, that acting out a coronation will really make him king. To John, as to Elizabeth, an attack on ceremony is an attack on royal supremacy.[20] John knows, however, that he does not have absolute control. He offers to reform whatever is not well and to hear and grant the lords' requests.

The lords demand, of course, what John will not be able to grant, release of Arthur. In Shakespeare's play, John is directly responsible for his young rival's death: fear of John motivates Arthur's attempted escape and subsequent death. He dies proclaiming, "My uncle's spirit is in these stones" (4.3.9). John tries to evade his responsibility by blaming Hubert's "evil" looks, in a scene certain to remind Eliz-abethan spectators of their queen's treatment of Francis Davison after the execution of Mary, Queen of Scots. Despite the circumstances, the lords are right to accuse their king of murder.

Our response to the hasty events of act 4 must be similar to the citizens' before Angiers. Neither side is right. The nobles' indignation is justified, but their revolt brings civil war. John's temporizing is as shameful as his order to Hubert. Yet, he is desperately trying to hold his kingdom together. Through this discord, no official ideology is privileged as it is in *The Troublesome Raigne.*

While Shakespeare has been criticized for not mentioning Magna Charta in his play, the text demonstrates his awareness of the power struggle between John and his nobles. Salisbury describes their revolt as a need to fight for their ancient "right." At the same time, Shake-speare seems more interested in the affective causes. Switching of feudal loyalties is an emotional response to the death of a child. Most of the play's decisions stem not from ideology but from personal loyalties and emotions. Melun, for example, confesses French treach-ery not simply because "My Grandsire was an Englishman" (both *TR* and *KJ*) but out of personal loyalty to Hubert (*KJ* 5.4.40–41).[21] Throughout *King John*, individual human beings subvert their collec-tive ideologies and contradict state and church expectations.

John cannot control his nobles, Pandulph cannot control Lewis, and the English lords cannot believe Lewis's sacred oath. Lewis puts secular chivalric goals—"To outlook conquest and win renown"—before his Church's command. As *King John* rushes to its conclusion, the three estates are in disarray. A foreign army invades England, and the "ordering of this present time" is left to a bastard.

How can the subversive forces released in Shakespeare's text be contained? For contained they must be if this chronicle history is to proffer some sense of an ending. First, women's subversive voice is silent after act 3. We are casually informed that both Elinor and Constance have died. Blanch seems to have disappeared. When the play ends, power is transmitted from dying father to first-born son with no women involved. After establishing that patrilineal inheri-tance is a legal fiction, Shakespeare resorts to it in the end. No nagging mother hovers over Henry III to raise doubts about his legitimacy. As the play closes, patriarchy is affirmed, a segment of genealogical time is complete.

Most of the play's dissidents have died or been dismissed. Blanch, who spoke against Lewis's war, is absent. John, who challenged the Church, has sickened and died. Arthur, who challenged John's (and therefore Henry III's) claims to legitimacy, dies without issue. One by one, the subversive voices are stilled.

Others are appropriated by the dominant authority and become spokesmen for official ideology. Melun convinces the English lords that they were wrong to rebel. In a metaphor of containment, they resolve that they will

> like a bated and retired flood,
> Leaving our rankness and irregular course,
> Stoop low within those bounds we have o'erlooked,
> And calmly run on in obedience
> Even to our ocean, to our great King John.
>
> (5.4.53–57)

Pandulph finally convinces Lewis to abandon his invasion (5.7.86). Henry will contain the disruptive forces unleashed by John's reign; Salisbury prophesies that Henry will "set a form upon that indigest / Which he [John] hath left so shapeless and so rude" (5.7.26–27).

Most startling in this rush to closure is the Bastard's transformation. The carnivalesque figure who delighted in puncturing rhetorical balloons of officialese now becomes authority's chief spokesperson, appropriating the jingoistic discourse of *The Troublesome Raigne* as his own. In lines lifted directly from the earlier play (the closest sustained borrowing in Shakespeare's text), the Bastard pronounces the lesson of Tudor homilies:

> This England never did, nor never shall,
> Lie at the proud foot of a conqueror,
> But when it first did help to wound itself.
> · · · · · · · · · · · · · · ·
> . . . . Nought shall make us rue,
> If England to itself do rest but true!
>
> (5.7.112–18)

This signifies closure. The audience can leave the theater on a burst of patriotism. But because this ideology has been subverted for four and a half acts, its imposition must be tenuous.

The image of the ideal state with its dissident elements safely contained dominates *King John's* last scene. It is a Renaissance image of England as independent and Protestant, subject to no foreign power. It is not the medieval ideal of a pan-European culture united by Roman Catholicism and a mission to reconquer the Holy Sepulchre. Having exploited both medieval and Renaissance perspectives throughout the play, Shakespeare closes on a contemporary note. King John's England lay in a distant past of feudal law and Roman

Catholic hegemony. England standing alone is Elizabeth's and Shakespeare's England.

Not surprisingly, few critics are satisfied with *King John's* conclusion. Sigurd Burckhardt suggested that "Shakespeare himself knew that he was not bringing the thing off—not because he was bored with a theatrical chore and wanted to finish it quickly and anyhow, but because he saw no way to put Humpty Dumpty together again."[22] Burckhardt spoke truer than perhaps he knew. Once Shakespeare had successfully deconstructed the received text, once he had restructured the play to show where ideology breaks down, he tried to end the play with the reimposition of ideology. The subversion of patrilineal inheritance that was so clear in act 1 lingers in our minds as we watch so much being made of Henry's lineal claim to the throne. Primogeniture works only when there are no obfuscations, no illegitimate sons, and no rival claimants. John's break from the Church, short-lived as it was, shows the contradictions at the core of that collective enterprise. The conflict between lords and king could be patched, but it was never fundamentally solved, as the events of Charles I's reign were to show. In other words, the conflicts embedded in *King John*, though set in the "past" (remember those cannons), were the conflicts of Shakespeare's own age. The shift from a medieval ideal of communal responsibility to modern individualism, the breakdown of the three estates, the spectacular rise of an upwardly mobile middle class, the end of the crusading ideal—all were characteristic of Shakespeare's cultural ethos. By not espousing one ideology over all others, Shakespeare's *King John* may seem less unified than earlier texts. But its disunity is clearly truer to the life that Shakespeare knew, and it speaks to us far more profoundly than the platitudes of his predecessors.

Notes

1. Graham Holderness, *Shakespeare's History* (Dublin: Gill and Macmillan, 1985), 31.
2. Allesandro Serpieri, "Reading the Signs: Towards a Semiotics of Shakespearean Drama," trans. Keir Elam, in *Alternative Shakespeares*, ed. John Drakakis (London: Methuen, 1985), 119–43; see particularly 125.
3. I am indebted here to Phyllis Rackin, whose discussion of anachronism in the history plays at the Columbia University Shakespeare Seminar (16 May 1986) inspired many of the ideas in this paper.
4. Written in 1965, John R. Elliott's "Shakespeare and the Double Image of King John" anticipates some of the ideas in this essay. His focus, however, is more on John's characterization. Mine is on the interplay of ideologies.
5. Lily Bess Campbell, *Shakespeare's Histories*, 126–67.
6. Elliott, "The Double Image," 68.

7. William Tyndale, *Obedience of a Christen Man* (London, 1535), 157r–v. I have silently regularized *j* and *i*, *u* and *v* in old spelling quotations.

8. See *The Homilie Against Disobedience and Wylfull Rebellion* (London, 1571), I2v–I3r.

9. Anthony Munday, *A Watch-woord to Englande* (London, 1584), 40. In his article, "Shakespeare and Munday," *Shakespeare Survey* 14 (1961): 25–33, I. A. Shapiro made the interesting suggestion that Munday may have written the plot of *The Troublesome Raigne*. Shapiro argued that it was likely Munday would write plays on patriotic and anti-papal themes around 1591.

10. I base much of my argument on the assumption that *The Troublesome Raigne* antedates Shakespeare's *King John*. For the most recent arguments, see Sidney Thomas, " 'Enter a Sheriffe': Shakespeare's *King John* and *The Troublesome Raigne*," 98–100 and the critical exchange of E. A. J. Honigmann, Paul Werstine, and Sidney Thomas in *Shakespeare Quarterly* 38 (1987): 124–30. For a detailed comparison of the differences between *The Troublesome Raigne* and *King John*, see my *The Drama As Propaganda* (published under the name Virginia M. Carr).

11. E. M. W. Tillyard, *Shakespeare's History Plays*. On p. 232, Tillyard notes, "In construction the play lacks unity. . . . The theme of rebellion may be prominent in the last two acts and give some coherence of subject matter, yet it does not arise naturally out of the peculiar virtues of the first three acts."

12. The most prominent exponent of *King John's* priority, E. A. J. Honigmann, notes in the Arden edition that "Shakespeare presents John as a usurper from the start" (*King John*, lxiv). See also Elliott, "The Double Image," 73–74.

13. Phyllis Rackin, "Anti-Historians," 329–44; see 341.

14. Sigurd Burckhardt, *Shakespearean Meanings*, 134.

15. Cannons are mentioned in 1.1.25, 2.1.37, 210, 251, 382, 461, and 462.

16. I disagree with Elliott ("The Double Image," 79) that Constance is a hysterical female who points to the self-dramatization of Richard II.

17. Maurice Keen argues that the crusading ideal "brought the church authorities, and in particular the reformed papacy of the late eleventh century, to terms with war and the warrior's place in society." See *Chivalry* (New Haven: Yale University Press, 1984), 45.

18. Cited from Geoffrey Bullough, ed., *Narrative and Dramatic Sources* 4 : 109–11.

19. Thomas Bilson, *The True Difference Between Christian Subjection and Unchristian Rebellion* (London, 1586), 348.

20. See Honigmann's footnote to 4.2.27 (New Arden *King John*, 97).

21. For an intriguing discussion of the relationship between Hubert and Melun, see Alan Dessen's paper, "The French Connection: Hubert and Melun in *King John*," presented at the second session of the *King John* seminar of the Shakespeare Association on 29 March 1986.

22. Burckhardt, *Shakespearean Meanings*, 134.

4

Patriarchal History and Female Subversion in *King John*

PHYLLIS RACKIN

'Zounds, I was never so bethump'd with words
Since I first call'd my brother's father dad.

(2.1.466–67)

HISTORIOGRAPHY IS A MAJOR CONCERN IN SHAKESPEARE'S HISTORY plays. Characters repeatedly allude to history, past and future, and define their actions as attempts to inscribe their names in the historical record. Like their playwright, these characters show an obsessive concern with the work of the historian—the writing, reading, and preservation of historical texts.

No woman is the protagonist of a Shakespearean history play. Renaissance gender role definitions prescribed silence as a feminine virtue, and Renaissance sexual mythology associated the feminine with body and matter in contrast to the masculine, which was linked to intellect and spirit. Renaissance historiography constituted a masculine tradition, written by men, devoted to the deeds of men, glorifying the masculine virtues of courage, honor, and patriotism, and dedicated to preserving the names of past heroes. Within that historical record, women had no voice.

The protagonists of Shakespeare's history plays, conceived both as subjects and as writers of history, were inevitably male. The women who do appear are often cast as opponents and subverters of the

Much of the material in this essay originally appeared in my article "Anti-Historians: Women's Roles in Shakespeare's Histories," *Theatre Journal* 37 (October 1985): 329–44, © 1985 by the Johns Hopkins University Press. Permission to reprint it here is gratefully acknowledged.

historical and historiographic enterprise. In the first tetralogy, Shakespeare depicts male protagonists defending masculine historical projects against female characters who threaten to obstruct those projects and feminine voices that threaten to discredit them. In *King John* the feminine voices become more insistent. They imply that before the masculine voice of history can be accepted as valid, it must come to terms with women and the subversive forces they represent. As soon as Shakespeare attempts to incorporate those feminine forces, however, historiography itself becomes problematic, no longer speaking with the clear, univocal voice of unquestioned tradition but represented as a dubious construct, always provisional, always subject to erasure and reconstruction, and never adequate to recover the past or determine the course of future events.

In considering the power of women to undermine the masculine historical enterprise, it is important to remember that Renaissance historiography was not only a masculine project, it was also patriarchal. More than a record of heroic names and glorious deeds or an aggregate of individual biographies, the Tudor chronicles told a connected story, tracing the passing down of land and titles from one man to another and validating the legitimacy of their current apportionment. Tudor historians constructed a myth of ancient descent and providential purpose to legitimate the new dynasty's claim to the throne. Genealogy lies at the base of the chronicle structure that constituted a narrative of patriarchal succession designed to legitimate the social order at the time in which the history was written and read.[1]

In a very important sense, chronicle history was not simply written without women: it was also written *against* them. Delineating a chain of inheritance passed down from father to son, it constructed a patriarchal mythology, which, like the strings of "begats" in the Old Testament, suppressed the roles of women. The son's name and entitlement and legitimacy all derived from the father, and only the father had a role in the historiographic text. Patriarchal history, then, was designed to construct a verbal substitute for the visible, physical connection between mother and child, to authenticate the relationship between father and son, and to suppress and supplant the role of the mother. An adulterous woman at any point could make a mockery of the entire story, and for that reason women were inevitably threatening to the historiographic enterprise. The verbal historiographic narrative suppressed women because it had to suppress the knowledge that all men and women have of the physical impossibility of ever discovering a sure biological basis for patriarchal succession.

A number of Shakespeare's history plays offer positive images of women in subsidiary roles, but none of them attempts to represent female authority, even though (or perhaps because) all but the last were written during the reign of Queen Elizabeth.[2] Shakespeare does not bring Elizabeth onto the stage until *Henry VIII*, a play written during the reign of her successor; and she comes in only at the end and only as a newborn baby, the object of the characters' hopes for the future, the audience's nostalgia for the past. Female authority is always absent in Shakespeare's histories, a dream of ultimate validation, an object of yearning as well as fear, which inevitably escapes the historiographic narrative.

Even such historically significant and consequential events as royal marriages are typically ignored (as in the case of Henry IV) or presented as disasters (as in the case of Henry VI or Edward IV). Only at the ends of the two tetralogies and in *Henry VIII*, the last of all his English history plays, does Shakespeare attempt to incorporate and transvalue the feminine. In *Richard III*, Margaret is transformed from a destructive French interloper whose marriage to the English king threatens to "cancel" English fame and blot English "names from books of memory" (*2 Henry 6*: 1.1.99–100) to the voice of Divine vengeance, descending upon the guilty Yorkists to purge England and make it ready for the glorious Tudor accession; and at the end of that play, it is the marriage of Richmond and Elizabeth that finally resolves the problems of the past and enables the prosperity of the future. Similarly, *Henry V*, the last play in the second tetralogy, culminates in the arrangements for the marriage of Henry to the French princess, and *Henry VIII*, the last play of all, ends with the birth of the Princess Elizabeth. In all these cases, however, the incorporation of the feminine represents the end of the historical process, a movement beyond the limits of the historiographic narrative. The marriages are announced, but they will not take place until after the plays have ended, and their announcements, like the announcement of Elizabeth's birth, are accompanied by prayers for future prosperity that go beyond the known facts of history, looking forward to the present time of the audience and even beyond it into an unknown future. The incorporation of the feminine can take place only at the point where history stops. A world that truly includes the feminine is a world in which history cannot be written.

Shakespeare's one attempt to depict such a world is *King John*. Separated from the temporal and genealogical chain that unites the two tetralogies, *King John* depicts a world where no actions are conclusive, neither the wills of fathers, nor the marriages of children, nor battles, nor papal decrees, nor the French king's repeated efforts at prospective history-making.[3] The French king swears he will put John down "Or add a royal number to the dead, / Gracing the scroll that tells of this war's loss / With slaughter coupled to the name of kings" (2.1.347–49). But the historical scroll he foresees will never be written, for he, no less than his English enemy, lives in a world where history-making is impossible. John, the English usurper, opposes the entire ethos of history. Seizing the English throne, he denies the patriarchal right that he knows belongs to Arthur. Having himself crowned a second time, he denies the permanence and efficacy of the ritual that made him king (4.2.1–34). Everything, even the supreme ritual by which patriarchal authority is passed down in temporal succession from one hand to another, is now endlessly repeatable and reversible. Only at the end, when he is about to die, does John associate his own being with a historical text, but the text he imagines is as fragile and mutable as he now sees his own life to be: "a scribbled form, drawn with a pen / Upon a parchment," shrinking up against the fire that will destroy it (5.7.32–35).

The image of the burning parchment completes Shakespeare's picture of John's estrangement from the tradition of Renaissance historiography. Tudor accounts of John's reign tended to emphasize his quarrel with the pope, collapsing the distance between John's world and their own to depict John as a heroic prototype of Henry VIII, a patriotic English king defying the foreign power of the papacy. Constructed in terms of difference and distance, Shakespeare's amoral portrait of John resists the patriotic appropriations of humanist historiography. John envisions his history as a fragile manuscript, the kind of text that was produced in his own medieval time, not as the kind of enduring monument that Renaissance humanists found in their classical sources and Renaissance historians tried to emulate in the printed books they produced. Moreover, when John envisions the manuscript shrinking up in flames, he anticipates what would happen when the monasteries were destroyed in the time of Henry VIII—who becomes, in this construction, not the heir and fulfillment of John's historical legacy, but its destroyer.

King John has been called the "most unhistorical" of Shakespeare's English histories, an "incoherent patchwork" where "the action is wandering and uncertain."[4] Rending the fabric of patriarchal history, Shakespeare opens a space where women can speak and act. In *King John* the roles of women are more various and prominent than in any of his other English histories, their subversive power to undermine the masculine historical project most fully revealed. Instead of playing subsidiary parts in a script written by men, the women in *King John* play crucial roles in determining the course of events. Driven by their own ambitions and by hatred and envy of each other, Elinor and Constance incite the war between England and France. The rivalry between the two women is an essential element in the story, in Holinshed, who states that John's establishment as king was "doone cheeflie by the working of the kings mother," who was "moved . . . by envy conceived against" Constance;[5] in *The Troublesome Raigne,* where Elinor claims that Arthur's "headstrong mother pricks him" on "so she may bring herself to rule a realm" (1.1.52–55); and in Shakespeare, who emphasizes the women's animosity as a motive force for their sons' quarrels from the very beginning, when Elinor reminds John, "What now, my son, have I not ever said / How that ambitious Constance would not cease / Till she had kindled France, and all the world, / Upon the right and party of her son?" (1.1.31–34) and Chatillion describes Elinor as "an [Ate,] stirring" John "to blood and strife" (2.1.63).

The traditional gender definitions that exclude women from the battles that form a major subject of patriarchal history are broken down. Elinor announces in the opening scene that she is "a soldier" (1.1.150), and her role is no anomaly in a play where "ladies and palevisag'd maids / Like Amazons come tripping after drums," changing "their thimbles into armed gauntlets . . . their needl's to lances, and their gentle hearts / To fierce and bloody inclination" (5.2.154–58). The blurring of gender distinctions also affects the men.[6] The English soldiers have "ladies' faces" (2.1.68), the Earl of Salisbury weeps, and the Dolphin declares that he values those "manly drops" above the "lady's tears" that have "melted" his heart in the past (5.2.47–49). Both contenders for the English crown—the bold and warlike John no less than his infant rival—are subjected to the domination of powerful mothers, and the French king bows to the threats of a mother church. Unwilling to break his truce with John lest they "make . . . unconstant children" of themselves (3.1.243), he finally agrees to do so after Pandulph threatens that "the Church, our mother, [will] breathe her curse, / A mother's curse, on her revolting son" (3.1.256–57).

The *Henry VI* plays depict a world where male right is threatened by female wrong; in the wicked world ruled by Richard III, the women line up on the side of heaven and the Earl of Richmond; but no such simple moral equations are possible in *King John.* Female characters take a variety of parts in the play's conflicts, they share in its moral ambiguities, and they also play a major role in their creation. Elinor and Constance back rival claimants for the English throne, and they wrangle openly on stage, adroitly subverting each other's claims and arguments. Blanch and Constance are both depicted as suffering victims, but neither can be consoled without wronging the other, and when they kneel together before the Dolphin (3.1.308–10) they do so to plead for opposite decisions. Earlier, Constance offers a stirring argument for a beloved son who is also the rightful heir to the throne, but she couches her speech in morally ambiguous terms: The "heaven-moving pearls from [Arthur's] poor eyes" will be taken by heaven "in nature of a fee," she says: "Ay, with these crystal beads heaven shall be brib'd" to do Arthur "justice" and do "revenge" on Elinor (2.1.169–72). And just in case the audience may have missed the impropriety of Constance's reference to "bribing" heaven for justice, Elinor pounces on it: "Thou monstrous slanderer of heaven and earth!" (2.1.173).

No longer categorized by their sex, female characters, for the first time, are sharply individualized. In the first tetralogy, the women characters fall neatly into groups, and their generic gender characteristics always transcend and subsume their individual identities. In *1 Henry VI*, although Joan is a peasant and the Countess of Auvergne and Margaret of Anjou are noblewomen, all three are united in nationality and in their roles as enemies to the English, male protagonists' struggle to preserve the legacy of Henry V. In *Richard III*, Margaret is a vengeful Lancastrian widow, and Elizabeth is a Yorkist queen; but before the play ends they too will be united with each other and with the Duchess of York in a chorus of distinctively female lamentation— all victimized and bereaved, all gifted with the power to prophesy and curse and articulate the will of Providence. In *King John*, by contrast, there is no way to reduce the female characters to a single class or category. Elinor is a soldier queen, a tough, Machiavellian dowager; Constance an outraged, lamenting mother; Blanch a compliant, helpless victim.

In a well-ordered patriarchal world, women are silent or invisible. First as daughters, then as wives, they are subject to male control, and their men speak and act on their behalf. But in *King John*, the fathers and husbands are dead, reduced to the status of names in history books, and the wives and mothers survive on Shakespeare's stage to dispute the fathers' wills and threaten their patriarchal legacies. In this play, female characters appear in their most threatening aspect—as the widowed mothers of sons, self-willed, controlling and vociferous. Elinor and Constance interrupt the parley between the two kings to accuse each other of adultery, each other's sons of bastardy (2.1.120– 33). Elinor impugns her grandson's birth in order to deny him the patriarchal right she knows is his (1.1.39–43). Constance, in the name of that right, impugns the legitimacy of her husband, subverting the patriarchal lineage that authorizes her son's claim to the throne. She proposes an alternate, female genealogical chain, deriving from Elinor and conveying a heritage of sin and suffering (2.1.179–82): "Thy sins are visited in this poor child, / The canon of the law is laid on him, /

Being but the second generation / Removed from thy sin-conceiving womb." She derives Arthur's ineffectual title from his father, but she incorporates the woman she hates in his genealogy to explain the reason for his actual predicament. And she refuses to hold her tongue, despite the men's commands.

Speaking with strong, irreverent voices, these mothers claim a place in the historical narrative and challenge the myths of patriarchal authority that the men invoke to justify their actions. When John answers the French king's threat with the conventional boast, "Our strong possession and our right for us," Elinor wittily and irreverently reminds him "Your strong possession much more than your right, / Or else it must go wrong with you and me" (1.1.39–41). When Pandulph claims that Constance lacks the "law and warrant" that give him the authority to curse John, Constance replies by challenging the law itself:

> when law can do no right,
> Let it be lawful that law bar no wrong;
> Law cannot give my child his kingdom here,
> For he that holds his kingdom holds the law;
> Therefore since law itself is perfect wrong,
> How can the law forbid my tongue to curse?
>
> (3.1.184–90)

In *King John*, Shakespeare subjects the masculine voices of patriarchal authority to skeptical feminine interrogation. No longer speaking with the clear, univocal voice of unquestioned tradition, the history he represents becomes problematic, an arena for contending interests rather than an authoritative voice to resolve their differences.

Instead of serving their traditional functions as creators of male bonds and validators of male identity, the women in *King John* speak and act for themselves, becoming sources and embodiments of conflict. The natural bonds that unite mother and child serve to divide Elinor and Constance, and the marriage of John's niece Blanch to the French Dolphin, which momentarily promises to unite the rival forces after their inconclusive battle for Angiers, becomes instead a source of further conflict when the Dolphin uses it as an excuse to claim the English throne. Blanch is the only woman in the play who is cast in the traditional feminine mold. Imported into the plot (as John, apparently, imports her into France) only for her ill-fated marriage to the Dolphin, she is placed in the archetypically feminine role of a medium of exchange between men.[7] Blanch is perfectly docile:

> My uncle's will in this respect [i.e., the marriage]
> is mine.

> If he see aught in you that makes him like,
> That any thing he sees, which moves his liking,
> I can with ease translate it to my will;
> Or if you will, to speak more properly,
> I will enforce it eas'ly to my love.
>
> (2.1.510–15)

With no will or agenda of her own, Blanch is ready to be used as an instrument of kinship arrangements, political alliance, and patriarchal succession. Perhaps taking his cue from the name of the historical character, Shakespeare depicts Blanch as a blank page awaiting the inscription of a masculine text.[8] Describing her living flesh as a text for male interpretation, John asks the Dolphin whether he can read "I love" in "this book of beauty" (2.1.484–85). To the Dolphin, Blanch is a "table" where his own image is "drawn" (2.1.503). And to all three men, she is a site for the inscription of a patriarchal historical narrative of military truce and genealogical succession.

Exercising a traditional patriarchal right by marrying his son to Blanch, the French king makes his strongest claim to historical authority: "The yearly course that brings this day about," he declares, "shall never see it but a holy day" (3.1.81–82). Blanch will serve as the inert female material of masculine history-making. But in *King John*, that female material also includes Elinor and Constance, recalcitrant and self-willed. Rejecting the French king's effort at prospective history-making, Constance demands,

> What hath this day deserv'd? what hath it done,
> That it in golden letters should be set
> Among the high tides in the calendar?
> Nay, rather turn this day out of the week. . . .
>
> (3.1.84–87)

And Constance's own appeal to the heavens—"Let not the hours of this ungodly day / Wear out the [day] in peace; but ere sunset, / Set armed discord 'twixt these perjur'd kings!" (3.1.109–11)—seems to be answered. Refusing to allow the marriage a place in the historical record, Constance rejects the news of it as a "tale" (3.1.5) "misspoke, misheard" (3.1.4) and demands to have the day on which it took place removed from the calendar. Denying the men's story and demanding the literal erasure of the date, she speaks for the forces that make the writing of patriarchal history impossible in the world of this play.

Constance is right, of course: the marriage will not make history. The peace the marriage is designed to secure is no sooner made than it is broken by the intervention of the papal legate Pandulph, a spokesman for a religious power as ambiguous as every other source of patriarchal authority in this play, who suddenly appears, as if in answer to Constance's furious demands. So instead of becoming a medium to unite the warring factions, Blanch becomes the victim of their divisions. Niece to the English king, wife to the French Dolphin, she pleads desperately for the peace her marriage was designed to secure; and, having failed in her plea, she cries,

> Which is the side that I must go withal?
> I am with both, each army hath a hand,
> And in their rage, I having hold of both,
> They whirl asunder and dismember me.
>
> (3.1.327–30)

The image of dismemberment makes Blanch the human embodiment of the many divisions that characterize this play—of the divisions among the female characters, of the division of the English throne between John's possession and Arthur's right, and especially of the divided allegiances that perplex the audience as they struggle with the ethical and political ambivalences that make *King John* the most troubling of all Shakespeare's English histories.[9]

In *King John*, Shakespeare leaves his audience, like the Bastard, "amaz'd" and lost "among the thorns and dangers" of an incomprehensible world (4.3.140–41), where every source of authority fails and legitimacy is reduced to a legal fiction. For the characters within the play, there is no clear royal authority. For the audience watching it, there is no unblemished cause and no unquestioned authority to claim their allegiance. None of these dilemmas is resolved until the end of the play when John's death ends the crisis of patriarchal authority and the Bastard adopts the idiom of historical faith and patriotic jingoism. The accession of Prince Henry, we are promised, will "set a form upon that indigest / which [John] hath left so shapeless and so rude" (5.7.26–27). It is significant, I believe, that before this can happen, the women's voices must be stilled. Blanch is removed from the stage, reduced to a genealogical pretext for the Dolphin's claim to the English throne. Elinor and Constance die, offstage and unhistorically, their deaths three days apart reported in a single speech of six lines (4.2.119–24) as if to suggest the containment of these bitter enemies within a single, genderically determined category, their reduction from vociferous actors to the silent objects of male narration.[10]

As long as the women live and speak, however, they set the subversive keynote for the other characters. John and the French king trade charges of usurpation (2.1.118–20), matching the women's mutual charges of adultery. Pandulph shares their distrustful vision of political process, embracing *Realpolitik* with a cynicism that matches their own. The Bastard shares their iconoclastic idiom, satirizing the heroic language that "talks as familiarly of roaring lions / As maids of thirteen do of puppy-dogs" and linking it to the patriarchal authority it claims to represent when he protests, "I was never so bethump'd with words / Since I first call'd my brother's father dad" (2.1.459–67). And it is the Bastard who best points up the problem of legitimacy—and who, by extension, demonstrates the power of female subversion.

In one sense, legitimacy is the issue in all Shakespeare's English history plays,[11] but nowhere is it so central as it is in *King John*. Like *1 Henry VI* and *Richard II*, the plays that begin the two tetralogies, *King John* looks back to a dead, heroic king, but while the legacies of Henry V and Edward III were opposed and endangered in the worlds their legitimate successors inherited but could not rule, those legacies remained intact and clearly defined, if increasingly remote, ideals. In *King John*, the legacy of the departed patriarch is problematized and dispersed. The division of Coeur de Lion's legacy among three defective heirs makes it impossible even to know who is the rightful king of England, and it gives rise to the crucial issue in *King John*—the problem of legitimacy. The entire action hangs on the unanswerable question: "Who is the legitimate heir of Coeur de Lion?"; and the presiding spirit of this play is not the king who gives it its name but the Bastard, the most powerful and dramatically compelling of the characters, the alter ego to whom John gives "the ordering of this present time" (5.1.77), and Shakespeare gives the last word in the play. The Bastard's literal illegitimacy characterizes the status of the king, the problems the play explores, and the curious nature of Shakespeare's creation.[12] The Bastard has no real place in history, neither in the chain of patriarchal succession, where he can never inherit his father's throne, nor in the historical record Shakespeare found in Holinshed. *King John* has the flimsiest of relationships to its historiographic sources, compressing and marginalizing John's dispute with Rome and the revolt of his nobles, ignoring Holinshed's account of Magna Charta, and centering instead on an unhistorical character invented for the sixteenth-century stage.[13]

A curious episode, which serves to introduce the Bastard, takes up most of the first act in *King John*, and it exposes, like nothing else in any of Shakespeare's histories, the arbitrary and conjectural nature of patriarchal succession and the suppressed centrality of women to it. The fictional quarrel between the two brothers over the Faulconbridge lands and title, like the historical quarrel between Arthur and John over the English throne, hinges on ambiguities and ruptures in the relationship between legal and biological inheritance. And both quarrels involve the mothers—but not the fathers—of the contending heirs. The Faulconbridge quarrel, in fact, centers on the mother, for Lady Faulconbridge's infidelity has created the nightmare situation that haunts the patriarchal imagination—a son not of her husband's begetting destined to inherit her husband's lands and title. Like Shakespeare's ubiquitous cuckold jokes, the Faulconbridge episode bespeaks the anxiety that motivates the stridency of patriarchal claims and repressions—the repressed knowledge of women's subversive power.

John's attempt to arbitrate the Faulconbridge quarrel exposes a deep contradiction in patriarchal law. "Sirrah," he says to Robert, "your brother is legitimate,"

> Your father's wife did after wedlock bear him;
> And if she did play false, the fault was hers,
> Which fault lies on the hazards of all husbands
> That marry wives. Tell me, how if my brother,
> Who, as you say, took pains to get this son,
> Had of your father claim'd this son for his?
> In sooth, good friend, your father might have kept
> This calf, bred from his cow, from all the world;
> In sooth he might; then if he were my brother's,
> My brother might not claim him, nor your father,
> Being none of his, refuse him. This concludes:
> My mother's son did get your father's heir;
> Your father's heir must have your father's land.
>
> (1.1.116–29)

According to the laws of patriarchy as expounded by John (and according to English law in Shakespeare's time), the woman, like a cow, is mere chattel, possession of the man. All her actions, even an act so radical as betrayal of the marriage bond, are totally irrelevant, powerless to affect her son's name, possession, legal status, or identity. Only the man's entitlement has significance under law. She is his possession, and any child she bears is his, even if he is not the biological father. Thus, the very absoluteness of patriarchal right provides for its own subversion.

By admitting that the relationship between father and son is finally no more than a legal fiction, John attacks the very basis of patriarchal history, as he does throughout the play. Relying on "strong possession" rather than "right" for his throne (1.1.40), John opposes the patriarchal authority that would legitimate Arthur. In this play, it is not John but the King of France who values history and wants to write it. The French king supports Arthur's lineal right to the English throne, and he describes Arthur as a "little abstract" of what "died in

Geffrey," which "the hand of time / Shall draw . . . into as huge a volume" (2.1.101–3). With this description of father and son as "volume" and "abstract," the French king grounds the historical record in nature. But John's verdict on the Faulconbridge controversy demythologizes that record, depriving it of the natural status implied by the French king's metaphor of man as volume and boy as abstract and exposing it as a social construct designed to shore up the flimsy and always necessarily putative connections between fathers and sons.

Elinor is the first to guess the Bastard's true paternity, for she can read the wordless text of his physical nature:

> He hath a trick of Cordelion's face,
> The accent of his tongue affecteth him.
> Do you not read some tokens of my son
> In the large composition of this man?
>
> (1.1.85–88)

But without Lady Faulconbridge's testimony, the Bastard's paternity would remain conjectural, and his name and title would belie the biological truth of the paternity they purported to represent. It takes one woman to guess the truth and another to verify it. In Holinshed, Coeur de Lion recognizes his bastard son, giving him "the castell and honor of Coinacke." In *The Troublesome Raigne*, the Bastard guesses his true paternity even before he asks his mother. In fact, he gets the news from Nature herself: "Methinks I hear a hollow echo sound," he says,

> That *Philip* is the son unto a King;
> The whistling leaves upon the trembling trees,
> Whistle in concert I am *Richard*'s son;
> The bubbling murmur of the water's fall,
> Records *Phillipus Regis filius;*
> Birds in their flight make music with their wings,
> Filling the air with glory of my birth;
> Birds, bubbles, leaves and mountains, echo, all
> Ring in mine ears, that I am Richard's son.
>
> (1.242–51)

Only in Shakespeare is he required to receive his paternity at the hands of women.

Lady Faulconbridge is an unhistorical character, but she is the only one who knows the truth about the Bastard's paternity. The Bastard's words are significant: "But for the certain knowledge of that truth / I put you o'er to heaven and to my mother" (1.1.61–62). The Bastard's ironic coupling of his adulterous mother with heaven as the only

sources of the elusive truth that no man can know on earth suggests a
deep affinity between them as keepers of the unwritten and unknow-
able truth never directly accessible to the knowledge of men, the
Others that delineate the boundaries of the male Self's kingdom of
knowledge and control. To incorporate women in the story, as Shakespeare does in *King John*, is to go beyond the patriarchal historical
narrative into the realm of the unwritten and the conjectural, the
inaccessible domain (literally a no-man's land) of the true paternity of
a child and the actual life that can never be fully represented in the
words of the historical text. As bearers of the life that names, titles,
and historical records could never fully represent, the women were
keepers of the unspoken and unspeakable reality that always threatened to belie the words that pretended to describe it.

Notes

1. Gabrielle M. Spiegel, "Genealogy: Form and Function in Medieval Historical
Narrative," *History and Theory: Studies in the Philosophy of History* 22 (1983): 47.
Spiegel is writing about late medieval French historiography, but, as scholars have
long recognized, the Tudor sponsorship of historiography was clearly motivated by
Tudor genealogical anxiety. David Riggs's observations (in *Shakespeare's Heroical
Histories: Henry VI and Its Literary Tradition* [Cambridge: Harvard University Press,
1971]) about Elizabethan nostalgia for the fast-vanishing ideal of the hereditary feudal
aristocrat are also relevant here, as are Lawrence Stone's demonstrations (in "Social
Mobility in England, 1500–1700," *Past and Present* 33 [1966] and *The Crisis of the
Aristocracy, 1558–1641* [Oxford: Clarendon Press, 1965]), that Shakespeare's contemporaries, living in an era of unprecedented social mobility, provided a thriving
business for the heralds who constructed the pedigrees by which they attempted to
insure their own places in a newly unstable social hierarchy. Another focus for the
Elizabethan genealogical anxiety that becomes such an important issue in *King John*
was Queen Elizabeth herself: The queen's refusal to marry had always provoked
anxiety about the succession, and by the time Shakespeare wrote *King John*, she was
well past the age of childbearing.
2. For a good account of Elizabethan anxieties and ambivalence about the queen's
authority, see Louis Adrian Montrose, "'Shaping Fantasies': Figurations of Gender
and Power in Elizabethan Culture," *Representations* 1 (1983): 61–94.
3. Sigurd Burckhardt argues in *Shakespearean Meanings*, 116–43, that every
source of authority fails in *King John* except the ties of blood and the simple human
decency that prevents Hubert from murdering Arthur. Burckhardt's demonstration of
the ways the play subverts religious and political authority is thoroughly convincing,
but I find it difficult to accept his claims about Hubert. In the chronicles, the reports
of Arthur's death were ambiguous, and although Shakespeare provides his audience
with eyewitness knowledge of the scene that no one but Arthur ever saw, he also shows
the false reports that kept even Arthur's contemporaries from true knowledge of the
circumstances of his death, and he shows the political and military effects of their
ignorance in the nobles' defection from John. The truth of Hubert's mercy has no
impact upon the plot of the play or the course of history.
4. E. A. J. Honigmann, ed., the New Arden *King John*, xxxi.

5. Raphael Holinshed, *Chronicles of England, Scotland and Ireland*, 2d ed., 1586 (London: J. Johnson et al., 1807), 2:274.

6. The reciprocal nature of the binary opposition that defined the difference between masculine and feminine gender was well understood in the Renaissance. Anxieties about masculine women inevitably involved the feminization of men. Cf. Caesar's accusation (*Antony and Cleopatra* 1.4.5–7) that Antony "is not more manlike / Than Cleopatra; nor the queen of Ptolomy / More womanly than he" and Linda Woodbridge's observation about the "*hic-mulier*" controversy of the early seventeeth century: "Whether praising or damning, comment on women in masculine attire was almost always accompanied by remarks on male effeminacy. . . ." (*Women and the English Renaissance: Literature and the Nature of Womankind, 1540–1620* [Urbana and Chicago: University of Illinois Press, 1984], 141).

7. See Gayle Rubin, "The Traffic in Women: Notes on the 'Political Economy' of Sex," in *Towards an Anthropology of Women*, ed. R. Reiter (New York: Monthly Review Press, 1975), 157–210.

8. See Susan Gubar, " 'The Blank Page' and Female Creativity" in *Writing and Sexual Difference*, ed. Elizabeth Abel (Chicago, Ill.: University of Chicago Press, 1982), 73–93, for a discussion of this traditional construction of women as blank pages awaiting the inscription of men's writing. See especially p. 75, where Gubar cites a number of examples of this image, ranging from Henry James's *Portrait of a Lady*, with its description of "the ideal *jeune fille* . . . as 'a sheet of blank paper,' " to Shakespeare's Othello, who asks whether his Desdemona, "this fair paper, this most goodly book, [was] / Made to write 'whore' upon" (4.2.71–72).

9. As Virginia Mason Vaughan has pointed out, Shakespeare uses "frequent turns of events [to] surprise the audience as well as the characters on stage," alternating "inflated claims of legitimacy and actions which undercut those claims" ("Between Tetralogies," 415).

10. I am indebted for the point about the women's silencing as a necessary condition for the restoration of patriarchal historical discourse to Lisa Sigler, a student in my 1984 graduate seminar on Shakespeare's history plays at the University of Pennsylvania.

11. As Herbert Lindenberger points out, "The action of historical drama is more precisely a struggle for legitimacy than a struggle for power as such. Dramas that depict a hereditary throne generally present sharply divergent readings of genealogies to justify the rights of various contenders for the throne" (*Historical Drama: The Relation of Literature and Reality* [Chicago, Ill.: University of Chicago Press, 1975], 160). Although Richard II is the undoubted heir of Edward III, his enemies invoke the law of primogeniture (2.3.122–24) and the rituals of royalty (4.1) to justify his deposition (see my article "The Role of the Audience in Shakespeare's *Richard II*," *Shakespeare Quarterly* 36 [Autumn 1985]: 262–81). Genealogical anxiety haunts Shakespeare's Lancastrian kings, and genealogical arguments rationalize the rebellions that plague them. Richard III follows what Robert Ornstein (*A Kingdom for a Stage*, 26n) has called the "time-honored custom for usurpers to bastardize those they overthrow" when he orders Buckingham to "infer [i.e., assert] the bastardy of Edward's children" (3.5.75); and Richmond's greatest achievement is not his victory at Bosworth Field but the marriage to the Yorkist princess by which he will "unite the White Rose and the Red" (5.5.19) and restore legitimacy to the royal succession.

12. For scholarly editors, the play has a problematic text and a clouded authorial genealogy. Not only does it include an abundance of fictional material absent from the historiographic sources, in addition, there is no way to know whether Shakespeare is the original author of that fictional material, since much of it is also found in a roughly contemporary play, *The Troublesome Raigne of Iohn King of England* (London, 1591),

and no one has been able to determine which play was written first (although, of course, many arguments have been advanced on both sides of the question). Estimates of the date of Shakespeare's composition range from 1591 to 1598.

13. If *The Troublesome Raigne* was a source for Shakespeare's play, the Bastard has a dramatic source there. The historical basis for the Bastard is confined to one sentence in Holinshed on "Philip bastard sonne to King Richard, to whom his father had given the castell and honor of Coinacke, [who] killed the vicount of Limoges, in revenge of his fathers death" (2:278).

5

The King's One Body

Unceremonial Kingship in *King John*

BARBARA H. TRAISTER

COMPARED TO SHAKESPEARE'S HISTORY PLAYS THAT PRECEDE IT, *KING John* is a play of reductions. Its cast of named characters is considerably smaller than those of the earlier plays. It has no fully staged battle scenes, despite the ongoing war between France and England. Many of its scenes and lines are devoted to private moments in its characters' lives. The panoply and ceremony that marked the first tetralogy have largely vanished. The crown itself has lost power as a symbol of majesty. The play presents homely kingship, a king who is a flawed and limited man rather than a divinely appointed public force. Only in the play's concluding scenes is lip service given to the "divinity [which] doth hedge a king" that produces so much ambivalence in weak king plays. In act 5 Faulconbridge, the returned nobles, and Prince Henry all attempt to invest England's monarch with his second body, the public image of majesty and power that has been absent from John's version of kingship.[1]

King John offers possibilities for spectacle and for elaborate stagecraft but does not urge them. Reporting on the play's stage history, Eugene M. Waith remarks of Macready's 1823 production, "The pageantry of court scenes and marching armies, the movement of large numbers of people across the stage, made it the equivalent of a Cecil B. DeMille extravaganza in the grand old days of film."[2] Macready had fifty-nine actors on stage when John spoke his opening lines, and eighty-eight people when the armies came together in act 2. Macready's very exaggeration, however, calls attention to the play's rather simple stage demands. Stage directions call for only six people to be on stage when the play opens—John, Elinor, the courtiers Essex, Salisbury, and Pembroke, who have no lines in the act, and the French messenger. The other fifty-three were Macready's elaboration, inspired no doubt by Shakespeare's earlier histories where courtiers, soldiers, and messengers crowd the stage. Acts 1 and 2 are each composed of a single scene, and though there are entrances and exits during those scenes, the effect is one of relative simplicity rather than of ceremonious activity.

Despite the international dimensions of its action, the play is unpretentious. As the armies of France, England, and Austria stand before the walls of Angiers (the stage direction "with forces" is an early editor's addition), the principals in the dispute speak directly to one another with no intervening ceremony or messengers. They are frequently interrupted, to be sure, by the irrepressible Faulconbridge and by the scolding women, but such interruptions can occur precisely because ceremony does not dominate the scene. The kings are not in control of those who accompany them any more than they are in control of the city of Angiers.

Though several rushes of armed men across the stage occur in the play, it contains no real battle scene. At one point Faulconbridge enters with Austria's head, and at another John is told to leave the battlefield. But there is no hand-to-hand combat by specified characters as there is in each of the plays of the first tetralogy.

Just as there are no formal battle scenes, there is little dramatized ceremony. Ritualistic occasions that might have been dramatized are merely reported: the wedding ceremony of Lewis and Blanch takes place offstage, as does John's second crowning ceremony. The one ritual that is dramatized—John's surrender of his crown to the papal legate—is an embarrassing one, lasting only for a few lines and witnessed only by "Attendants." Macready's panoply was indeed primarily of his own creation.

In lieu of ceremony and ritual, *King John* presents informality and personal drama.[3] The king himself is constantly criticized and upbraided by characters who show no fear of reprisals. The play opens with an ambassador who addresses John as "borrowed majesty," and only a few lines later his mother corrects John's claim to have right on his side in the contest for the crown. Faulconbridge speaks his mind before the king with no fear or restraint. John's nobles, curiously silent in his presence except when expressing opposition, directly criticize his insistence on a second coronation. The citizens of Angiers display no fear of the opposing kings and their armies.

Other Shakespearean kings, most notably Henry VI, also receive a good deal of criticism within their plays, but John, unlike Henry VI, is not "weak" except in his claim to the throne. In the play's early acts he is decisive, a good judge of character, and not afraid to act or to fight. But except for a few moments in act 5, John acts and is treated more like an important man than like an untouchable king, apparently inspiring and demanding very little awe. John sets the tone for his relationships with those around him, and he repeatedly encourages a man-to-man straightforwardness; though he himself becomes devious when he attempts to persuade Hubert to murder Arthur in act 3, scene 3. This attempt, interestingly enough, is John's first serious misstep.

As a result of this lack of ceremony—apparent even in his speech (see Joseph Porter's essay, chapter 9)—the symbols of majesty and power normally associated with a king carry little weight when John attempts to use them for political advantage. For example, as he stands before Angier's walls John offers his crown as proof of his legitimacy as king: "Doth not the crown of England prove the King?" (2.1.273). But evidently recognizing his crown's weakness as a proof, John does not even pause for an answer before continuing with less symbolic but more practical proofs: "Twice fifteen thousand hearts of England's breed" (2.1.275).

John's own lack of belief in what should be his ceremonious second body becomes clear to the audience as well as to his nobles when he chooses to be crowned a second time. According to Tudor theory, the king as present in his second body never died or erred. By ordering a second coronation, John implies that he had not formerly been properly king, that he had not been invested from the moment of the previous sovereign's death with the ceremonial body of kingship. Thus he weakens rather than strengthens his position by betraying insecurity about his kingship. As Faulconbridge demonstrates in the first act, what is important in this play is not so much who is legitimate (for titles and legalities are all subservient to commodity) but rather who is confident enough to base his claim to power on his own merits: "And I am I, howe'er I was begot" (1.1.175).[4]

King John portrays individuals' responses to power and political reality. Repeatedly, characters are judged not on their pedigrees or their positions but on their physical appearance. When Faulconbridge first arrives at court, Elinor and John find in his face, his voice, his build, and his spirit evidence that he is son to Coeur de Lion. Before Faulconbridge forces his mother to admit that he is Coeur de Lion's son, the king has accepted him as a kinsman on the basis of appearance alone. No other proof is necessary.

Constance claims that she pushes her son's claim to the throne of England because he is fair and looks like a king. If he were ugly, "I would not care, I then would be content, / For then I should not love thee; no, nor thou / Become thy great birth nor deserve a crown" (3.1.48–50). Later, Arthur describes Hubert's change of heart about blinding him as a change in appearance: "O now you look like Hubert!

All this while / You were disguis'd" (4.1.125–26). When John believes that Hubert has murdered Arthur and regrets ordering him to do so, John blames his own moral lapse on Hubert's appearance:

> How oft the sight of means to do ill deeds
> Make deeds ill done! Hadst not thou been by,
> A fellow by the hand of nature mark'd,
> Quoted, and sign'd to do a deed of shame,
> This murther had not come into my mind.
>
> (4.2.219–23)

Once Hubert makes clear that he has not followed the king's order to murder Arthur, John's vision of Hubert suddenly changes:

> Forgive the comment that my passion made
> Upon thy feature, for my rage was blind,
> And foul imaginary eyes of blood
> Presented thee more hideous than thou art.
>
> (4.2.263–66)

Judgments made on the basis of appearance and manner are, of course, as error-ridden as those based on social position and title. But in this play history is made by individuals on the basis of physical evidence. Given that basis for judgment, John's lack of "majesty" becomes a serious political handicap.

John's style of kingship is apparently to lead his people on the strength of the personal bonds he forges with them. Almost every aspect of his relationships with those around him focuses on the personal. Despite Faulconbridge's subordinate position, John frequently addresses him as "cousin." When he persuades Hubert to kill Arthur, John gives him no direct order. In their fifty lines of dialogue, John addresses Hubert three times as "friend," once as "gentle Hubert," twice as "good," and says that he "owes" Hubert, "respects" him, and "loves" him. He also takes his hand. Not once in the scene does John say anything to break the illusion that this conversation is taking place between two old and dear friends. Hubert remains aware, however, that despite his friendly approach John is still "your Majesty" (3.3.29–64). When Shakespeare's kings hire or command subjects to eliminate their enemies, they conventionally address the murderers-to-be in friendly terms, but this scene goes far beyond what is required to keep an employee happy. John might have commanded as a monarch; instead he begs as a friend.[5]

John is not the only character in the play to stress the personal and individual. Burckhardt's penetrating analysis of the death of Melun points out the personal emphasis in that scene, Melun's two reasons for revealing Lewis's plans to destroy the English nobles being strikingly personal: his grandfather was an Englishman, and he loves and respects Hubert.[6] Hubert himself, kept from blinding Arthur by the boy's pleading, does not rationalize his decision by appeals to morality or a greater good. Instead, his decision seems purely *ad hominem;* he cannot bear to hurt the child who stands before him "for the wealth of all the world" (4.1.130).

Earlier in the play, the arguments thrown back and forth across the stage by Constance and Elinor are painfully personal. The women seem to feel that the kingship should be decided on the basis of who was faithful or unfaithful to whose husband; each implies the other is an adulteress. Even Lewis, whose responses to the question of whether he will have Blanch for a wife are Petrarchan clichés, does not define an obviously political decision in political terms. Instead, he personalizes his response, speaking to Blanch as to an individual woman—though one he barely knows. Compared to Henry V's similar attempt to personalize a political liaison, Lewis's response here seems colorless. Yet both political wooers attempt to turn the public political deal into a semblance of personalized romance.

The central question in the plot of *King John*—who is the legitimate English monarch, embodying majesty?—brings the issue of the king's second body to the fore. Two physical bodies, John's and Arthur's, vie for the right to be the English monarch. John holds the position "by possession." But, as we have seen, he rarely invokes the perquisites of his position. The great exception is, of course, his prompt defiance of Pandulph:

> What earthy name to interrogatories
> Can taste the free breath of a sacred king?
> . . . .
> But as we, under [God], are supreme head,
> So under Him that great supremacy,
> Where we do reign, we will alone uphold
> Without th' assistance of a mortal hand.
>
> (3.1.147–58)

But his claim here only earns him excommunication and loss of the alliance with France. Eventually he submits to Pandulph, in what Faulconbridge terms an "inglorious league" (5.1.65). John's chief attempt to invoke his sacred kingship, his second body, fails; no one pays attention.

The second claimant, Arthur, is even less persuasive than John as an embodiment of sacred majesty. In the first place, he is only a boy and does not particularly want to be king. His claim is supported by foreign powers who clearly see in his kingship a political advantage to themselves. He is dominated by his scolding mother who expects to be the power behind Arthur's throne. Only in his captivity and despair, separated from his mother, does Arthur win sympathy, not so much for his claim to the throne as for his personal eloquence and courage. The words that Faulconbridge speaks over Arthur's dead body— "How easy dost thou take all England up / From forth this morsel of dead royalty! / The life, the right, and the truth of all this realm / Is fled to heaven" (4.3.142–45)—suggest that Arthur may have had the "majesty" that John lacks, but this suggestion comes only after Arthur's death. As the realist Faulconbridge clearly sees, if "majesty" is to live on in England, it can only be in John now that the rival claimant is dead.

In *King John* Shakespeare examines kingship in a way explored by earlier Tudor dramatists in what is sometimes called "romantic" or "comical" history.[7] Such drama is perhaps best exemplified by the "historical" plays of Robert Greene: *James IV, Friar Bacon and Friar Bungay,* and *George a Greene*. There the monarch mingles with his people on more or less equal terms, discarding ceremony and pomp. In *King John,* such unceremonial kingship is removed from the holiday world of the comical history and placed instead in the arena of international politics. Can rulers deal successfully with one another and with their subjects without the trappings of ceremony and "sacred kingship?" Apparently not easily. By the end of act 4, Faulconbridge sees only "the bare-pick'd bone of majesty" and the "imminent decay of wrested pomp" (4.3.148, 154).

Maintenance of kingship on the basis of the king's personal qualities is possible only so long as that king performs well. For a while, John's vigor, determination, and wise choice of subordinates (namely Faulconbridge) carry him along. But when he tires, slows, and makes bad judgments, he has nothing to fall back on. His kingship becomes a bone to be fought over. To emphasize the low point to which John's rule has fallen, act 5 opens with his handing his crown, "the circle of my glory," to Pandulph. From this point, John's personal leadership as king is at an end. But as though by common consent, his followers begin to invoke not the king as individual but the king as sacred majesty. King John gives the reins of command to Faulconbridge— "Have thou the ordering of this present time" (5.1.77)—who begins to speak in the voice of the "English King," though not necessarily in the voice of John:

> Now hear our English King,
> For thus his royalty doth speak in me:
> . . . .

> . . . . Know the gallant monarch is in arms,
> And like an eagle o'er his aery tow'rs,
> To souse annoyance that comes near his nest.
>
> (5.2.128–50)

The image of kings, the eagle, here appears in the play for the first time, and Faulconbridge's description of John is clearly not of the man as he is but of the king as he should be.

A similar response comes from the nobles who, upon learning of Lewis's plans to kill them after the battle is won, prudently decide to return to "our ocean, to our great King John" (5.4.57). Ironically, the physical body to which this allegiance is pledged is wracked by both fever and poison. But the final scene, despite the painful and rather ignominious death of John, is the most ritualistic of the play. As John dies, his son offers a traditional *ubi sunt* response: "What surety of the world, what hope, what stay, / When this was now a king, and now is clay?" (5.7.68–69), and Faulconbridge promises—as do Kent and Horatio at the death of their lords—to follow his monarch into death. Later in the scene Faulconbridge and the nobles kneel and pledge their loyalty to Prince Henry, a gesture of fealty stronger than any John received in the play.[8] Prince Henry has done nothing to show himself more worthy than his father of such a response. But John's lack of success in embodying "majesty" suggests that ceremony and ritual, the continuing acknowledgment of the king's second body, are a necessary part of kingship.

However attractive the informal, unceremonious, man-to-man style of leadership may seem, its pitfalls are real. The *Henry VI* trilogy suggests that the monarchy cannot stand unless the man who embodies it has a certain personal strength and ability. Sacred majesty is not enough. But *King John*, examining the other side of the coin, suggests that a strong and vigorous man who lacks majesty is not enough either. The individual must be bolstered by the ceremonies and awe owed to the king's second body. The informality of the comical history will not work in the world of *Realpolitik*. The king needs both his bodies.

The proper use of both those bodies is explored at length in the Lancastrian tetralogy to which Shakespeare turned next.[9] The reason why Shakespeare chose to dramatize the reign of John in the midst of his War of the Roses histories has often been a matter for critical speculation. If indeed he wished to explore a kingship in which the man and not the "sacred majesty" dominated, then perhaps he had to move back in time, away from his own age in which divine right was so familiarly invoked.[10] *King John* was written at a time when the question of the succession was very much in the minds of the Elizabethan audience.[11] Which physical body was to embody "sacred majesty" once the old queen died was not at all clear, and that uncertainty must have called into question, for those who understood it, the whole concept of the undying second body of the monarch. *King John* depicts a king without a second body, whose physical presence alone proves inadequate to maintain loyalty in his subjects and order in his kingdom. The solution, at least for Faulconbridge and the nobles, is to establish ceremony, to convince themselves and all England that the emperor is wearing his clothes and the king his two bodies.

Notes

1. Ernst H. Kantorowicz, *The King's Two Bodies: A Study in Medieval Political Theology* (Princeton: Princeton University Press, 1957), has written the seminal work on this theme. In *The Queen's Two Bodies: Drama and the Elizabethan Succession*, Marie Axton explores how Elizabethan dramatists at the Inns of Court and in the public theaters used this theme to offer veiled advice on the succession. My essay is informed throughout by both discussions.

2. Eugene M. Waith, *"King John* and the Drama of History," 204.

3. There is considerable critical disagreement on this point. Alexander Leggatt, in "Dramatic Perspective in *King John*," sees a change from public to private occurring after act 2: "Instead of great massed public movements, we are more aware of private intrigue, and private feeling. Many scenes involve only two speakers" (8). Larry S. Champion, " 'Confound Their Skill in Covetousness,' " sees the play as public: "Inevitably the spectators' interest is directed, not to single individuals, but to the broad sweep of events characterizing critical moments during John's reign" (39).

4. John R. Elliott, "Shakespeare and the Double Image of King John," 64–84.

5. Ralph Berry, *The Shakespearean Metaphor*, writes of this scene: "There are limits to the obedience a king can exact of a subject, and the play explores them" (26). But John claims the duty of a friend, not the loyalty of a subject.

6. Sigurd Burckhardt, *Shakespearean Meanings*, 116–43.

7. M. C. Bradbrook, *The Growth and Structure of Elizabethan Comedy* (1955; rpt. Baltimore: Penguin, 1963), 76–83.

8. Philip Edwards, *Threshold of a Nation*, reads Faulconbridge's efforts in act 5 to restore majesty to the English kingship with similar emphasis (120–21).

9. Kantorowicz finds *Richard II* the *locus classicus* of this concern.

10. Edwards, *Threshold*, 115.

11. Axton reads *King John* as one of a number of plays that comment upon the question of the succession (*The Queen's Two Bodies*, 107–11).

6

"So Jest with Heaven"

Deity in *King John*

DOROTHEA KEHLER

BOTH MONARCH AND CHURCH ARE DISCREDITED THROUGH *KING JOHN'S* depiction of murderous Erastian John and warmongering Catholic Pandulph. Is faith discredited too, shown to be no more than a desperate hope? In our post-Holocaust age, the absence of God has become an available meaning. Was it also (unofficially) available to Shakespeare and his 1590s audience? The history of the thirteenth century as Shakespeare reinscribes it bears a perilous resemblance to that of his own time.[1] While *King John* does not lack anti-Catholic propaganda value to serve the Anglican cause, the drama, as origin and as site of contemporary beliefs, may exceed its surface meaning: the audience may not only reject Machiavellian ecclesiastical politics but also interrogate all churches as corruptible temporal powers and ultimately the faith that churches institutionalize.

Many critics have addressed themselves, therefore, to a central interpretive question *King John* poses: Is Shakespeare presenting a world from which God has withdrawn? The play's debate structure is echoed by debate among the critics. For some, God's presence can be inferred from the conclusion of *King John*. According to E. M. W. Tillyard, "By his firmness the Bastard prevents the country from collapsing before the French, and God showed his forgiveness by uniting it very shortly under Henry III."[2] M. M. Reese concurs: "The final promise of unification under the young Prince Henry marks God's forgiveness of the former acts of revolt; a forgiveness made possible only by Faulconbridge's decision not to be a rebel too."[3] For James L. Calderwood, "once human decisions have been made, a supernatural judgment is pronounced upon them."[4] Other critics, however, find that in *King John* God ceases to show His hand in history. John F. Danby sees a change in Shakespeare's attitude towards

99

history between the writing of the first tetralogy and *King John*: history becomes "a process not controlled by God, nor subject to the scheme of His revenges. History is no longer divine. . . ."[5] H. M. Richmond argues that John's swift, successful retreat from France "shatters the conventional belief that violation of the code of religious sanctions is necessarily followed by the appropriate divine retribution. . . ," and concludes that "the play offers no evidence for a simple providential judgment by God, either against the 'immoral' John, or for him."[6] Sigurd Burckhardt states, "God may still be there, but He can no longer be effectively invoked in the affairs of men, since He has neither voice nor sanctions."[7] Little wonder that these divergent views have led to more recent discussion of *King John* as deliberately ambivalent or open-ended.[8]

What has not yet received sufficient attention in this critical debate is the quality of faith evident in the characters' use of religious language. An examination of the contexts within which *King John*'s characters refer to religion should clarify the extent to which faith influences their behavior. Because *King John* is dialectical and emphasizes talk over action, because Elizabethans went to "hear" rather than to see a play, language is primary in creating the dramatic context from which meaning unfolds. Expletives grounded in Christianity, invocations of heaven and the deity, oaths, and references to salvation and damnation and to sin and blessedness—indeed the entire vocabulary of religion as a response to specific situations is integral to the spectator's sense of the play's informing world view. I do not claim that piety demonstrates God's presence or that irreverence or religious hypocrisy demonstrates God's absence; nevertheless, piety creates a dramatic ambience supporting providentialism, whereas hypocrisy supports secularism.

There are few characters in *King John* who do not at some point "jest with heaven" (3.1.242); young Arthur for the most part and Prince Henry stand out as exceptions. The others bear out Sir Walter Raleigh's observation on the gulf between religious discourse and actual practice: "We are all (in effect) become comedians in religion; and while we act in gesture and voice divine virtues, in all the course of our lives we renounce our persons and the parts we play."[9] The religious utterances through act 3, scene 4—where Constance apprehends Arthur's death—are without exception jests with heaven, and are instrumental in establishing the strongly secular tone of the first half of *King John*.

From Elinor's first reference to heaven through the Bastard's last adversions to hell and sin in act 1, scene 1, divinity is trivialized to the point of losing all force as a guide to right action. The de-ethicizing of religion begins with Elinor's rejoinder to John, who insists on "Our strong possession and our right" (1.1.39):

> Your strong possession much more than your right,
> Or else it must go wrong with you and me;
> So much my conscience whispers in your ear,
> Which none but heaven, and you, and I, shall hear.
>
> (1.1.40–43)

The claims of Elinor's conscience extend only far enough to alert her son to his weak suit. Heaven becomes party to political chicanery; God is on the side of the bigger battalions, a co-conspirator winking at the maneuvers of *Realpolitik*. The same heaven that overlooks sin in the public sphere winks at venial sin. The Bastard at first relies on a heaven that has conveniently guarded the secret of his parentage: "But for the certain knowledge of that truth / I put you o'er to heaven and to my mother" (1.1.61–62). He hopes for continued heavenly protection—"Heaven guard my mother's honor, and my land!" (1.1.70)— while breezily thanking heaven for his good looks: "O old Sir Robert, father, on my knee / I give heaven thanks I was not like to thee!" (1.1.82–83). Knighted but landless, he rests secure in his easy relationship with a leering divinity. His mother's adultery becomes a holy occasion: "Now blessed be the hour by night or day / When I was got, Sir Robert was away!" (1.1.165–66).[10] A sin that bears its privilege on earth is no sin, as the Bastard proves by turning Christian doctrine upside down in defense of his mother:[11] "And they [my kin] shall say, when Richard me begot, / If thou hadst said him nay, it had been sin. / Who says it was, he lies, I say 'twas not" (1.1.274–76). Implicit in the Bastard's jocularity is a denial of God as a moral force. For the Bastard as for Elinor—who likes him well—God is an accomplice. For the Renaissance audience, however, a god who smiles upon public and private misdeeds is no god.

If the first scene depicts the Bastard as irreligious, the second shows his conversion: "Gain, be my lord, for I will worship thee" (2.1.598). Since each character's every speech invoking the concept of deity is uttered in the context of self-interest, the Bastard is merely assimilating to the majority culture. Even Arthur disappoints, for his first words, admittedly spoken at King Philip's urging, bespeak a compromise with commodity ill-befitting innocence: "God shall forgive you Cordelion's death / The rather that you give his offspring life, / Shadowing their right under your wings of war . . ." (2.1.12–14). Arthur's speech also implies that he knows God's intention towards Austria and knows God's reasons. Remarkably, God's will corresponds exactly to Arthur's—or to his mother's. In spite of his declaration that he is "not worth this coil that's made for me" (2.1.165)—an embarrassed, tearful response to Elinor's and Constance's bitter contest over him—Arthur's initial appreciation of Austria's "wings of war" endorses a bloodbath in God's name.

The military leaders are quick to take their cues from Arthur. Austria speaks for all: "The peace of heaven is theirs that lift their swords / In such a just and charitable war" (2.1.35–36). John—now "God's wrathful agent" (2.1.87) notwithstanding the intimations of Elinor's conscience—and King Philip—"most divinely vow'd" (2.1.237) to protect Arthur—proceed to a trial by combat in which their subjects' lives are food for powder:

> *King John.* Then God forgive the sin of all those souls
> 　　That to their everlasting residence,
> 　　Before the dew of evening fall, shall fleet
> 　　In dreadful trial of our kingdom's king!
> *King Philip.* Amen, amen! Mount, chevaliers! To arms!
>
> 　　　　　　　　　　　　　　　　　　(2.1.283–87)

When insufficient lives are lost on either side to define a decisive victory, the Bastard cavalierly offers his plan to increase the devastation by destroying Angiers as a prelude to "Mak[ing] work upon ourselves, for heaven or hell" (2.1.407), a plan which wins the approval of the moral majority.

The kings leave the Bastard's plan untried only because of Hubert's[12] alternative, a marriage of policy between Blanch and the "blessed" Dolphin (2.1.437), whose patently false protestations of love earn the Bastard's parody. The marriage arranged, King Philip admits to John that "God knows" (2.1.549) he is forsworn for his own advantage.[13] The Bastard knows this too. Earlier, he had heard Constance prophesy a kind of supernatural simony as she declaimed on Arthur's tears, "Which heaven shall take in nature of a fee; / Ay, with these crystal beads heaven shall be brib'd / To do him justice, and revenge on you" (2.1.170–72). What can the Bastard conclude but that where "have is have, however men do catch" (1.1.173), lipservice may be given to God, but the wise worship Gain.

The religious rhetoric of the ensuing scenes similarly delineates the victims' piety as self-serving or hypocritical. Pathetic as Constance and Blanch are, it is difficult to applaud their devotion. Constance dominates the scene, but the altruism of her invocations of God grow suspect once she expresses her most heartfelt concern: "France friend with England, what becomes of me?" (3.1.35). Out of frustrated ambition, fear, and despair, Constance denounces the wedding day as

"A wicked day, and not a holy day" (3.1.83). Hers is the victim's image of God—a powerful protector who at any cost to others evens the score. Thus, she demands war as divine aid:

> Arm, arm, you heavens, against these perjur'd kings!
> A widow cries; be husband to me, heavens!
> Let not the hours of this ungodly day
> Wear out the [day] in peace; but ere sunset,
> Set armed discord 'twixt these perjur'd kings!
> Hear me, O, hear me!
>
> (3.1.107–12)

For Constance, Elinor (who would profit from peace) is a "devil" (3.1.196), and Blanch is another: "O Lewis, stand fast! the devil tempts thee here / In likeness of a new untrimmed bride" (3.1.208–09). If Philip makes war, he will be saved and "hell lose a soul" (3.1.197). Yet when Constance kneels in prayer, it is not to God but to Lewis. Again, she mistakenly puts her faith in princes. Lewis, she implies, is able to defeat what she knows to be God's will—a double theological fallacy: "I do pray to thee, / Thou virtuous Dolphin, alter not the doom / Forethought by heaven!" (3.1.310–12). In crises Constance's faith wavers, exposing a "mistrust of heavenly justice."[14] While we are likely to believe with Blanch that "The Lady Constance speaks not from her faith, / But from her need" (3.1.210–11), the same can be said of Blanch. The sounds of war only now become "clamors of hell" (3.1.304) because this is Blanch's wedding day. Her loyalties divided, she gives way to self-pity: "Husband, I cannot pray that thou mayst win; / Uncle, I needs must pray that thou mayst lose . . ." (3.1.331–32). Life is easier when one knows whom to pray for and whom to pray against. Blanch rues her own hard lot. Not faith but need moves both betrayed women. Victims no less than victimizers juggle religious language and precepts for their own purposes.

The victimizers are, of course, far more unappealing in their implicit negation of a higher ethical power. After having heard Elinor deny the legitimacy of her son's claim in the first scene, it is impossible to accept John's "sacred king" speech at face value. In light of his false claim, John's use of divinity to serve his own ends is transparent:

> What earthy name to interrogatories
> Can taste the free breath of a sacred king?
>
> . . . .
>
> But as we, under [God], are supreme head,
> So under Him that great supremacy,
> Where we do reign, we will alone uphold
> Without th' assistance of a mortal hand.

> So tell the Pope, all reverence set apart
> To him and his usurp'd authority.
>
> (3.1.147–48, 155–60)

Granted the supremacy of Church over State, the pope's authority is legitimate. Granted the supremacy of State over Church, John's authority is still "usurp'd."

The papal legate is not interested in the question of John's right. Since John holds England, initially he is included in Pandulph's acknowledgment of power: "Hail, you anointed deputies of heaven!" (3.1.136). But once his "holy errand" (3.1.137) is thwarted, Pandulph mandates war between France and England, providing King Philip with a justification for breaking his oath to John. Given his premises, his argument may be "irresistible,"[15] but it is couched in language that anticipates Polonius at his most devious: "though indirect, / Yet indirection thereby grows direct, / And falsehood falsehood cures . . ." (3.1.275–7). Almost as much as his warmongering, the casuistical tone of Pandulph's argument leads us to discount his talk of "heaven" (3.1.266), "religion" (3.1.279, 280), and "pray'rs" (3.1.293) and to see him, at our most charitable, as just another power broker.[16]

King Philip again emerges equally if not more tarnished than his fellows. Reluctant to undo "the conjunction of our inward souls / . . . link'd together / With all religious strength of sacred vows" (3.1.227–9)—and to forgo Blanch's magnificent dowry—he begs Pandulph to reconsider. But when Pandulph is adamant, Philip bows to the pope's more secure power, now breaking faith to John as he had to Arthur. To the questions Philip asks Pandulph—Shall he and John (and Austria and Lewis, and later the lords and Melun) "Play fast and loose with faith? so jest with heaven?" (3.1.242)—the answer is a resounding "yes."

Act 3, scene 2, moving swiftly from the Bastard's flippancy through John's seduction of Hubert, marks a nadir in the corruption of religious rhetoric. The Bastard gives Gain priority over God as, setting out to plunder abbeys, he takes leave of Elinor: "Grandame, I will pray / (If ever I remember to be holy) / For your fair safety . . ." (3.3.14–16). Elinor, most likely aware of John's purpose, conveniently takes Arthur aside while John commissions Hubert to assassinate the boy. Then she bids John farewell: "My blessing go with thee!" (3.3.71). John's gradual insinuation of his purpose to Hubert is an exercise in evil, made even more loathsome by his references to religion. He mingles the spiritual with the mercenary: "There is a soul counts thee her creditor, / And with advantage means to pay thy love . . ." (3.3.21–22). He invokes heaven to witness his love: "By heaven, Hubert, I am almost asham'd / To say what good respect I have of thee" (3.3.27–28). Although he cannot bring himself to speak openly because "The sun is in the heaven" (3.3.34), he could "If this same were a churchyard where we stand" (3.3.40). And Hubert, who swears "By heaven" (3.3.58) to die for John, within a few lines unflinchingly agrees to kill for him. Shakespeare's tone in this scene is at its most sophisticated and ironic.

Although this pattern of irreverent, egotistical, warped use of religious language can be traced throughout the second half of the play as well, it is not the only pattern. Elliott claims that "piety in *King John* is almost always tainted with hypocrisy,"[17] but that "almost" is significant. In act 3, scene 3, another pattern of religious reference is initiated, opposed to what we have seen so far, suggesting that religion does have a place in a political world. The road forks, one leg being a continuation of the main, one a new path of sincerity. Both are traveled. Some characters—Pandulph, Lewis, the English rebels— remain committed to the old way of insincerity. But as many other characters sooner or later strike out on the new path. This alternative to religious hypocrisy creates a sense of division within *King John*[18] and contributes to its ambivalence.

The alternative strand of allusions to deity originates among the unsuccessful. The change in circumstance that Constance undergoes, from potential winner to loser, motivates her use of religious language now void of manipulation. Even Philip appears moved to genuine compassion by the sight of the prescient widow: "Look who comes here! a grave unto a soul, / Holding th' eternal spirit, against her will . . ." (3.4.17–18). Perhaps he, like Constance, learns sincerity in defeat just before disappearing from the play. Constance, mourning her son, forgets ambition and becomes a Niobe: "I am not mad, I would to heaven I were!" (3.4.48). Desperately she hopes "That we shall see and know our friends in heaven" (3.4.77), and fears, "When I shall meet him in the court of heaven / I shall not know him . . ." (3.4.87–88). She concludes her most moving speech ("Grief fills the room up of my absent child") by crying, "O Lord, my boy, my Arthur, my fair son!" (3.4.103), a cry torn from her heart.

Once removed from the instruction of King Philip and the ambition of his mother, Arthur is all innocence.[19] Reminiscent of Henry VI, Arthur wishes he were a homely swain: "By my christendom, / So I were out of prison and kept sheep, / I should be as merry as the day is long" (4.1.16–18). Ironically, he wishes that Hubert were his father: "I would to heaven / I were your son, so you would love me, Hubert" (4.1.23–24). Learning that he must be blinded, the boy attempts religious resignation: "If heaven be pleas'd that you must use me ill, /

Why then you must" (4.1.55–56); but the sight of the irons is too much for him: "For heaven sake, Hubert, let me not be bound!" (4.1.77). He cries out, "O heaven! that there were but a mote in yours [Hubert's eyes] . . ." (4.1.91) and believes that God has heard him and has cooled the coal: "The breath of heaven hath blown his spirit out, / And strew'd repentant ashes on his head" (4.1.109–10). When Hubert is won over, Arthur remembers God in his exclamation: "O heaven! I thank you, Hubert" (4.1.131). Reese points out that in *King John* Arthur does not argue theologically against Hubert as the character does in *The Troublesome Raigne*.[20] Instead, Shakespeare's Arthur, whose dying words are a prayer—"Heaven take my soul, and England keep my bones!" (4.3.10)—comes to represent simple and innocent faith.

Even John has moments of religious honesty, ushered in by Pembroke's reminder of the final judgment: "This must be answer'd either here or hence" (4.2.89). However much John squirms, attempting to displace his guilt onto Hubert—"But thou didst understand me by my signs, / And didst in signs again parley with sin . . ." (4.2.237–38)—John cannot forget his soul's destiny: "O, when the last accompt 'twixt heaven and earth / Is to be made, then shall this hand and seal / Witness against us to damnation!" (4.2.216–18). In his death throes, his unconscious unlocked, he describes his physical state *here* as a metaphor for his spiritual state *hence:* "Within me is a hell, and there the poison / Is as a fiend confin'd to tyrannize / On unreprievable condemned blood" (5.7.46–48).

Once he feels secure in his integrity, Hubert uses religious language as he had not in his scene with Arthur. Now, thinking Arthur alive, he tells John, "I'll make a peace between your soul and you" (4.2.250). Innocent of Arthur's death, Hubert defends his life against Salisbury—"By heaven, I think my sword's as sharp as yours" (4.3.82)—and protests his innocence "Upon my soul" (4.3.125). "If I in act, consent, or sin of thought / Be guilty . . ." (4.3.135–36), he says, staking his salvation on his truth, "Let hell want pains enough to torture me" (4.3.138).

But the character whose language is most instrumental in infusing the latter part of the play with piety is the Bastard. Shocked into a new seriousness by Arthur's death, he finally remembers to be holy. His response upon discovering Arthur's body is judicious and sincere: "It is a damned and a bloody work, / The graceless action of a heavy hand— / If that it be the work of any hand" (4.3.57–59). Alone with Hubert, the Bastard speaks more passionately: "Beyond the infinite and boundless reach / Of mercy, if thou didst this deed of death, / Art thou damn'd, Hubert" (4.3.117–19). Then, having lost his way, the

Bastard considers his situation and England's and decides to follow John—a decision from which the awareness of a higher power is not absent: "The life, the right, and truth of all this realm / Is fled to heaven" (4.3.144–45). Now that "heaven itself doth frown upon the land" (4.3.159), the Bastard will serve his country. Thus, to John, still unaware of Arthur's death, the Bastard extends a charitable (or politic) benefit of the doubt. Arthur has been killed "By some damn'd hand" (5.1.41); the Bastard knows only "on my soul" (5.1.43) that it was not Hubert's.

Whereas Arthur's death is irrevocable, England's defeat need not be. The Bastard's prayer may be for England, or for himself, or for both: "Withhold thine indignation, mighty heaven, / And tempt us not to bear above our power!" (5.6.37–38).[21] Arthur's death, the nobles' revolt, the king's physical and mental collapse, the unpromising prognosis of the war—all teach what can happen when men "bear above" their power. Pushed to the limit—"The Dolphin is preparing hitherward, / Where [God] he knows how we shall answer him . . ." (5.7.59–60)—the Bastard falls back on loyalty to sustain him: "my soul shall wait on thee to heaven, / As it on earth hath been thy servant still" (5.7.72–73). We may quarrel with the Bastard's disposition of John's soul but not with his generosity of spirit: after all, John has shown the Bastard only kindness and advancement, and the Bastard has just watched him die in agony. Faith and altruism shine through the convention of the squire's speech. Although the Bastard's character narrows when he becomes a "King's man," it deepens as well.[22]

Also important for sharply delineating a religious alternative to the irreligious content of the first half of the play is the appearance of two new characters. Both not only speak devoutly but are godsends to England. Melun, who "must die here and live hence by truth" (5.4.29), asks only that he be borne where he may "part this body and my soul / With contemplation and devout desires" (5.4.47–48). He is a "ficelle,"[23] his sole function being to confess and so bring the rebels back to John. Prince Henry, a *deus ex machina*, is necessary to provide England with a legitimate ruler. An innocent and pious child,[24] he is a second Arthur. Unlike Arthur, however, he is free from foreign domination and has a stronger claim by virtue of possession and inheritance from the *de facto* king. Prince Henry's inquiring mind promises intellectual strength: grieved by John's death, he yet observes parenthetically that it is the brain "Which some suppose the soul's frail dwelling-house" (5.7.3). He is moved to reflect on his father's end: "'Tis strange that death should sing," listening as John "from the organ-pipe of frailty sings / His soul and body to their lasting rest"

(5.7.20, 23–24). We remember Arthur as Prince Henry wishes his tears "might relieve" his father (5.7.44–45). He weeps again as the Bastard and Salisbury swear fealty to him: "I have a kind soul that would give thanks, / And knows not how to do it but with tears" (5.7.108–09). This, the penultimate speech of the play, provides a vital context for the Bastard's martial music.[25] The Bastard ends the play affirmatively by drowning out the memory of the mad king's song. But Prince Henry gives to England his innocent soul.

This providentialist reading is further supported by the significant role given to the supernatural in the latter part of the play. Alexander Leggatt calls attention to "the workings of chance" that leave the characters "at the mercy of forces greater than themselves, forces whose action is erratic but irresistible."[26] Manheim notes that Shakespeare departs from *The Troublesome Raigne*, making the omen of the five moons "a message from God to John."[27] And Calderwood asserts that "the loss of his [the Bastard's] army has personal as well as military implications, that this check of power also represents a form of divine injunction against any attempt to seize power for himself."[28] Humanity may jest with heaven, but heaven will assert itself. Through the new genuineness of references to divinity and the workings of the supernatural in the last two acts, Shakespeare makes a providentialist interpretation tenable.[29]

And yet, Shakespeare does not employ so simple and schematic a division as secular first half and providentialist second half. From act 3, scene 4 to the play's final moments, the path leading to a secular interpretation is still traveled. Keeping to the old way, using religious language for his own ends, is Pandulph, who plots with Lewis to exploit John's fear and Arthur's vulnerability. Like Edmund, he cynically mocks supernatural interpretations of natural occurrences, explaining that once John kills Arthur, the disaffected English will inevitably construe natural events to John's disadvantage as "tongues of heaven" (3.4.158). When John is forced to submit to Rome, he lies: "But (heav'n be thank'd!) it is but voluntary" (5.1.29). Not unexpectedly, Lewis, far less green and fresh than Pandulph thinks him, holds his own in this company of experienced reprobates. Lewis has his pact with the rebellious lords inscribed so that both sides "May know wherefore we took the sacrament, / And keep our faiths firm and inviolable" (5.2.6–7), although all the while he intends their deaths. When Salisbury weeps over being forced to rebel, Lewis finds "This show'r, blown up by tempest of the soul" (5.2.50) as startling as the sight of meteors covering "the vaulty top of heaven" (5.2.52); then he promises the doomed lords shares of booty equal to his own. Lewis speaks piously of Pandulph, thinking him an enemy to England who comes "To give us warrant from the hand of heaven, / And on our actions set the name of right / With holy breath" (5.2.66–68). But when Lewis learns that Pandulph comes to make peace, he swears by his soul to defy Rome: "And shall I now give o'er the yielded set? / No, no, on my soul, it never shall be said" (5.2.107–08).

Like Pandulph and Lewis, Salisbury treads the path of hypocrisy. As chief spokesman for the English lords in act 4, Salisbury seems as unconvincing in his religiosity as the leaders he betrays. Kneeling before Arthur's corpse, Salisbury makes a "holy vow" (4.3.67) to avenge Arthur, which Pembroke and Bigot "religiously confirm" (4.3.73). Religiously Salisbury leads the lords to Lewis: [30] "Away with me, all you whose souls abhor / Th' uncleanly savors of a slaughter-house, / For I am stifled with this smell of sin" (4.3.111–13). Later, just as religiously, he leads them back to John. Although Salisbury declares that to fight against England "grieves my soul" (5.2.15), not until he learns of Lewis's perfidy does he "untread the steps of damned flight" (5.4.52). Whether Salisbury is motivated by his waning influence over John (evidenced by John's proceeding with his second coronation), by considerations of safety, by fears for Arthur's life, or by some combination of these factors is open to speculation. Nevertheless, religion in the mouth of one who turns and turns again is invariably suspect. More likely than not, the lords are time-servers seeking to clothe themselves in some shreds of honor.

And, then, there is the powerful presentational image of Arthur's fall "at the centre of events."[31] The death of a child, England's rightful heir, strengthens the impression that the world of commodity is one in which humanity is separated from God. Arthur's falling to his death is anticipated by Pandulph's prediction—"That John may stand, then Arthur needs must fall" (3.4.139)—and emphasized by Lewis's repetition—"But what shall I gain by young Arthur's fall?" (3.4.141). Arthur's fall both literalizes or "unmetaphors" (to use Rosalie Colie's term) the *de casibus topos*, and, at the same time, as a culminating pictorialization suggests the fallen world of *King John*. Both Edward I. Berry and Virginia Mason Vaughan describe *King John* as a portrait of a fallen world.[32] John Wilders posits a broader thesis: in the history plays Shakespeare portrays "in social and political terms the theological idea of a 'fallen' humanity."[33] In *King John* the fall of innocence is visually enacted before us.

In answer, then, to the question at the heart of this essay—Has God withdrawn from the world of *King John*?—it appears from the way characters use the language of faith (as well as from key supporting stage images) that *King John* is open to a secular interpretation no less than to a providential one. Providentialists are likely to weight the last part of the play more heavily than the first, arguing that although the world of *King John* is beset with godlessness, in the end it is not devoid of acts of God or of the godly through whom the Deity works His will. Secularists are likely to be influenced by the proportion of irreligious to genuinely religious speeches. There are more of the former, and they are found throughout the play, thus creating a prevailing tone not easily undermined by the lines of the devout. The play's devout may be unconvincing, either because of mixed or ambiguous motives or because they are underdeveloped characters, seemingly "tacked on." Then, too, John's assassination attempt and Arthur's consequent death pose the problem of evil as baldly as does the murder of Macduff's family: "Did heaven look on / And would not take their part?" Ambivalence would seem an appropriate mode for Shakespeare, a maturing, insightful, and politically cautious writer, to adopt in approaching John's reign, a reign dominated by hegemonic political and religious problems. Conflict between a *de jure* and a *de facto* king vitiates the concept of divine right. Sectarian quarrels opposing Catholicism to what most members of Shakespeare's audience would regard as early Protestantism may cast all in doubt. That Shakespeare allows his audience a choice of interpretations is not surprising in light of the intensification of the conflict between the politically disaffected and the divine-right monarchists, between secularism and fideism, in the 1590s. Shakespeare wrote for the church censor, humanist Puritan, Catholic recusant, closet agnostic, and School-of-Night atheist, apparently without offending.

Yet if spectators of varying opinions could think that the play confirmed their beliefs, ambivalence regarding the vital religious concerns of the play and of its audience makes for a potentially weak ending. *King John* risks leaving those spectators to gaze at a stage whose heaven and hell can be seen as demystified emblems, constructs shorn of authority, between which kings and would-be kings, graceless men and vulnerable boys, vie for power. Hence at the end of act 5, the question of God's presence or absence is displaced. *King John* concludes with the Bastard's rousing clarion call:

> Come the three corners of the world in arms,
> And we shall shock them. Nought shall make us rue,
> If England to itself do rest but true.
>
> (5.7.116–18)[34]

What matters in the end are not spiritual but military needs, not the soul's but the nation's survival through the common bond of patriotism. The need to worship, inherent or learned, is dangerous when left unfulfilled. The Bastard's final speech provides an answer to that need and a dramatic distraction from *King John's* ambivalence. Bellicose nationalism is the new faith in Shakespeare's vision of the modern political world.

Notes

1. Some parallels: The official church—Catholic in the thirteenth century, Anglican in the sixteenth—was threatened both theologically and politically. The Catholic church taught that Elizabeth had supplanted Mary, the rightful ruler; similarly John supplants Arthur. In *Narrative and Dramatic Sources,* Geoffrey Bullough notes that like John Elizabeth was excommunicated, was invaded by a foreign power sympathetic to Rome, had wished for her competitor's assassination, and had made a scapegoat of her agent in the execution proceedings (4:1–2).

2. E. M. W. Tillyard, *Shakespeare's History Plays,* 226.

3. M. M. Reese, *The Cease of Majesty,* 278.

4. James L. Calderwood, "Commodity and Honour in *King John*" in *Shakespeare: The Histories,* ed. Eugene M. Waith, 92.

5. John F. Danby, *Shakespeare's Doctrine of Nature,* 69.

6. H. M. Richmond, *Shakespeare's Political Plays,* 113 and 118.

7. Sigurd Burckhardt, *Shakespearean Meanings,* 133.

8. "Accordingly, *King John* appears to be the play in which Shakespeare commits himself to the development of this powerfully ambivalent perspective for his history plays, a perspective combining the elements of depth and breadth, of engagement and detachment, which will ultimately produce *Henry IV* and *Henry V*" (Larry S. Champion, " 'Confound Their Skill in Covetousness,' " 38). In "*King John* and Problematic Art," Jonathan Reeve Price observes that Shakespeare "brings the play to a definite conclusion—and yet leaves it open to interpretation" (28). And Douglas C. Wixson states, "By refusing particular views, Shakespeare encourages us to devise our own" (" 'Calm Words Folded Up in Smoke,' " 122).

9. Raleigh, "Preface" to *The History of the World* (1614) in *The Works of Sir Walter Ralegh, Kt.,* 8 vols., 1820 (rpt. New York: Burt Franklin, 1965), 2:xxxii.

10. In light of Kökeritz's observation that "hour" and "whore" were homophonic in Elizabethan English, the couplet is all the more ribald; see E. A. J. Honigmann's note in the New Arden *King John,* 12.

11. After a futile attempt at concealment, Lady Faulconbridge admits Philip's paternity. Despite her expletive, she speaks less out of penitence than out of fear of his anger and the desire to exonerate herself:

> Heaven! lay not my transgression to my charge,
> That art the issue of my dear offense,
> Which was so strongly urg'd past my defense.

> (1.1.256–58)

12. I accept the conclusion of J. Dover Wilson in his Cambridge edition of *King John* (xlv–xlvii) and of Honigmann in the New Arden edition (xxxvi–xxxvii) that Hubert and the Citizen of Angiers are one and the same.

13. John R. Elliott regards King Philip as a model Machiavel: "Thus, just as Machiavelli . . . note[s] that a Prince 'should seeme with great reverence to extoll and imbrase Pittie, Fayth Honestie Courtesie & Religion, and speciallie the laste,' so Shakespeare's Philip is careful to interlace his address with pious words and phrases—

'divinely,' 'religiously,' 'zeal,' 'clouds of heaven'—and to deal liberally in 'Amens'"
("Shakespeare and the Double Image of King John," 77).

14. Elliott, "Double Image," 79.

15. Samuel Johnson's argument is quoted in full by Reese, *Cease of Majesty,* 272 n. 1.

16. This is the view of John Palmer in *Political Characters of Shakespeare,* 331; on the other hand, Gunnar Boklund sees him as the "archpolitician" ("The Troublesome Ending of *King John,*" 183); and Champion sees him as "chilling" ("'Confound Their Skill,'" 48).

17. Elliott, "Double Image," 77.

18. Julia C. Van de Water finds a break between the first three acts and the last two with regard to the development of the Bastard ("The Bastard in *King John,*" 144). In "Dramatic Perspective in *King John,*" Alexander Leggatt also notes this change (10) as well as a change in the design of the scenes after Angiers: "The play is broken down into a series of shorter scenes with fewer characters" (8). The change in the way religious rhetoric is employed is one facet of a larger development.

19. In fact, Arthur is associated with innocence in three passages—4.1.25 and 64, and 4.2.259. Nevertheless, suspicious of the friendship between Arthur and Hubert and of Arthur's denial that his is "crafty love" (4.1.53), Richard Levin questions Arthur's innocence; he suggests that "Arthur's love may well be 'crafty' [politically calculating]" ("*King John*'s Bastard," 34). See also Honigmann on "a child forced into duplicity" (New Arden *King John,* lxvii). I cannot believe that a theater audience would find Arthur anything but pathetic in this scene.

20. Reese, *Cease of Majesty,* 281 n. 1. See also Burckhardt's reply to Reese in *Shakespearean Meanings,* 119–23.

21. Although Honigmann cites *I Corinthians* 10:13 to clarify line 38 (New Arden *King John,* 141), it remains ambiguous, perhaps deliberately; it may mean no more than "do not test us with intolerable suffering," but the possibility of the Bastard's usurpation enriches the play by creating a parallel to John's situation vis-à-vis Arthur.

22. Leggatt, "Dramatic Perspective," 10.

23. Van de Water so designates the Bastard ("The Bastard in *King John,*" 146), but insofar as he has the most lines in the play and becomes the commander of the English forces, the identification is questionable for his character.

24. Shakespeare's Prince Henry appears more mature than a nine-year-old, whereas sixteen-year-old Arthur is an "infant . . ." (3.4.132).

25. See Michael Manheim's discussion of the Bastard's "fourth" voice in his essay "The Four Voices of the Bastard" (Chapter 8).

26. Leggatt, "Dramatic Perspective," 12.

27. Michael Manheim, *The Weak King Dilemma in the Shakespearean History Play,* 140.

28. Calderwood, "Commodity and Honour" in the Waith anthology, 100.

29. Such a reading is fleetingly suggested in the opening scene when John voices his amusement at the Bastard: "Why, what a madcap hath heaven lent us here!" (1.1.84). If "us" refers to Elinor and John, the Bastard is heaven-lent, for he rescues Elinor (3.2.7–8) and stands by John despite Arthur's death. If "us" is understood as the royal possessive, John's exclamation suggests that heaven's purpose is to preserve England. Notwithstanding John's jesting tone, the Bastard may be considered as much a godsend to England as Melun or Prince Henry. Although the Bastard neither wins a decisive victory nor establishes a just peace, his spirit, at its best insouciant, courageous, and loyal, appears to hold England together. In the first scene there is a presentational image of the Bastard's knighting that also supports a providentialist reading. While too abrupt to convey immediately a sense of personal consecration to

duty, for some spectators the remembered image may later develop such resonances. But even at the start of the play, the truncated ritual is enough to remind the audience that the creation of a knight was intended as more than a mere promotion, i.e., it signified a contract to which God was a party.

30. We should not forget that the lords were in communication with Lewis and were planning to join him (4.3.11–20) even before they found Arthur's body.

31. Boklund, "Troublesome Ending," 175.

32. See Edward I. Berry, *Patterns of Decay*, 118, 122; and Virginia Mason Vaughan, "Between Tetralogies," 420.

33. John Wilders, *The Lost Garden: A View of Shakespeare's English and Roman History Plays* (London: Macmillan, 1978), 10.

34. David Scott Kastan observes that the speech is conditional and that in fact the nobles were not loyal to Henry III for long (*Shakespeare and the Shapes of Time*, 53). On the basis of similar observations, Philip Edwards concludes that *King John* portrays "the frustrations of the search for true royalty in the national community, when the condition of life is one of self-wounding caused by new ambitions extinguishing old sanctity" (*Threshold of a Nation*, 122). Even so, the force of the Bastard's rhetoric and the small chance of the spectators' familiarity with the early years of Henry's reign suggest that the final speech is a coup de théâtre.

7

Blots, Stains, and Adulteries

The Impurities in *King John*

JOSEPH CANDIDO

> To solemnize this day the glorious sun
> Stays in his course and plays the alchymist,
> Turning with splendor of his precious eye
> The meagre cloddy earth to glittering gold.
>
> (3.1.77–80)

THE VOICE IS THAT OF PHILIP OF FRANCE, AND THE SUBJECT IS THE FAIR expectation of a royal father on the marriage of his son to the niece of a newly made ally. Yet Philip's resolution—soon dashed—to forge a "blessed" and "holy" (3.1.75, 82) moment from the dross of human experience ("cloddy earth to glittering gold") provides not only a metaphor for the sacramentally transforming force of Christian marriage and the hope for political renewal, but also an instructive focal point for much of the tension and "ambivalence" that critics have seen in *King John*.[1] For Philip's hopes, futile though they prove to be, nevertheless evince a psychological longing for "purity" that is one of the most avid preoccupations of the play. This longing, whether expressing itself in a desire for political or personal legitimacy, clear conscience, or right behavior, helps invest the play with a tonal quality rather distinct among Shakespeare's histories, and may even account for some of what we find so disquieting and indeed so "different" about *King John*.

From the very outset of the play we find ourselves in a moral environment betraying something like a Hamletesque obsession with sullied purity and, as in Hamlet's case, with adultery. This concern is, of course, serio-comically evoked in the Bastard's confrontation with Robert Faulconbridge in act 1, where the tangled question of personal

114

legitimacy reflects ominously the larger political problem of royal right. Here, as elsewhere, accusing another of personal defilement (in this case bastardy) becomes no more than a bald exercise in self-interest; but just this sort of accusation can also function at other points in the play, perhaps less cynically, to underscore the moral gap that separates an engaging ideal of purity from a defiled political world. When, for example, Philip challenges John's right to the English throne by announcing his determination to "look into the blots and stains of right" on behalf of the "boy" Arthur (2.1.114–15), he raises, metaphorically at least, the dilemma of the undefiled innocent in the corrupt world of "strong possession." Indeed, simple purity, when invoked in *King John*, is almost always seen as set perilously in an adulterate world that pays it moral lip service at one moment and sullies it the next.

Nowhere is this situation more apparent than in the events immediately following Philip's open challenge of John's legitimacy, where the silent Arthur gets caught in a verbal crossfire between his mother and his grandmother that defiles his legitimacy along with that of his uncle:

Elinor. Out, insolent, thy bastard shall be king
  That thou mayst be a queen, and check the world!
Constance. My bed was ever to thy son as true
  As thine was to thy husband, and this boy
  Liker in feature to his father Geffrey
  Than thou and John in manners, being as like
  As rain to water, or devil to his dam.
  My boy a bastard? By my soul I think
  His father never was so true begot—
  It cannot be, and if thou wert his mother.
Elinor. There's a good mother, boy, that blots thy father.
Constance. There's a good grandame, boy, that would blot thee.

(2.1.122–33)

The pun here on "blot" (to stain and to eradicate) is instructive, for as Constance is quick to notice, the grim fact of such internecine accusation is that blood will spoil blood.[2] Arthur's "crystal beads" may indeed prove to be "heaven-moving pearls" (2.1.169, 171) but they have little salutary effect in an earthly environment adulterated by the "sin-conceiving womb" (2.1.182):

  [Arthur] is not only plagued for her sin,
    [i.e., Elinor's supposed adultery]
  But God hath made her sin [i.e., John] and her the plague
  On this removed issue, plagued for her,
  And with her plague, her sin; his injury

> Her injury, the beadle to her sin—
> All punish'd in the person of this child,
> And all for her. A plague upon her!
>
>   (2.1.184–90)

The same problem is delineated in far less convoluted fashion in the incidents surrounding the marriage of Lewis and Blanch. Amidst the swirl of rapidly shifting priorities at Angiers, Hubert proposes the match in rhetorical terms that hearken back to the "crystal beads" and "heaven-moving pearls" of Arthur. He sees the young couple as two "silver currents" that when joined will "glorify the banks that bound them in" (2.1.441–42). Cynicism answers pragmatism with the Bastard's reply that "Here's a stay / That shakes the rotten carcass of old Death / Out of his rags!" (2.1.455–57); but the remark, like Philip's metaphor of the sun, does nonetheless hint at some genuine hope for new—and pure—beginnings.[3] Pandulph's appearance, however, smothers that hope; and Philip's response to the sudden breach of amity again articulates metaphorically the tenuous status of purity in a soiled moral landscape that labors—not always cynically—to sustain it. Philip begins by asking Pandulph to see things from his perspective, particularly in the light of a truce made

>   but new before,
> No longer than we well could wash our hands
> To clap this royal bargain up of peace,
> Heaven knows they were besmear'd and over-stain'd
> With slaughter's pencil. . . .
>
>   (3.1.233–37)

But such incipient cleansing is not to be; and it is Blanch (her name acquires a sad irony as this pattern unfolds) who finds a metaphor for nature's alchemy that speaks far truer than Philip's: "The sun's o'ercast with blood; fair day, adieu!" (3.1.326).

It is Constance, however, who most fully enunciates the perils of innocence in John's adulterate court. Shaken with grief over the proposed marriage of Lewis and Blanch, she begins by equating Arthur's beauteous appearance with moral purity: her son is "fair," in no way "sland'rous to [his] mother's womb," and utterly without the "unpleasing blots and sightless stains" (3.1.44–45, 51) that in her imagination at least would somehow remove him from her love and the right to rule. She then goes on to depict the young boy's political misfortune metaphorically as a form of sexual betrayal:

>   at thy birth, dear boy,
> Nature and Fortune join'd to make thee great.

Of Nature's gifts thou mayst with lilies boast,
And with the half-blown rose. But Fortune, O,
She is corrupted, chang'd, and won from thee;
Sh' adulterates hourly with thine uncle John,
And with her golden hand hath pluck'd on France
To tread down fair respect of sovereignty,
And made his majesty the bawd to theirs.
France is a bawd to Fortune and King John,
That strumpet Fortune, that usurping John!

(3.1.51–61)

The characterization of Fortune as a strumpet is, of course, conventional; but the familiar association of political impurity with failed marriage or adultery is no less meaningful on that account. Furthermore, this odd and persistent joining of politics and adultery in *King John*, as in *Hamlet*, helps locate the play morally in a sort of unweeded political and personal garden that sets it apart tonally from Shakespeare's other histories. The sense of defilement and corruption in *King John* is of a markedly different sort from that found, say, in *Richard III* or even in the plays of the second tetralogy; it is in a far more basic, indeed more literal sense, adulterate.

The feeling of psychological enclosure that derives from being tainted by a corrupt, debased, or illegitimate stock—whether real or imagined—is one of the most strongly realized aspects of *King John* and does, quite clearly, haunt the title character.[4] This anxiety manifests itself in John's case in an almost compulsive strategy of concealment and deception as regards the facts of his moral nature. Elinor's famous "whisper" to John in the opening scene urging him to emphasize his "strong possession" rather than his weaker "right" (1.1.40–43) is perhaps the most obvious expression of the root cause of this anxiety, and helps set the moral and behavioral tone for much of the play. But listen also to the language of the English lords in response to John's controversial second coronation:

Pembroke. You were crown'd before,
    And that high royalty was ne'er pluck'd off;
    The faiths of men ne'er stained with revolt;

· · · · · · · · · · · · · · ·

Salisbury. Therefore, to be possess'd with double pomp,
    To guard a title that was rich before,
    To gild refined gold, to paint the lily,
    To throw a perfume on the violet,
    To smooth the ice, or add another hue
    Unto the rainbow, or with taper-light

To seek the beauteous eye of heaven to garnish,
Is wasteful and ridiculous excess.

. . . .

[Your behavior] Makes sound opinion sick, and truth suspected,
For putting on so new a fashion'd robe.
Pembroke. When workmen strive to do better than well,
They do confound their skill in covetousness,
And oftentimes excusing of a fault
Doth make the fault the worse by th' excuse:
As patches set upon a little breach
Discredit more in hiding of the fault
Than did the fault before it was so patch'd.

(4.2.4–34)

The sense of strain, excess, and over-embroidery that pervades the passage points instructively to the essential difference between John's response to a nagging moral impurity and those of most other characters in the play. Even so pragmatic a politician as Philip occasionally entertains the hope of turning base human matter into moral gold, of somehow cleansing impurity or in some measure reaching beyond it to recapture a lost original of innocence and the hope for new beginnings. John, however, simply lays on a sort of moral makeup that instead of hiding his gnawing corruptions blazons them with bad art. The point here is not merely that cheap appearance is a poor moral substitute for purgation, but that John has absolutely no will—or worse still—capacity to take the nobler course. He is the one king in all of Shakespeare's histories morally inferior to his foreign opposite. The quite unmistakable odor of decadence that surrounds such activities as gilding gold, painting lilies, or perfuming violets is nowhere associated with Philip. In John we have an *English* king with so diminished a moral sensibility that his most ardent response to guilt is the psychological equivalent of putting on a newly made robe or patching worn cloth. His essential ugliness as a character is linked, not as many have supposed, merely to his capacity for evil, but also to his tawdry attempts at coverup.

There is, therefore, a grisly yet metaphorical appropriateness to John's last moments, for the king bodies forth in death the very moral condition he tried so strenuously to conceal in life. Much, quite rightly, has been made of John's ordeal as reflecting the state of a corrupted body politic, but hardly to be missed here is the metaphorical relationship of this particular poisoning to the whole question of personal impurity that the play is everywhere at pains to enforce. Indeed, the repeated comments on the precise details of John's death amount to something like a choric anatomy of moral pollution, and as such call to mind plays like *Doctor Faustus* and even the late medieval moralities:[5]

> It is too late, the life of all his blood
> Is touch'd corruptibly; and his pure brain
> (Which some suppose the soul's frail dwelling-house)
> Doth by the idle comments that it makes
> Foretell the ending of mortality.
>
> (5.7.1–5)

> I am a scribbled form, drawn with a pen
> Upon a parchment, and against this fire
> Do I shrink up.
>
> (5.7.32–34)

> Within me is a hell, and there the poison
> Is as a fiend confin'd to tyrannize
> On unreprievable condemned blood.
>
> (5.7.46–48)

In this rhetorical context the king's dilemma becomes the grim literalization of a moral condition that both defines the world of *King John* and colors it tonally. He is quite literally seared to death beneath the "wasteful and ridiculous excess" (4.2.16) of his moral disguise.

The idea of a hostile and inevitably destructive opposition between purity and adulteration is everywhere apparent in *King John;* but it is not the only attitude expressed in the play regarding these seemingly irreconcilable forces. For example, when Constance, luxuriating in sorrow, alludes to the "sound rottenness" of "amiable lovely death" (3.4.25–26), she touches upon the strange and oxymoronic connection of wholesomeness with decay. Her "fair affliction" (3.3.36), like Cleopatra's under different circumstances, excites in her a desire for a tenacious lovers' embrace that shackles accidents and bolts up change. Highly embroidered as Constance's remarks often tend to be, they are seldom without thematic point. In this instance her attempt to yoke wholesomeness with rottenness, indeed to perceive a sort of tense but inevitable inseparability between the two, has clear implications for the play as a whole and in particular for the Bastard, its most psychologically and physiologically divided character.

From the very outset of the play we are aware of a strange quality of authenticity in the Bastard that exists somehow untainted by the clear fact of his illegitimacy. This idea is one way expressed by John when he argues that the Bastard is "legitimate" (1.1.116) on the grounds that he was born in wedlock into the household of a man with a perfect right to claim him (1.1.116–29), a nice legalism soon brushed aside when the king further authenticates his kinsman by investing him with his natural father's name: "Sir Richard, and Plantagenet" (1.1.162). On these grounds the Bastard emerges as a witty and engaging impurity who can be translated into "perfect Richard" (1.1.90) on royal impulse, whose legitimacy is tied, as is that of so many others in *King John*, to royal will rather than to moral right. Moreover, at the beginning of the play the Bastard appears to endorse, at least in part, this pragmatic view of authenticity. In language that disturbingly anticipates John's attitude of moral concealment, he gives his own twist to the familiar relationship of inner corruption with fair show:

> And not alone in habit and device,
> Exterior form, outward accoutrement,
> But from the inward motion to deliver
> Sweet, sweet, sweet poison for the age's tooth,
> Which though I will not practice to deceive,
> Yet to avoid deceit, I mean to learn;
> For it shall strew the footsteps of my rising.
>
> (1.1.210–16)

But the Bastard also shows signs of an attitude more complex and morally sophisticated than John's strategy of gilding poison with sweetness yet one which is nevertheless more practical than Philip's dream of moral transmutation. In his brief meeting with Lady Faulconbridge he gives voice to the idea of a synthetic relationship between purity and adulteration that relies neither on moral coverup nor on airy hopes for retrieving lost innocence:

> Some sins do bear their privilege on earth,
> And so doth yours: your fault was not your folly;
>
> .   .   .   .
> With all my heart I thank thee for my father!
> Who lives and dares but say thou didst not well
> When I was got, I'll send his soul to hell.
> Come, lady, I will show thee to my kin,
> And they shall say, when Richard me begot,
> If thou hadst said him nay, it had been sin.
> Who says it was, he lies, I say 'twas not.
>
> (1.1.261–76)

Here is a quite different view of adultery from that expressed by any other character in the play, for it sees purity and adulteration not as hostile and inevitable opposites but rather as curiously interrelated—

indeed often shifting—elements in the practical affairs of life: "If thou hadst said him nay, it had been sin." I do not mean to suggest here that the Bastard is endorsing a position of simple moral relativism; I am suggesting, however, that he is the spokesman in this instance for a synthetic and clear-eyed view of social man that accepts the fact that good can not only often be linked to evil but can also grow out of it. Furthermore, it is this awareness on the Bastard's part that frees him later in the play from the simplistic and self-defeating thinking of the English lords, allowing him to remain loyal to John while at the same time entertaining no naïve illusions about the king's moral goodness. Viewed from this perspective the Bastard—himself a trustworthy, engaging, and morally sensitive product of adultery—becomes a walking embodiment of the ethical position he first expresses here and continues to define and refine as the play proceeds.[6]

The ultimate moment in this process of definition comes shortly after the death of Arthur, as the Bastard, the English lords, and Hubert all meet by chance near the young prince's corpse.[7] In the moments before the body is discovered, the Bastard tries to persuade the "distemper'd lords" (4.3.21) to incline to the king's party. Salisbury speaks for the rebel faction:

> We will not line his thin bestained cloak
> With our pure honors, nor attend the foot
> That leaves the print of blood where e'er it walks.
>
> (4.3.24–26)

In addition to elaborating negatively upon his earlier metaphor of the newly fashioned robe ("thin bestained cloak"), Salisbury here insists once more upon the essential irreconcilability of purity and impurity—at least as he chooses to define the terms. Pure honors (self-interested as their adherents may appear to be) can in no way attach themselves to the filthy garment of John's majesty; good cannot blend productively with evil. Echoing and emphatic consent comes instantly from Pembroke with the discovery of Arthur's body:

> O death, made proud with pure and princely beauty!
> The earth had not a hole to hide this deed.
>
> (4.3.35–36)

> All murthers past do stand excus'd in this;
> And this, so sole and so unmatchable,
> Shall give a holiness, a purity,
> To the yet unbegotten sin of times.
>
> (4.3.51–54)

Poised between the shrill self-righteousness of the lords and the unde-
niable fact of John's moral ugliness is the Bastard. He cannot deny
what looks like "a damned and a bloody work, / The graceless action
of a heavy hand" (4.3.57–58), but he wants to know more. And when
Hubert (supposed by all to be the murderer) soon appears, we have
one of those trenchantly emblematic scenes so characteristic of the
early Shakespeare. As the Bastard stands over the dead body of Arthur
he struggles to mediate between opposed moral and political imperatives. On the one hand are the lords, apparently taking up the "right"
cause in sympathy with the plight of a slaughtered innocent but
treasonous nonetheless; on the other is Hubert, apparently the murderer of Arthur yet loyal to his sovereign in a desperate hour. Here, as
at Angiers, we are aware of swirling and confusing priorities; but we
are also aware of a "bastard to the time" determined to forge his way
through such moral entanglements on some basis other than that of
pure commodity. For Salisbury, typically, ambiguities are easily resolved:

> Trust not those cunning waters of [Hubert's] eyes,
> For villainy is not without such rheum,
> And he, long traded in it, makes it seem
> Like rivers of remorse and innocency.
> Away with me, all you whose souls abhor
> Th' uncleanly savors of a slaughter-house,
> For I am stifled with this smell of sin.
>
> (4.3.107–13)

The lords' outraged exit from the "uncleanly" circumstance at hand is
the final expression of their belief in the irreconcilability of purity and
impurity. But the Bastard stays on, determined through the admoni-
tions he directs at Hubert to sift out loyalties, to clarify where good
and evil reside in an attempt to establish some tenable moral course. It
is an exercise that forces one to eschew idealistic extremes for an
impure but workable ethical compromise—indeed a sort of morally
defensible "bastardy" with none of the pejorative overtones the term
carries for so many purists in the play. Fundamental to this position is
the rejection of John's strategy of cheap coverup in favor of a synthetic
accommodation of good and evil that allows one to locate "right"
priorities in an imperfect political world:

> The life, the right, and truth of all this realm
> Is fled to heaven; and England now is left
> To tug and scramble, and to part by th' teeth
> The unowed interest of proud swelling state.
> . . . .

> Now happy he whose cloak and center can
> Hold out this tempest. Bear away that child,
> And follow me with speed. I'll to the King.
>
> (4.3.144–57)

This is an extraordinary statement, particularly in light of the Bastard's earlier ironic pronouncement on the age's taste for "sweet,
sweet, sweet poison" and his own professed "worship" of the
"smooth-fac'd gentleman, tickling commodity" (2.1.573). Like Salisbury before him, he raises the issue of the royal "cloak and center,"
but instead of expressing anger at its impurities he wonders only if it
can protect the beleaguered king suffering outside from tempest and
inside from the "imminent decay of wrested pomp" (4.3.154). He can
view the dead innocent ("Bear away that child") at the same time that
he recognizes the loftier importance of national duty ("I'll to the
King"). His movement toward John here—in clear contrast to the
movement of the lords away from him—demonstrates a mature loyalty,
honed on an unsentimental awareness of the facts of political man, that
allows him to locate a meaningful good in a manifest evil. His actions,
in short, exemplify precisely those values of which he is the tangible
embodiment—wholesome impurity, "good" adulteration. In this
sense he becomes a sort of moral oxymoron—in Sigurd Burckhardt's
shrewd term an example of "innocent cynicism"—who represents the
best we can expect from political man, particularly in the unweeded
garden.[8] He is himself, in a much fuller and more meaningful sense
than he had earlier imagined, a true bastard to the time.

I should like in conclusion to return to the question of "ambivalence" raised at the beginning of this essay. In a cogent and
carefully argued study of "meaning" in Shakespeare, Norman Rabkin
confronts this problem squarely.[9] Dismissing on the one hand the
reductive thematists so efficiently assailed by Richard Levin, and on
the other the adherents of ambiguity who would place dramatist,
character, and scholar alike in a critical no-man's-land where meaning
is impossible to locate, Rabkin argues instead for a dynamic complex-
ity in Shakespearean drama that implies meaning at the same time that
it resists neat critical formulas:

> The good Shakespeare critic must point out the patterns of the dance. He
> must find terms in which the oppositions and conflicts and problems
> within a play can be stated while recognizing the reductiveness of those
> terms. He must fight the temptation to proclaim what it boils down to; he
> must fight against the urge to closure which, as a gifted audience, he feels
> with particular intensity. He must learn to point to the centers of energy

and turbulence in a play without regarding them as coded elements of a thematic formula. (P. 25)

And later, in a now seminal treatment of *Henry V* in which he argues that the play gives us two "rival gestalts" that cannot be reconciled with each other, Rabkin observes that

> If what happens in *Henry V* is a version of the fundamental ambiguity that many critics have found at the center of the Shakespeare vision, it is nevertheless significantly different here. Such ambiguity is not a theme or even the most important fact in many plays in which it figures. . . . Though one perceives it informing plays as different from one another as *A Midsummer Night's Dream* and *King Lear,* one cannot say that it is what they are "about," and readings of Shakespearean plays as communicating only ambiguity are as arid as readings in which the plays are seen to be about appearance and reality. . . . (P. 61)

My purpose in quoting so extensively here is to suggest that the Bastard's dilemma in *King John* has some tantalizing affinities with that of the Shakespearean critic who comprises the "gifted audience" posited by Rabkin. The Bastard, like Rabkin's critic, must also find terms in which the oppositions and conflicts and problems in his world can be stated even as he recognizes the reductiveness of these terms. And he must learn, to borrow Rabkin's phrase, to point to centers of energy and turbulence without regarding them as coded elements of an immutable or paradigmatic moral formula. And, of course, his dilemma is ours. This does not mean, however, (as it does not mean for Rabkin's critic), that the Bastard's position is hopelessly "ambivalent" or that he (or we) are unable to formulate clear moral choices in the midst of such complexities. To borrow yet again from Rabkin, the Bastard's dilemma need not necessarily communicate a paralyzing "ambiguity" to him or to his gifted audience; yet it can and does show that audience precisely the sort of moral complexities through which the mature and clear-sighted politician must chart a reasonable moral course.

What I am suggesting here is that the concept of "ambivalence" in Shakespeare, particularly as it manifests itself in *King John,* need not always imply an inability (on our part or on the part of any Shakespearean character) to arrive at clear moral choices. The Bastard, unlike Hamlet, is not a man to double business bound, although he is, in a far more immediate and psychologically compelling sense than Hamlet, a double man—like Hamlet aware of disturbing physical and emotional dualities, but unlike him in failing to be daunted by them. The Bastard is, moreover, unusually sensitive to such dualities—he knows them, so to speak, from within—and perhaps just because he feels them so close to the bone, so inextricably bound up with all aspects of life, he is able to press on despite them. He understands, as Hamlet does not until the very end, that we are wedded to the contraries that lie in wait to paralyze us. His ability to confront these contraries and to act in the face of them can thus be seen as the triumph of an informed and unblinkered political realism over a naïve political purity unattainable in the real world. In this context his ideological bastardy becomes the touchstone of his political superiority as well as of his symbolic stature as national leader after John's death. Such is the ideological trick the English lords must learn, and one that Henry V, at once Shakespeare's most triumphant politician *and* the mirror of all Christian kings, masters so artfully in the plays of the Henriad.

Notes

1. See particularly John R. Elliott, "Shakespeare and the Double Image of King John," 72; Ronald Berman, "Anarchy and Order in 'Richard III' and 'King John,'" 56; Eamon Grennan, "Shakespeare's Satirical History," 34; Douglas C. Wixson, "'Calm Words Folded Up in Smoke,'" 120–22; James L. Calderwood, "Commodity and Honour in *King John*" in *Shakespeare: The Histories*, ed. Eugene M. Waith, 85–101; Virginia Mason Vaughan, "Between Tetralogies," 411–20; Larry S. Champion, "'Confound Their Skill in Covetousness,'" 36–55.
2. See also her comments at 3.1.2.
3. E. A.J. Honigmann, in the New Arden *King John*, follows J. Dover Wilson in interpreting the Bastard's remarks as referring "to the sudden check in a manage, which shakes the rider (Death) from his seat" on a horse (46 n). The precise meaning here, however, as Honigmann points out, is much discussed. See also the variorum edition of *The Life and Death of King John*, ed. Horace H. Furness, 138–42.
4. Harold Jenkins, in the introduction to the New Arden edition of *Hamlet* (London: Methuen, 1982), probes this idea as it pertains to Hamlet and helps define the world of the play; see particularly 147–49.
5. The affinities between *King John* and the late Tudor morality play are perceptively explored by Emrys Jones, *The Origins of Shakespeare*, 236–46.
6. The presence of innate tensions in the Bastard and their political significance has been examined by many scholars. See particularly, Ronald Stroud, "The Bastard to the Time," 154–66; Calderwood, "Commodity and Honour" in the Waith anthology, 97–101; Julia C. Van de Water, "The Bastard in *King John*," 137–46; Charles Stubblefield, "Some Thoughts About *King John*," 25–28; Kristian Smidt, *Unconformities in Shakespeare's History Plays*, 79–80; and E. Jones, *Origins*, 246–52.
7. I am indebted here to the introductory remarks of William Matchett in his edition of *King John* in the Signet Classic Shakespeare, xxxi–xxxiii.
8. Burckhardt, *Shakespearean Meanings*, 133. In this regard see also M. M. Reese, *The Cease of Majesty*, 284–85; and Robert Ornstein, *A Kingdom for a Stage*, 94–95.
9. Norman Rabkin, *Shakespeare and the Problem of Meaning* (Chicago: University of Chicago Press, 1981); all subsequent references to Rabkin's study will be noted parenthetically in the text.

8

The Four Voices of the Bastard

MICHAEL MANHEIM

ALMOST TWENTY YEARS AGO JOHN DANBY OBSERVED THAT *KING JOHN* is a transition between the first and second tetralogies,[1] but because of problems over dating and the dominance of Tillyardian thinking before the 1970s, little has been done with the idea. The figure who Danby suggests constitutes the bridge between the tetralogies is the Bastard. But since Danby is largely interested in the generation of the character of Edmund in *Lear*, he never comes to grips with the split between what Julia C. Van de Water calls the "thinly disguised vice" figure of the play's first three acts and "the English patriot" of the last two.[2] That split, as we shall see, involves other splits.

To understand what happens to the Bastard in *King John* and why his image changes so drastically in the course of the play, we need to consider first that the Bastard's character is a response to the image of the king presented not only in *King John* but in most of the history plays of the period.[3] It is an image of human weakness borne of the constant vacillations and uncertainties the flesh is heir to. As Lily Bess Campbell pointed out, when one thinks of the histories, one thinks not of strong kings but of weak ones:[4] of Marlowe's Edward II, of the two (at least) versions of Richard II, of Henry VI, and of the several versions of John. When the history plays of the early 1590s are considered as a group, our response to the royal figure is highly ambivalent. In scenes where the king is protected and seemingly invulnerable, he is either too frivolous or too fearful to correct the wrongs his reign has caused, and he elicits reactions from us running from indifference to contempt. But when he is vulnerable—especially to the point where deposition and even death seem probable—our reactions turn to those of compassion and, still more important, guilt. We feel, often with the subjects in the play, that our earlier antagonism has helped bring about a royal downfall. We have given our "soul's consent / T'undeck the pompous body of a king" (*Richard II* 4.1.249–

50). But despite these feelings of guilt late in the play, neither of our two prevailing responses is finally dominant. Our recollection of the royal abuses in retrospect strongly counters our compassion at the play's conclusion.

In *King John* our reactions to the royal figure run the gamut.[5] First he seems a fair adjudicator between the brothers Faulconbridge, next a crude dealer willing to give up the better half of his kingdom to win clear possession of a crown he can never in good conscience call his own, next the heroic pre-Protestant opponent of arrogant papal authority, next a child-torturer. By the last act, John seems hopeless. Unless we blind ourselves to the whining, guilt-ridden self-justification of the John of the final scenes, it is impossible for us to think of loyalty to a crown in the possession of such a figure. Not ambivalence but disgust characterizes our response to a king who sells out to the pope and then is overcome by paroxysms of guilt and fear as others fight to maintain his right. Were it not for the Bastard, the play would end with a whimper. Instead, it ends with one of the most resolutely patriotic-sounding speeches in English drama.

Solely because of the Bastard, then, this play about the weakest of medieval English kings ends on a seemingly positive note. To see what the Bastard sees and to sense the feelings that prompt his reactions throughout requires a consideration of what his lines and simply his presence may reveal about the great changes that take place in his perspective between acts 1 and 5, changes which bring him to defend and even become spokesman for so sorry a piece of royalty as John becomes by the last act.

The Bastard speaks successively in four distinct voices in *King John*, roughly representing stages of what might today be called his political coming-of-age. Three of these voices are identified by his three important soliloquies in the play, while the fourth is the cumulative effect of the new and different language he unexpectedly uses in the last act. The first three of these voices indicate the increasing degree of knowledge of the world and of himself that Shakespeare intends this young man to acquire; the fourth, that of the new Machiavel, shows how the Bastard uses his newly acquired knowledge.

The Bastard we see and hear in the first act is an Elizabethan soldier-of-fortune. As such, his image is made up of a number of contradictory components. He is a mixture of chivalry, intelligence, surface cynicism, brilliance, arrogance, egotism, personal charm, and almost total indifference to the uglier realities of the world around him. The fortune he is after involves wealth, of course, but it also involves adventure, i.e., the discovery of ever-more-daring challenges to his honor. He has obviously determined sometime before his confrontation with his brother to seem the "madcap" the king calls him; and he uses language which, far from making him seem the legitimate son of old Sir Robert Faulconbridge, will convince his royal listeners that by no stretch of the imagination could he possibly be the son to so dull a gentleman. At the same time, he says, he deserves the inheritance by virtue of gifts of personality alone—especially when he is contrasted with his physically unappetizing brother (1.1.138–47). From the beginning he seems to be inviting those around him to believe that he may indeed be Coeur de Lion's son. His colloquialisms, used so offhandedly before royalty, seem calculated to suggest that he too is of the blood royal. The Bastard first persuades John to grant him the Faulconbridge fortune practically on the grounds of charm alone; then he prompts Elinor to urge him to give up that fortune on the same grounds. But in all this he is unreflecting about the moral implications of what he does—and uninquiring about the moral implications of the military adventure Elinor so winningly invites him to join.

An Elizabethan audience, or an audience familiar with verse satire of the 1590s, might understand what Shakespeare is doing with the Bastard in the first act more quickly than a modern audience. The Bastard's first soliloquy, which embodies the first of his four "voices," describes how he plans to behave now that he is to become a courtier. He reveals his contempt for the empty affectations of courtiers, especially those who ape the manners and dress of foreign lands:

> Now your traveller,
> He and his toothpick at my worship's mess,
> And when my knightly stomach is suffic'd,
> Why then I suck my teeth, and catechize
> My picked man of countries.
>
> (1.1.189–93)

So, too, does the fictional young parasite Ruffio satirized by Joseph Hall in 1597 subtly parody the much-traveled courtier. Like the Bastard, Ruffio picks his teeth, converses effusively, and affects even as he condemns foreign fashion. But the aim of both these sprightly youths is not so much to reform pretentious manners as to "knave" what they can out of their courtly gulls. What has been overlooked in the Bastard's soliloquy here is the degree to which rather than simply being satirist, he is also being satirized. Shakespeare's treatment of his young parasite is not so biting as Hall's, but he does create the similar image of a still-shallow if quite talented and attractive young man bent on getting what he can out of the rich and powerful. The similarity suggests that we may see the Bastard early in the play as a would-be courtier seeking to conform to the fashions of the times. Despite his intention to "deliver / Sweet . . . poison for the age's tooth" (1.1.212–13), this figure is not so aware of the larger dimensions of human corruptibility as he claims to be and is soon to become.

There is another component to the Bastard's voice in act 1 that is closely related to the voice we shall hear from him in act 5. Though he could hardly be called a Machiavel at this point, the seeds for such a figure are evident:

> And not alone in habit and device,
> Exterior form, outward accoutrement,
> But from the inward motion to deliver
> Sweet, sweet, sweet poison for the age's tooth,
> Which though I will not practice to deceive,
> Yet to avoid deceit, I mean to learn. . . .
>
> (1.1.210–15)

The striking phrases here are "inward motion" and "to avoid deceit, I mean to learn." He is talking about a state of mind he plans to achieve by self-conditioning. And in a sense that is applicable in all ages, it is a Machiavellian state of mind. While he "will not practice to deceive," he wishes to learn the skills of deception so well that they will become second nature, an "inward motion." His stated desire not to practice deceit is at best slippery, since he is constantly aware of the effects his appearance and statements will have on others. He did not deliberately seek to deceive John and Elinor into thinking he was Coeur de Lion's son, yet his language was such that the idea could occur to them. The Bastard thus possesses the proper requisites to be a Machiavel, though the type he will ultimately become was a new kind on the Elizabethan stage—not the "stage Machiavel" of yore but something subtler and more complex.

Nevertheless, the Bastard is not yet a true Machiavel at this point in the play because he is not particularly interested in the acquisition of power so essential to Machiavellianism. His goals are those of the soldier-of-fortune: inexhaustible money, an active life, and a good time. The Machiavel he ultimately becomes grows out of what happens in the play during the four acts to follow. All we see in the Bastard here are the qualities needed for one to assume such a role.

The Bastard's reactions as the events in France unfold early in act 2 begin the transformation in his outlook. What we observe, of course, is the great game of international politics played at its crudest. The Bastard hears King Philip of France swear and break oaths of chivalric loyalty to young Arthur, whose altogether justified claim to the English throne is the source of all the conflict. He hears the two kings,

John and Philip, lay their cases before the leading citizen of Angiers, who, as the important scholarship of J. D. Wilson and E. A. J. Honigmann makes clear,[6] is actually Hubert de Burgh, "a fellow" John elsewhere describes as "by the hand of nature mark'd, / Quoted, and sign'd to do a deed of shame" (4.2.221–22). This supposedly unprejudiced judge reveals from his later associations with John that he had been working secretly for the English side all along. And finally, the Bastard hears King Philip jump at the "deal" whereby John will relinquish his huge French holdings if Arthur's claims are put aside.

All of this leads to the Bastard's most famous speech, his soliloquy on commodity, his second "voice" in the play. That the speech reveals genuine outrage at the way political affairs are conducted has been amply discussed, but what it also shows is the degree of shallowness underlying his first act soliloquy. The self-conscious wit of that earlier speech gives way to the immense gap he finds yawning between what men say and what they mean. He is now genuinely appalled by the hypocrisy that he has claimed to be appalled by all along. The Bastard had no specific courtier in mind earlier, and his spoof of an imaginary courtier was itself an affectation. Here the Bastard has the actions and statements of two live kings to work with, and the result is his most monumental attack upon human corruption.

But the conclusion the Bastard draws from what he has witnessed is not what one expects. Far from opposing himself to the corruption he has experienced, he decides to take part in it. The end of the commodity speech suggests the response of the callow youth who has been jolted into cynical manhood. He decides to "worship gain," to become part of the rotten system he has seen in operation. Though there remains a gnawing contempt for himself for doing so—one part of the Bastard remains the idealist—he behaves in what follows in a manner far removed from idealism.

What we see from here on in the play is the Bastard's sober, controlled, fully calculating commitment to a course he knows is dishonorable. He becomes one form of the Machiavel. Since silence is the most notable characteristic of the Bastard immediately following the commodity speech, it is difficult to assess his motives; and it is that silence in the third and fourth acts, in contrast to his earlier volubility, which has made him seem inconsistent to many critics. But that silence can indicate patience and caution, standard attributes of the Machiavel before his leap for power. It is the same silence that characterizes the Bolingbroke of *Richard II* during his climb to the throne. It is what the Bastard does rather than what he says during this period that is more important. And what he does is to become King John's trusted and knowing ally in political perfidy. He plunders abbeys and seeks on the king's behalf to flatter or intimidate leading lords of the realm. He never again comments on what he is doing, but it is not difficult to infer his motives from what we see. He lives and acts in a thoroughly "political" manner, a Machiavellian manner, in which all statements and actions are dedicated to attaining and retaining power.

But if the Bastard in act 4 has learned the uses of Machiavellian silence, he has still not found his Machiavellian "voice." That discovery and the concomitant assertion of his real power in John's reign must wait until act 5. The voice we do remember from act 4 is that of the Bastard's soliloquy (4.3.140–56) commenting on the violent death of Prince Arthur, which John has indirectly brought about; and that voice tells us both of the Bastard's idealism and his determination never again to act on that idealism. This remarkable speech helps develop our sense of the contrast that exists between the Bastard's opposing states during the latter part of the play. The first state, what some might call his "inner" state, is indicated by his "amazement" at the treachery and peril of political life and his unqualified reference to the dead Arthur as "The life, the right, and truth of all this realm" (144); the second, or "outer," state is indicated by his flat conclusion, "I'll to the king" (157).[7] Political reality, as the Bastard sees it, as Shakespeare apparently saw it—painfully—and as the Elizabethan theater audience was coming to see it, necessitated political expediency. For all his compassion, and despite his keen awareness of "the right," the Bastard must either return to the king more strongly renewed than ever in his commitment to the surest avenue to power, or he must disappear as a political force. There was no alternative. The message of *The Prince* was taking hold in the 1590s.[8]

The Bastard's fourth and final voice is not limited to any single speech but is rather the cumulative effect of all his major speeches in act 5. It is a voice that previews the political pageant of *King Henry V.* Shakespeare endows the Bastard with a new language in the play's final act, and it is through this language that the Bastard becomes a new kind of stage Machiavel.

I have elsewhere discussed in detail the nature and effect of the Bastard's new language,[9] but I failed to observe the important parallel between the Bastard's final voice and his first. Gone is the juvenile bravado and the satirical tone of that earlier voice. The Bastard's tone in making his utterly deflated monarch seem the terror of the earth[10] is always serious and decorous. But his purpose in the final act is quite comparable to what it was in the opening act. Then, the Bastard was "selling" himself to a king; now, he is selling that king to a hostile nobility. Then, we heard an articulate, uninhibited youth through the mastery of a studied diction create the image of himself necessary to make his fortune. Now, through the mastery of another studied diction—one that will help win wars and assure domestic unity—he creates an image capable of making his country's fortune. The Bastard, in other words, has transformed his earlier verbal versatility into an art requisite for the new Machiavellian state, where brutalities and deceptions must take place beneath an attractive veneer.

Most discussions of the kind of heroic diction the Bastard uses in act 5 have focused on the better-known use of that diction in *Henry V.* But the Bastard masters it with little less facility than does the hero of Agincourt. A good example occurs in act 5, scene 1 when the Bastard exhorts his flagging monarch:

> be fire with fire,
> Threaten the threat'ner, and outface the brow
> Of bragging horror; so shall inferior eyes,
> That borrow their behaviors from the great,
> Grow great by your example and put on
> The dauntless spirit of resolution.
>
> (5.1.48–53)

The special stamp of this rant is not only its vigor but the homespun quality the Bastard, and later Henry V, work into it. Henry's "We are but warriors for the working-day" (*Henry V* 4.3.109), and the Bastard's engaging harmony of Amazons and thimbles (5.2.154–58) are notable examples. Both the Bastard and Henry make such diction a powerful instrument of political image-making, both use it to impress followers and frighten enemies, and both use it to disguise some of the more unpleasant realities with which each is forced to deal.

Discussing *Henry V,* Michael Goldman describes Henry's speeches of that play in terms that are also well-suited to the Bastard's speeches in act 5. Goldman describes them as "arias" that

> stimulate us to share his noticeable effort, to be aware of the glory and labor involved in making authoritative sounds. They carry with them, in the most patent and seductive form, the pleasures, the rewarding effort of persuasive, masterful public performance. Their verse is wonderfully suited to the accents of a man speaking to a crowd, a confident man, practiced in exertion but working hard, raising his voice, stilling and exhorting the group around him.[11]

But Goldman, concerned as he is with the politics implicit in good theater, neglects the actual politics of the play, the politics of state. He correctly sees these speeches as part of the author's contrivance in creating a character, but he does not see that they are also the character's contrivance in creating a sought-after image of himself. Both characters are aware that they are making authoritative and seductive sounds, and both know the effect that the practice and adept use of such sounds may have on listeners who might otherwise have to face weakness and ugliness masked by authority and seduction.

Both Henry V and the Bastard of act 5 act in conformity with a "good" deriving roughly from the phrase "good politician" rather than from the phrase "good man." Both are in the process of learning a new political ethos and unlearning an old one. Both are good men, of course—we have just considered the genuine humanity of the Bastard's third voice and there is ample evidence of Henry's essential decency—but both have eschewed the older good in favor of a newer one, a "pragmatic" good that has as its goal the achieving and maintaining of a strong state. Both have turned away the good implicit in a figure like Henry VI of the first tetralogy in favor of the more immediately effective "good" of *The Prince*. And the chief political instrument of both is the brightly lit language that has provided their nation a full set of patriotic utterances suited to times of national crisis.

The Bastard's discovery of a new diction by means of which the king's weakness may be disguised and the state renewed, outwardly at least, is our discovery of the nature of the transition between Shakespeare's two historical tetralogies. Richard III of the first tetralogy was the stage Machiavel, the super-villain who provided a vent for all varieties of audience hostility toward ruthless government. But the ideas essential to the new Machiavellianism were coming to be accepted by popular audiences of the 1590s, in spite of their hatred of the name, as those ideas had already been tacitly accepted by the Elizabethan ruling class. The plays of the first tetralogy suggest the genuine outrage of audience and playwright at the apparent acceptability, if not respectability, of coercion and duplicity in place of justice and mercy as instruments of leadership. But the new politics was becoming deeply ingrained in Elizabethan public life, and the same audience that hooted the old stage-Machiavel would cheer the real Machiavel on stage as long as he was properly gifted and adorned. The Bastard possesses the necessary gifts from the start, and the adornment is his seemingly spontaneous, highly energetic new language, the legacy he passes on to Henry V. By means of linguistic artifice, Machiavellian tactics, so despised in the earlier history plays, are made attractive in both theatrical and political terms.

From the fiercely emotional exposé of political perfidy and the cannibalization of moral leadership, which constitutes the first tetralogy, we move, through the political chaos of *King John*, to a (perhaps bitter) acceptance of coercion and deception brilliantly dis-

guised. We move to the political science of "the Bolingbrokes." From
outrage at the victimization of the good though ordinary man trying to
rule well (Henry VI), and at the concomitant rise of England's blood-
iest tyrant, we pass, through the eye of the Bastard's needle, to
pleasure and approval of the maturation and triumph of a great and
glorious king whose concern for justice and mercy seem somehow
overlooked amid all the verbal music, pageantry, and military victories. Without the Bastard, the two tetralogies seem inconsistent, in
tone as well as theme. With the Bastard, and in the course of his own
transition, as marked by his four voices, we come to understand the
larger transition apparently being made by the public theater audience
of the late 1590s to an increasing political pragmatism.[12]

Notes

1. John F. Danby, *Shakespeare's Doctrine of Nature*, 68–80.
2. Julia C. Van de Water, "The Bastard in *King John*," 143.
3. For a fuller discussion of this image, see my study *The Weak King Dilemma in the Shakespearean History Play*.
4. Lily Bess Campbell, *Shakespeare's Histories*, 11.
5. In "*King John* and Problematic Art," Jonathan Reeve Price sees all of *King John* as a study in shifting perspectives (25–28). Our sympathies, he feels, are drawn from one character or position to another, with no fixed intention on Shakespeare's part as to where they should finally reside.
6. J. Dover Wilson, in his preface to the Cambridge edition of *King John* (xlv–xlvii), and E. A. J. Honigmann, in the New Arden edition (xxxvi–xxxvii), base their conclusion on the fact that the character the folio later identifies (in speech prefixes) as "Hubert" is identical with the character who earlier appears as "A Citizen of Angiers."
7. This point is made most clearly by William Matchett in "Richard's Divided Heritage in *King John*" in *Essays in Shakespearean Criticism*, ed. James L. Calderwood and H. E. Toliver, 152–70. Matchett's conclusion, however, that the Bastard's political nature is central to the play is anticipated by James L. Calderwood in "Commodity and Honour in *King John*" in *Shakespeare: The Histories*, ed. Eugene M. Waith, 85–101. Both Matchett and Calderwood, in finding the Bastard the play's leading figure, are guided, as I have been, by Adrien Bonjour's "The Road to Swinstead Abbey," 253–74.
8. This contention is supported most notably by Felix Raab in *The English Face of Machiavelli* (London: Routledge and Kegan Paul, 1964). He makes clear that for all their official detestation of Machiavelli, men in public life were positively influenced by him, both in behavior and, obliquely, in statements. By the 1590s, the citizenry was also becoming subject to the appeal of Machiavellian thought. Various critical studies have seen the positive influence of *The Prince* on the popular drama of the period: among them, the works of Wilbur Sanders (*The Dramatist and the Received Idea* [Cambridge: University Press, 1968]), Una M. Ellis-Fermor (*The Frontiers of Drama*), and H. B. Charlton (*Shakespeare, Politics, and Politicians*).
9. Manheim, *The Weak King Dilemma*, 155–59.
10. Philip Edwards, while more a defender of the Bastard's true patriotism than I, suggests that the Bastard here "puts up the magnificent pretense that there is a fierce

and warlike John behind him, [and] pretends that his own stirring eloquence is an index of John's continued strength," (*Threshold of a Nation*, 121).

11. Michael Goldman, *Shakespeare and the Energies of Drama* (Princeton: Princeton University Press, 1972), 58.

12. David Scott Kastan suggests that the Bastard's great paean to national unity which closes the play fails to bring about the "stable resolution" the actual terms of the Bastard's speech imply (*Shakespeare and the Shapes of Time*, 53–55). The kingdom will now be led by the child-king Henry III, and that fact alone, Kastan points out, would hardly be settling to an audience still mulling over the fate of the kingdom under the child-king Henry VI in the first tetralogy. While Kastan may be right, the new heroic diction of the Bastard's speeches in the last act nevertheless does much to gloss over the very real trouble in which the kingdom remains at the close of the play.

9

Fraternal Pragmatics
Speech Acts of John and the Bastard

JOSEPH A. PORTER

AS VERBAL ACTORS JOHN AND THE BASTARD STAND IN NOTABLE CON-
trast, each with his own significantly characteristic range of speech
acts. At the same time, as the following pragmatic reconnaissance
attempts to suggest, certain similarities in the things the two men do
with words manifest a deep and troubled fraternality between them.
Hence *King John* provides one of the earliest examples of a configura-
tion Shakespeare returns to often.[1]

Among the features of John's verbal action that make him "uncom-
municative . . . laconic and reserved"[2] is the general inexplicitness of
his speech acts. Bolingbroke, the "silent king" (whose comparatively
inexplicit verbal action stands in significant contrast to that of Richard
II with its ceremonial explicitness), still has more performatives than
John's two, "I do defy thee, France" (2.1.155), and

> Then do I give . . .
> . . . five provinces,
> With her to thee, and . . .
> . . . thirty thousand marks . . . .
>
> (2.1.527–30)

His one ceremonial act—the knighting of the Bastard—is of a sort that
seems as a rule to have been inexplicit, as it is in John's case.[3] John's
speech in fact may well be the least illocutionarily explicit of any
Shakespearean monarch's. And within John's own play, contrastive
examples modestly heighten the effect. The explicitness of Pandulph's
repeated performative,

> I Pandulph . . .
> Do in his [Innocent's] name religiously demand

136

Why thou against the Church, our holy mother,
So willfully dost spurn . . . .
This, in our foresaid Holy Father's name,
Pope Innocent, I do demand of thee

(3.1.138–46)

seems appropriate to the gravity of his errand, and is perhaps more predictable in a public figure than John's inexplicitness. While these are Pandulph's only two performatives, coming as they do in his first speech they have a peculiar prominence that makes them contribute to and partake of his general Romish ceremony and officiousness. John's speech has a kind of nakedness in contrast.

When John is attempting to shrug all responsibility for Arthur's supposed death off onto Hubert he characterizes himself as having earlier spoken "darkly," without "express words," about "The deed, which both our tongues held vild to name" (4.2.232, 234, 241), thus touching on the general quality of which his illocutionary inexplicitness is a special case. The earlier scene, act 3, scene 3, has been widely praised, and much of the praise is for the quality of John's verbal action.[4] In the last two-thirds of the scene (the first third of which I return to below) John comes to the point slowly and peculiarly with Hubert. The promises of unspecified rewards for as-yet-unspecified services (19–22, 30–32, 68) are standard enough softening-up techniques, as may be the admixture of polite imperatives in the opening gambit (19, 25) and the weightier "Remember" (69) as the last word in private after the contract has been sealed. So too may be a certain amount of preliminary digression, but John beats about the bush in his own quite distinctive way, elaborating with alarming vigor on his hatred of "that idiot, laughter" (45) and his alienation from the proud day's gauds. When he finally comes to the point, he does so with the crucial question "Dost thou understand me?" (63) followed by so uninformative a statement—"Thou art his keeper" (64)—that it could serve as a textbook example of H. Paul Grice's "conversational implicature," i.e., the flouting of a conversational maxim in order to convey an unstated message to the hearer. Knowing that Hubert already knows he is Arthur's keeper, and that he knows that John knows it (John in the preceding scene having instructed him, "Hubert, keep this boy" [3.2.5]), John clearly means something other than what he says. Hubert understands, or at least claims to understand, a fairly general adjuration, as he signifies with "And I'll keep him so / That he shall not offend your Majesty" (64–65). Whereupon John says simply "Death." Here, while the substantive is more specific (and more extreme) than anything Hubert seems prepared for, at the same time not merely the illocutionary force but also the entire sentential framework is left unexpressed. Like someone who can't believe his ears, Hubert requests verification with "My lord?"[5] which prompts John to "A grave," the substantive just as specific and the speech act just as inexplicit.

In contrast to a character like Bolingbroke/Henry IV, whose illocutionary inexplicitness manifests a certain cautiousness, and hence may seem a kind of disguise, John in his inexplicit verbal action seems not generally to be hiding anything. His speech seems unclothed rather than disguised because of its brusqueness and impulsiveness, and also importantly because he has no soliloquy, so that to us the audience it seems he has kept nothing hidden from other characters. And I think this peculiar nakedness appears even in the scene where he speaks with the most clearly ulterior motives, act 3, scene 3, where he persuades Hubert to agree to murder. It appears in John's lurching changes of subject, and also in what he says about what he has to say. "I had a thing to say, / But I will fit it with some better [time]" (25–26) sounds controlled enough, but immediately as John changes the subject he seems inadvertently almost to reveal uncontrolled feelings about this thing: "By heaven, Hubert, I am almost asham'd / To say what good respect I have of thee" (27–28). John's "thing" obtrudes itself into his response to Hubert's expression of indebtedness, "thou has no cause to say so yet / But thou shalt have . . ." (30–31), which seems addressed almost as much to himself as to Hubert. Two lines later in John's reiteration, "I had a thing to say, but let it go" (33), the last verb's ambiguous mood manifests a kind of verbal nakedness. If used as an imperative—"But let's let it go"—the verb shows the controlled manipulator, whereas in the indicative—"But I let it go"— it shows a kind of weird helplessness, as if there might never be another opportunity to say a thing.

Finally, John's questions seem to distinguish his verbal action. Here it is a question of real, not rhetorical, questions, and John begins asking them as early as the opening line of the play.[6] While the Bastard has the most lines, and the most utterances, John has the most questions, and the predominance of John's questions in the first two scenes establishes the interrogative mood as particularly his.[7] Several of his questions in act 1, scene 1 nicely illustrate John's distinctive use of the interrogative:

> What follows if we disallow of this?
>
> (16)

> What men are you?
>
> (49)

> What art thou?
>
> (55)

> Why, being younger born,
> Doth he lay claim to thine inheritance?
>
> (71–72)

> What is thy name?
>
> (157)

Inasmuch as these questions are without any explicit element of command, and hence without reference to the speaker's position of authority (except via the pronouns), and inasmuch as they are otherwise unembellished and often unaccompanied by other contiguous utterances of the speaker, they contribute to what I have been calling the nakedness of John's verbal action, giving it kinds of immediacy, directness, vulnerability, and even a certain loneliness. When an element of command is expressed with John's questions:

> Now, say, Chatillion, what would France with us?
>
> (1)

> Sirrah, speak,
> What doth move you to claim your brother's land?
>
> (90–91)

the utterances are still relatively unceremonial and direct, compared for instance with John's pure imperatives in the same scene (e.g., 19–20, 23–30). It is a bit as if in these moments John's need to know is too urgent to permit more than the briefest expression of his own authority in the imperative clauses. John's last question in the play,

> How goes the day with us? O, tell me, Hubert.
>
> (5.3.1)

is also linked with an imperative. Here the interrogative by its precedence supersedes still further, and the imperative has become merely grammatical, with the illocutionary force of a plea.

In many respects the Bastard's verbal action contrasts with John's. His soliloquies give him a psychological wholeness unique in the play, and his interruptions, challenges, expostulations, defiances, mockeries, expressions of incredulity, and other verbal excursions are almost universally taken to be foundations for the attractiveness that also distinguishes him from John and from the other characters. A full-dress analysis of his verbal action would need to take into account other idiosyncratic features, such as his predilection for quotation of real or imagined speech.

At the same time his speech bears interesting affinities with John's. He has nearly as large a total number of questions, if not so large a percentage. His questions, clustered near the beginning and the end of the play, have some of the nakedness and urgency of John's. In act 1, scene 1, where he in fact asks more real questions than John, the one that seems most to resemble John's speech acts in its deep urgency is the repeated question to his mother,

> Therefore, good mother,
> To whom am I beholding for these limbs?
>
> (238–39)

and

> Then, good my mother, let me know my father;
> Some proper man, I hope. Who was it, mother?
>
> (249–50)

The Bastard's speech also has an immediacy reminiscent of John's that shows, for instance, in their abrupt changes of subject and in their common ability to change direction of address in midspeech.[8]

These affinities in verbal action seem to manifest a more general deep affinity, a kind of fraternality or identification between the two characters, such that, for all their differences of station and character, the curve of the action of the play is one of a passing of the torch.[9] Early on, John speaks for himself, and the fact is emphasized in

> [Hubert.] Who is it that hath warn'd us to the walls?
> King Philip. 'Tis France, for England.
> King John.   England for itself.
>
> (2.1.201–2)

and

> King John. In us, that are our own great deputy,
>   And bear possession of our person here . . . .
>
> (2.1.365–66)

But by act 5 the Bastard has become the royal deputy, prefacing his defiance of Lewis and accusation of the English nobles with

> Now hear our English King,
> For thus his royalty doth speak in me . . . .
>
> (5.2.128–29)

Having been given the ordering of the present time by John, in act 5 the Bastard often speaks with an authority at least as great as John's in the beginning of the play. The interrogative mood also passes from John, with his last significant cluster of real questions in act 4, scene 2, to the Bastard, who asks seven questions in the final scene of act 5.

That this passing of the torch from one male to another is burdened with unacknowledged guilt is suggested by Constance's gratuitous mention of "Cain, the first male child . . ." (3.4.79), and by the psychologically charged act 3, scene 2, whose ten lines, beginning with the Bastard's entrance with his father's killer's head, contain such peculiarities as Shakespeare's "curious conflation"[10] transferring credit for Elinor's rescue from John to the Bastard, and the Bastard's and John's anomalous uses of the Bastard's original name, Philip. Out of these murky waters rises John's "Death" and "A grave," the core of a command accepted but never enacted by Hubert, feared yet accidentally enacted by the victim himself, condemned yet never correctly attributed by the Bastard. And at John's own death (as later at the deaths of Hotspur and Laertes) out of the troubled depths of Shakespearean fraternality comes a release of affection signaled by the shift into the intimate second person:

Bastard. Art thou gone so? I do but stay behind
  To do the office for thee of revenge,
  And then my soul shall wait on thee to heaven,
  As it on earth hath been thy servant still.

(5.7.70–73)

Notes

1. As with Romeo and Mercutio, Hal and Hotspur, or Hamlet and Horatio. See the investigations of doubling and fratricide by René Girard, *"To Double Business Bound": Essays on Literature, Mimesis, and Anthropology* (Baltimore: Johns Hopkins University Press, 1978) and Joel Fineman, "Fratricide and Cuckoldry: Shakespeare's Doubles," *Psychoanalytic Review* 64 (1977): 409–53.

A word about speech acts and pragmatics may be of use here. *Pragmatics*—the term formed in obvious parallel to phonetics, syntactics, and semantics, the traditional levels of linguistic analysis—is the study of speech acts, or verbal action, or "the relation between linguistic signs and their users" (see Geoffrey N. Leech, *Explorations in Semantics and Pragmatics* [Amsterdam: John Benjamins, 1980], 2). *Speech acts*, or illocutionary acts, are acts performed in speech, acts such as asserting, denying, naming, and thanking. They may be inexplicit, as when I say "I wasn't there," or explicit, as when I say "I deny that I was there," in which latter case they are called *performatives*. Speech acts may or may not be addressed to specified hearers. Any two speech acts may or may not share any of a number of such features as commitment on the part of the speaker. Pragmatics includes conversation analysis (of such features as

control and uptake), in addition to the analysis of discrete speech acts and families of
speech acts. These analytic approaches have their foundations in J. L. Austin's *How
To Do Things With Words*, ed. J. O. Urmson (Oxford: Clarendon Press, 1962), and in
later works of H. Paul Grice and John R. Searle, and have been used by Stanley E.
Fish ("How To Do Things With Austin and Searle: Speech Act Theory and Literary
Criticism," *Modern Language Notes* 91:5 [1976]: 983–1025), and Joseph A. Porter
(*The Drama of Speech Acts: Shakespeare's Lancastrian Tetralogy* [Berkeley and Los
Angeles: University of California Press, 1979]). See also Heather Dubrow's *Captive
Victors: Shakespeare's Narrative Poems and Sonnets* (Ithaca, N.Y.: Cornell University
Press, 1987); Keir Elam's *Shakespeare's Universe of Discourse: Language-Games in the
Comedies* (Cambridge: Cambridge University Press, 1984); and Mary Louise Pratt's
Toward a Speech Act Theory of Literary Discourse (Bloomington: University of Indiana
Press, 1977). For a summary of pragmatic theory with special attention to its use in
Shakespeare study, see my "Pragmatics for Criticism: Two Generations of Speech Act
Theory," *Poetics* 15 (1986): 243–57.

  Finally, while I have kept *The Troublesome Raigne* in general view, and made the
occasional specific comparison in passing, I have carried out no systematic detailed
comparison.

  2. G. G. Gervinus, *Commentaries*, 357, quoted in Horace H. Furness, ed., *The
Life and Death of King John*, 558.

  3. "Hee that is to be made Knight, is stricken by the Prince with a Sword
drawne, upon his back or shoulder: The Prince saying, *Soys Chevalier*, and in times
past was added *S. George*. And when the Knight riseth, the Prince saith, *Avance*. This
is the manner of dubbing Knights at this present. . . ." (Sir William Segar, *The Booke
of Honor and Armes* [London: 1590, University Microfilms 15451] Q3).

  4. "There is a moral significance in the suspended construction of the language.
The mind of the dastard king hovers over the subject of the ungodly act and dares not
alight upon it; and the verse, in its uncadenced movement, admirably registers the
speaker's state of mind" (Furness, ed., *King John*, 242).

  5. G. Blakemore Evans accepts (as do editors generally) Rowe's emendation here,
altering the punctuation from a period (F1) to a question mark. The emendation and
its acceptance reflect general discomfort with the ambiguity of the original punctuation's implied pragmatic analysis of the line. While the period could imply an
expression of incredulity much as does the question mark, the period could also give
the speech the same unquestioning acquiescence we find in Hubert's speeches immediately before and after. I am grateful to Alan Dessen for drawing my attention to the
distinction.

  6. In the play's opening line, "Now, say, Chatillion, what would France with
us?", John has a kind of hybrid command ("Now say, Chatillion") and question
("what would France with us?"). Questions are themselves commands or "directives"
of a sort (see Kent Bach and Robert M. Harnish, *Linguistic Communication and Speech
Acts* [Cambridge, Mass.: MIT Press, 1979], 40–49). But questions, unlike such other
directives as "requirements," "prohibitives," and "permissives" (Bach and Harnish,
40–47), entail no authority of speaker over hearer. John's opening line could without
metrical disruption have been purely command, as "Now say, Chatillion, what France
would with us."

  7. By my rough count (including a few judgment calls on the difference between
real and rhetorical questions), the numbers of real questions and of other utterances,
and the resultant percentages of interrogatives for prominent speakers in act 1, scene 1
are as follows:

	Real questions	Other utterances	Interrogative (%)
John	8	43	16
Bastard	11	108	9
Elinor	3	18	14
Robert Faulconbridge	1	13	7
Lady Faulconbridge	7	6	54
Chatillion	0	6	0

Since Lady Faulconbridge's sample is small, and since she does not reappear, her high percentage of questions may be discounted. Elinor does, of course, reappear, but she has no more questions in the play. Of the two most prominent speakers in the scene, John has less than half as many utterances as the Bastard so that, while he also has a smaller total number of questions, his percentage is nearly twice the Bastard's. John's early interrogativeness is further established in the second scene (2.1), where he has five questions to the Bastard's three, although here too the Bastard is more verbose. John's other high concentration of questions is in act 4, scene 2. Questioners and an approximate count of their questions are as follows: John, 23; Bastard, 22 (clustered at the beginning and end); Hubert, Philip, 9; Lady Faulconbridge, 7; Constance (with the third largest number of lines), Arthur, 5; Elinor, Lewis, 4; Salisbury, Bigot, 3; Austria, Pandulph, 2; Robert Faulconbridge, Pembroke, Prince Henry, 1.

8. Ability to change addressee, i.e., to finish addressing one person and to begin addressing another, is of course in part a function of authority or power. So it is that Philip's five mid-speech address changes outnumber Constance's four despite her far larger number of lines. These two characters have the largest number of address changes after John and the Bastard, who have nineteen and twelve, respectively. While with John the large number derives partly from his authority, and the Bastard's large number manifests in part a certain insubordinateness, the speech of both men has a resultant immediacy that makes them kindred.

9. My image of passing the torch is prompted partly by 5.7.30–48, where John's vivid extended imagery of the poison's burning him prepares for the Bastard's entrance line, "O, I am scalded with my violent motion. . ." (49). I am grateful to Deborah Curren-Aquino for pointing out the way in which the imagery here thus supports the kind of deep identification between the two men that I find in their speech acts.

10. E. A. J. Honigmann, ed., the New Arden *King John*, 74n.

Constance

A Theatrical Trinity

CAROL J. CARLISLE

As with any other Shakespearean character, the stage interpretations of Constance in *King John* have varied from one period to
another, reflecting changing tastes, ideas, social customs, and theatrical styles; they have necessarily varied within periods, too, according to the personal attributes of each actress. The differences involve
aspects of Constance's personality and manner as well as her degree of
prominence in the play. Such variations are most strikingly manifested
in an analysis of three Constances: the late eighteenth/early nineteenth-century Sarah Siddons, the Victorian Helen Faucit, and the
modern-day Claire Bloom. True to her name, however, the Constance
of the English stage has remained much the same in her basic
character. Whatever the differences, all three actresses in this study
have made maternal love, not personal ambition, the mainspring of the
character.

Another kind of "constant" also needs to be noted, a theatrical
problem which, though inseparable from this role, may account—
ironically enough—for some of the differences among the three portrayals. Constance has long been recognized as an unusually challenging part. To represent her ever-changing, ever-extreme emotions with
"harmony and propriety," to keep from crossing the "boundary between poetry and frenzy," to avoid becoming "either too sentimental
or too shrewish"—this, according to critics of various periods
(Thomas Davies in 1784, William Hazlitt in 1817, and Westland
Marston in 1888), is the difficult task Shakespeare set for the actress
who undertakes his most extravagantly depicted heroine.[1] The problem has taken on somewhat different dimensions from one period to
another (and, recently, from one medium to another), but it has
remained a basic consideration for every Constance. The individual

solutions to this theatrical dilemma have done much to determine the variations in Constance's personality.

Mrs. Siddons introduced her interpretation to the London public at Drury Lane Theatre on 10 December 1783. This was a propitious time for an actress to do justice to Constance. In her passionate devotion, her strong distress, and her rhetorical eloquence, Shakespeare's character resembled the heroines of the "she-tragedies," still popular in the late eighteenth century—Isabella, for example, in *Isabella, or The Fatal Marriage*, which had given Mrs. Siddons her first London success in 1782. Constance's role was less obviously designed for a leading actress, of course, than were the heroines' parts in the dramas of Southerne, Otway, and Rowe; but, despite its relative lack of prominence, it similarly challenged a star performer because of its potential ability to arouse admiration and excitement and to elicit sympathetic tears. Both in the literary criticism and the stage practice of that period the "just delineation" and forceful expression of "the passions" were highly valued.

In general the eighteenth-century critics admired Shakespeare's depiction of Constance's emotions and found her despairing speeches touchingly effective. Although Dr. Johnson noted that "a passion so violent cannot be borne long," his discussion of Constance's grief was wholly sympathetic.[2] Several critics deplored her indecorous scolding match with Elinor, but they apparently admired her lofty tirades. Thomas Davies, always sensitive to stage effects, remarked that in the early part of the play Constance appears more of a virago than an afflicted mother but that she takes on, in the third act, "the dignity of just resentment and majesty of maternal grief."[3]

Just as the literary critics approved Constance's passionate hyperboles, so the acting style that had been popularized by David Garrick (only recently retired, in 1776) encouraged the exploitation of her heightened emotions in all their variety. In doing so, however, it probably exaggerated a basic problem of the role. For this was a style that emphasized dynamic portrayals of distinct, often opposing, passions, yoked together with sudden and exciting "transitions." The difficulty was in keeping a performance from being simply a series of unrelated bravura exhibitions. The best actors (like Garrick himself), though not concerned with such later ideals as consistently revealed motivation and gradual development, evidently succeeded in giving their characters an overall identity; they recognized, too, the importance of preserving, even in the "whirlwind" of passion, the kind of "temperance" and "smoothness" advocated by Hamlet.[4] Few representatives of Constance seem to have met such standards, however. According to Davies, only Susannah Cibber (the most eminent of

Mrs. Siddons's predecessors in the role) had completely succeeded in depicting Constance's varied passions with "harmony and propriety."

Davies's phrase could aptly describe the acting style of the Kembles, including Mrs. Siddons, who would dominate the London stage from the mid-1780s for years to come. By taking a single "ruling passion" as the key to a character, they would give unity and artistic shape to the performance, however strong and varied the secondary emotions might be.[5] The Kembles' style has often been termed "artificial" in contrast to the "natural" style of Garrick and, later, Edmund Kean; at its best, however, in the acting of Mrs. Siddons, it was impressive and emotionally powerful. When asked whether a character "should be acted above the truth of Nature" in order to "produce an effect on the audience," Mrs. Siddons replied, "No, Sir, but undoubtedly up to Nature in her highest Colors."[6] This was obviously the ideal that governed her own portrayal of Constance.

Mrs. Siddons was well aware of the extraordinary challenge presented by "this grand creature" (as she called the character) and her "gorgeous affliction." She could think of no more difficult role in all dramatic literature. The Constance of her imagination required a commanding appearance and manner, an unusually expressive face, a harmonious, widely ranging voice, and the ability to suggest nobleness of mind. This description might have applied just as well to the actress herself: her imposing figure, her brilliant dark eyes and strong classical features, the effortless power and harmonious modulation of her voice—all equipped her to represent her ideal Constance. But there was a further difficulty. As Mrs. Siddons pointed out, this role demands unremitting concentration on the character and her situation, for there is no chance of working up to an emotional climax—Constance must enter the stage already in "the plenitude of her afflictions." Mrs. Siddons solved this problem by keeping her dressing-room door open when she was offstage so that she could hear the machinations of the other characters; during the kings' march to Angiers to ratify the marriage that would destroy her hopes, she used to stand in the wings, holding Arthur's hand, and the "sickening" sounds of that march would bring to her eyes "bitter tears of rage, disappointment, betrayed confidence, and . . . agonizing . . . maternal affection."[7]

Grandeur—that is the characteristic that remains in one's mind after all the descriptions of Mrs. Siddons's acting have been read. Macready spoke admiringly of her "grand and massive style"; Hazlitt wrote that she seemed "to belong to a superior order of beings, to be surrounded with a personal awe, like some prophetess of old."[8] The descriptions of her Constance fit the same pattern. Leigh Hunt was particularly impressed by the actress's ability to portray Constance's "violence" and "majestic excess" without loss of dignity.[9] Although maternal love was meant to be the character's ruling passion and although variety certainly characterized the acting, the mode seems to have been mainly heroic. "With what unutterable tenderness was her brow bent over her *pretty Arthur* at one moment," writes Campbell, "and in the next how nobly drawn back, in a look at her enemies that dignified her vituperation." Here is the flexibility of fine acting, but here, too, is the idealizing quality of the Kemble style. One thinks immediately of sculpture—the "embodied image" of Motherhood, replaced a moment later by that of Righteous Indignation. Mrs. Siddons's costume, with its careful artistry, must have enhanced her statuesque effect: she wore a graceful gown of black satin, whose skirt extended into a train behind but curved upward in front to reveal a white underskirt, "disposed in certainly the most tasteful folds of that day"; her magnificent arms were bare below the elbow. On her head was a crown, with a long veil falling from it. In Constance's last scene, according to James Boaden, Mrs. Siddons "disheveled even her hair with graceful wildness."[10] Yet the analogy with sculpture is misleading: Mrs. Siddons's acting did have an element of the statuesque and the abstract, but it was far from static. Indeed the dynamic quality of her Constance was what distinguished it most from the later portrayal of her niece Fanny Kemble. Miss Kemble, wrote Leigh Hunt, was "almost stationary in her grief. Mrs. Siddons used to pace up and down, as the eddying gust of her impatience drove her."[11] Vigor and grandeur stand out as the hallmarks of her Constance.

One of Constance's most memorable moments occurs in the first scene of act 3 when she refuses to go with Salisbury to the kings and, seating herself upon the ground, exclaims:

> To me and to the state of my great grief
> Let kings assemble; for my grief's so great
> That no supporter but the huge firm earth
> Can hold it up. Here I and sorrow sit;
> Here is my throne, bid kings come bow to it.
>
> (3.1.70–74)

Mrs. Siddons delivered this speech "with an energy of sorrow so mighty" that the bare earth seemed more majestic than a throne, and she "marvellously reconciled the mad impulse of it, with habitual dignity." The effect on the audience was "electrical."[12]

Concerning the next sequence, Constance's tirade of curses on the "wicked day," Mrs. Siddons explained: "Goaded and stung by the treachery of her faithless friends, and almost maddened by the injuries they have heaped upon her, she becomes desperate and ferocious as a hunted tigress in defence of her young" as she utters this "frantic and appalling exclamation." After denouncing Philip for his perfidy, Constance cries, "Arm, arm, you heavens, against these perjur'd kings!" (3.1.107). Mrs. Siddons, who spoke these words with head thrown back and hands clasped bosom-high, strove to make the audience feel what she described as the "awful, trembling solemnity, the utter helplessness of that soul-subduing, scriptural, and prophetic invocation."[13] She considered it difficult to speak what followed with "tempered rage and dignified contempt," but she was much admired in doing so. Boaden praises both her "furious demand" of "War, war, no peace!" (3.1.113–29) and her "withering" sarcasm to Austria.[14] In Constance's reply to Cardinal Pandulph when he rebukes her for trying to add her curse to Rome's, Mrs. Siddons's "lofty indignation came into play with all its nobleness."[15] But her acting in the passage where Constance tries to counter Blanch's plea to Lewis not to fight her kinsman John is puzzling. The text indicates that both women are kneeling as Blanch asks, "what motive may / Be stronger with thee than the name of wife?" and Constance replies, " . . . His honor. O, thine honor, Lewis, thine honor!" (3.1.316). One might expect Constance's words to be spoken in an urgent, pleading tone, but Mrs. Siddons, who must have been standing at this point, spoke them with a laugh and patted Lewis on the breast. Campbell found "sublimity in the laugh of her sarcasm."[16]

In commenting on Mrs. Siddons's performance of her final scene, Boaden explained: "Constance is too impassioned for hope; she sees the future in the instant: Arthur in the power of her enemy is already dead to her. . . . She therefore does not linger in expectation but expires in frenzy. . . ." At Constance's exit, he wrote, even an actress who is "not highly intellectual" can make some effect simply with the "sharp shrillness of the voice," but Mrs. Siddons, not content with an "inarticulate yell, the grief of merely savage natures," gave meaning to the words themselves.[17] Thus, even in her most frenzied moment, there was a dignity that other actresses did not have.

Mrs. Siddons's final performance of Constance was on 8 June 1812. Her comments on the character were not published until 1834, however, when Thomas Campbell incorporated them in his biography of her. Both her stage portrayal—or the memory of it—and her written criticism remained influential for years to come. Aside from Mrs. Siddons's remarks, the most notable literary criticism of Constance in the first third of the nineteenth century was the essay by Anna Brownell Jameson in her widely known book *Characteristics of Women* (1832). Since Mrs. Jameson had been a friend and admirer of Mrs.

Siddons, it is not surprising that she should also emphasize maternal love rather than selfish ambition and recognize a haughty spirit, "excited into frenzy by sorrow and disappointment." Mrs. Jameson's most original contribution was her idea that, whatever Constance's motivation and emotions, the "prevailing tone" of the character comes from the "predominance of imagination." Thus Constance loves her young son not simply with a mother's fondness but also with a "poetical imagination" that makes her idolize him, exulting in "his beauty and his royal birth" and envisaging "his infant brow already encircled with the diadem."[18] This interpretation sorts well with the ideality of Mrs. Siddons's portrayal.

In 1843, however, a critic named George Fletcher took issue with Mrs. Jameson on two points: he found no haughtiness in Constance (only the "indispensable self-respect of the woman, the mother, and the princess"), and he insisted that she is far more intellectual and rational than Mrs. Jameson supposed. (He pointed out, for example, her well-reasoned speeches in both scenes with Pandulph.) Indeed, he particularly admired Constance's "moral and intellectual beauty." Fletcher had formed his conception under the influence of the actress Helen Faucit: he had seen her as Constance in William Charles Macready's production of *King John*, which opened at Drury Lane on 24 October 1842 and had the last of its twenty-six performances on 15 May 1843. His essays on the women characters in *King John* and their representation in Macready's production, first published in the *Athenaeum* and later reprinted in his book *Studies of Shakespeare* (1847), helped to publicize Miss Faucit's interpretation and extend its influence.[19]

Helen Faucit had first attempted Constance at Covent Garden on 6 October 1836, just nine months after her London debut, and had performed it fourteen times that season. In later years she would occasionally revive this role (though much less frequently than most of her others), the last time being at the Theatre Royal, Glasgow, in 1855. But her most important performances of Constance, by far, were in the production that so impressed Fletcher. For Macready's *King John*, with its beautiful scenery, its historically accurate costumes, and its strong cast (Macready himself as John, for example, and Samuel Phelps as Hubert), was not only one of his most splendid revivals but also one of the most notable productions of this play in theater history. Although Constance did not loom large in Helen Faucit's career, it may have represented a milestone for her: according to the *Morning Chronicle* (25 October 1842), this was the character in which she first proved she "really was a Shakespearian actress."

The costume that Miss Faucit wore in Macready's production was based on an effigy of the year 1211 but was adapted to suit Constance's character and situation. It consisted of a plain, long-sleeved gray gown with a gold collar and gold belt, a black cloak lined with rose, and a red, crown-like headdress with a black veil hanging from it.[20] This somber apparel with touches of brilliant color might suggest that the wearer had a stern personality with a streak of violence—and indeed the artist's sketch of the costume does show a woman with a grim, uncompromising look. But the actress's slender figure and piquant face, with its dark-lashed, luminous gray eyes and its dimpled chin, would have considerably modified this effect. When Helen Faucit tore off the headdress in her last scene, releasing her long black hair, this Constance must have looked unusually young and vulnerable.

Miss Faucit's acting style, strongly influenced by Macready's, combined a new "psychological" approach with some of the Kembles' "ideal" methods. For example, the cadence of the blank verse might be broken occasionally with pauses, sighs, or other naturalistic devices to suggest unspoken thoughts or half-suppressed emotions (producing, as unfriendly critics complained, a "staccato" sound), but at other moments a transcendent, almost symbolic effect would be created by some attitude, expression, tone, or gesture that made a "poetic" appeal to the imagination. Despite the mixed styles, the performance as a whole would give the impression of unity because the keynote was sounded early and its theme was developed in the unfolding characterization. Not only her manager's influence but also her own physical problems—a delicate constitution and limited vocal resources—had converted Helen Faucit from an early leaning toward uninhibited, tempestuous acting, which quickly showed the signs of strain, to a more artistic shaping of her performances that saved her strength for the big moments. Such vocal artistry, together with her stately carriage, enabled her to achieve lofty if not forceful effects.[21]

Both her appearance and her best acting style made Helen Faucit a peculiarly fine representative of the "womanly woman," a type idolized by her Victorian contemporaries—charming, tender, highminded, devotedly loving; dependent on man, yet inspiring and guiding him; capable of heroic self-sacrifice. Sooner or later Miss Faucit adapted most of her characters to this ideal, or to some aspects of it; her Rosalind, for example, retained its playful wit but took on a new refinement and depth.[22] Thus it is not surprising that she put special emphasis on Constance's "womanly" characteristics. True, the ideal demanded a reticence foreign to Constance's character, but even the "womanly woman" could be stirred by circumstances to ringing declarations of noble sentiments. By emphasizing Constance's tender moments and by moderating the vehemence of her tirades, Helen Faucit could not only bring the character closer to the feminine ideal of her day but also accommodate a difficult role to her own abilities.

Early critiques of Helen Faucit's Constance varied widely, from praise to condemnation. The usual verdict was that her conception was admirable, as were parts of her performance, especially the tender and pathetic passages, but that the strain on her voice in Constance's violent speeches had resulted in shrillness and rant. The highstrung Miss Faucit was usually at her worst on the opening night of an important part, and in this case a recent bout with influenza had exacerbated her vocal difficulties. But her most serious problem was the specter of Mrs. Siddons. Although the great actress's Constance had not been seen for thirty years, it was still recalled as the ideal portrayal. Challenged by accounts of Mrs. Siddons's magnificent delivery, Helen Faucit had marred the effectiveness of her own by a "constant effort to attain the unattainable." Naturally her performance suffered from comparisons with the "sublime" Constance of her predecessor. One critic wrote, for example, that parts of the new impersonation were unrivaled "for grace, and for true unadulterated pathos" but added, "there has been but *one* Constance."[23]

As the production continued its run, however, Helen Faucit evidently improved in strength and confidence. Most important, she "found herself" in the role, moderating the violence and placing greater emphasis on those passages best suited to her talents. A playgoer who saw her Constance at this time and never forgot it wrote years later: "Indignation, irony, scorn, tenderness, affection, and sorrow were depicted by her in the most natural manner, and she had the advantage of a grand presence, great flexibility, clearness, and mellowness of voice, somewhat of a low pitch, but very distinct, with a passionate expression. . . ."[24] Although nostalgia might have glorified the remembered performance in this case, the description is consonant with the one written by George Fletcher while the production was still running. Miss Faucit's physical powers were "adequate" rather than "great," he said, yet she was able to achieve the "elastic force" of an "intellectual . . . poetical, and essentially feminine character" because of her effective use of the principle of contrast, aided by her "exquisite modulation of tone and flexibility of feature."[25]

As Fletcher explained, Helen Faucit made "*feeling*, not *pride*, the mainspring of the character." Although she tried at some points in the play to be "imposing, stately, grand" in the manner of Mrs. Siddons (see her annotations on her prompt-copy of Constance), she gave expression to the softer emotions much more frequently than her predecessor had done. The softness did not connote weakness, however. Helen Faucit particularly admired women who, with all the tender feelings of their sex, had also a noble spirit, a daring devotion to some beloved person or revered principle. Evidently she had built up such a conception of Constance. In her usual manner of sprinkling her promptbooks with quotations from literature, intended apparently as oblique stage directions to herself, she wrote on her prompt-copy of Constance two poetic passages dealing with characteristics she wished to portray: self-knowledge (a virtue not everyone would attribute to Constance) and—of course—constancy ("Be constant—and thou chainest time forever").[26] When Fletcher called Miss Faucit's Constance "intellectual" as well as "poetical" and "feminine," he was paying tribute to the qualities usually associated with her "noble" impersonations.

According to the same critic, Helen Faucit showed somehow that Constance's "effusions of bitterness" were repugnant to her natural character and that she found relief in every look or word that she addressed to her beloved Arthur. One example of the contrast between Constance's abnormal bitterness and her natural tenderness occurred in the midst of her angry exchange with Elinor (2.1), when Miss Faucit gave a gentle and delicate quality to the passage "His gran-dame's wrongs, and not his mother's shames, / Draws those heaven-moving pearls from his poor eyes" (168–69). Another such transition was made in the first scene of act 3, after Constance learned of the marriage that ruined her hopes for Arthur. "Her burst of indignation" at "Gone to be married?" (1) was "very grand," but her tone changed in the midst of her reply to Arthur's plea that she be "content." At the words "But thou art fair" (51) there was a "wonderful tenderness and pathos and change of voice and manner." In this "exquisitely touch-ing" passage Helen Faucit's "faltering pauses" were, for a sympathetic listener, "more eloquent than the finest declamation."[27]

In Constance's most famous passage (3.1.67–74), when Salisbury said he could not go without her to the kings, Faucit's Constance turned on him and declared with "withering scorn," "Thou mayst, thou shalt, I will *not* go with thee. . . ." She had spoken the last line of the preceding speech—"And leave those woes alone, which I *alone* / Am bound to underbear"—as if "drawing herself within herself," and she was once again speaking "to herself" when she said "I will instruct my sorrows to be *proud*." She turned to Salisbury, however, and looked him in the eye as she commanded, "To me and to the state of my great grief / Let kings assemble. . . ." Here, Faucit reminded herself, she must express "dignity—power—imperial majesty." She drew her mantle about her and allowed it to envelop her figure with its folds. Then "she seemed gradually to sink into the ground—never taking her eyes off Salisbury—with a kind of long sweeping curtsey, and never dropping her voice until her body rested on the stage," she spoke with "mournful cadence" the words "Here I and sorrow sit; / Here is my throne, bid kings come bow to it."[28] A spectator who was only a boy at the time wrote more than forty years later that he could "still hear in imagination the pathetic tones of Helen Faucit" as she spoke these lines.[29] Here the actress introduced another of her contrasts. In the midst of her regal representation of Grief, she looked up to see her little boy "drooping over her" and raised her hand to play with his ringlets.[30]

In her denunciation of Philip for his perfidy, Helen Faucit once again juxtaposed two opposite effects: when she spoke the words "And our oppression hath made up this league" (106), she bent down and clasped her son; then, as if drawing a strong stimulus from his embrace, she rose, "as it were, to more than the natural height" and lifted "high her hands to heaven in the majestic appeal—'Arm, arm, you heavens, against these perjured kings. . . .'"(107). At "A widow cries; be husband to me, heavens," Helen Faucit wrote in her prompt-copy: "as she would pull the heavens down to her." In her imprecations she again used pauses very effectively: here they seemed to show Constance "at a loss for expressions adequate to the intensity of her unwonted bitterness." Her "taunting sarcasm" to Austria was accompanied with hysterical laughter. When she appealed to Lewis, however, she knelt and spoke "O, thine honor . . ." with "noble and generous fervour."[31]

In her final scene (3.4) Helen Faucit's Constance was obviously distracted. Arthur was gone, and she knew she would never see him again; yet she kept looking about for him in contradiction to her own words, and "occasionally [she] put out the hand as if expecting to meet his." In Macready's text the invocation to Death as a bridegroom (25–36) had lost its most grotesque lines. Its effect when Miss Faucit spoke it tended toward pathos, but she warned herself not to make it "*too* pathetic More despairful [underlined twice]." When Philip urged her to bind up her tresses, "She look[ed] at him enquiringly": her reply, "To England, if you will"(68), which Helen Faucit noted as a non sequitur, was spoken "wildly."[32] When she tore off her headdress, exclaiming, "I will not keep this form upon my head / When there is such disorder in my wit" (101–2), her voice was "crazed with grief."[33] For all her air of distraction, however, Helen Faucit played most of this scene quietly. Even on opening night she was "much more moderate" here than elsewhere and, according to the *Morning Herald*, "touchingly effective" (25 October 1842). The tone changed dramatically, however, for Constance's last three lines—"O Lord, my boy, my Arthur, my fair son! / My life, my joy, my food, my all the world! / My

widow-comfort, and my sorrows' cure!" (103–5). In her prompt-copy
Helen Faucit wrote here, "Think of seeking & calling for him,"[34]
suggesting, whether intentionally or not, a shocking parody of a
mother's calling her little boy. Oddly enough, one early critic considered her too tame at this point; if so, she later became increasingly
violent here, even while moderating her effects in other passages.
These lines, recalled one spectator, were an "agonizing cry"; when
Helen Faucit left the stage he was glad her part was over, for his nerves
were "overstrung" with the reality of her whole performance.[35] Even
Fletcher admitted that her voice rose "almost into a scream" here. But
he added: "What . . . are the whole three lines themselves but one
long scream of intensest agony?"

In the 1840s Constance was still considered by most critics a sympathetic character as well as a remarkable dramatic creation. Only occasionally would someone write, as did a critic for *Bell's Weekly Message*
(29 October 1842), "She is the heroine of terror of the school of
scolding tragedy, and is so full of invective and fierce abuse that she
reduces to a very low ebb that sympathy and compassion which she
would otherwise excite." Negative opinions were expressed more
frequently, however, as the century went on. J. O. Halliwell believed
that her maternal affection was mixed with "dangerous ambition," as
did the influential German critic G. G. Gervinus. H. N. Hudson, who
deplored her "redundancy of rhetoric and verbal ingenuity," declared
that she had been overrated because of Mrs. Siddons's genius in
portraying her. Later critics did not scruple to accuse her of outright
rant. In the present century she has fared no better—at least until
recently. Frederick Boas even questioned the purity and normality of
her love for Arthur. Constance did find some defenders in this case.
Stopford Brooke, for example, saw her as a depiction of "primeval
motherhood," "the deep agony of the female in animals and in humanity." In general, however, critics have shown little interest in her.[36]
Mark Van Doren called her "the last and most terrible of Shakespeare's wailing women," and several other writers have emphasized
her generic rather than her individual character. Margaret Webster,
though more sympathetic than some, gives her short shrift, calling her
"another Margaret, with a mellower tone and some strain of moving
nobility, but an equal tendency to dull our ears and hearts with
repetition of her griefs."[37]

In very recent years feminist criticism has created new interest in
the position of women in Shakespeare's plays. Juliet Dusinberre, in
Shakespeare and the Nature of Women, relates Constance to other
"women trapped in the political world" as portrayed by Shakespeare
and his fellow dramatists:

A woman suffers continually from the impotence which is exceptional in a man. . . . At moments of crisis women in the drama are painfully aware that their only weapon is words. . . . Women use words to create the illusion of action. . . . The theatricality of Constance's grief . . . comforts her; like Richard II lacking an army, she peoples her imagination with subjects. . . . Her appeal to the Heavens to fight on her behalf looks forward to Lear. . . . The effect of impotence is to turn women against each other rather than against the men who injure them. The famous slanging match between Eleanor and Constance in *King John*—sometimes cut as unseemly—is psychologically apt.[38]

Margaret Loftus Ranald echoes Dusinberre but gives more attention to the character of Constance, viewing her as both a "professional figure of lamentation" and a psychologically understandable woman who uses rhetoric "as a means of attack" and also as "a way of clinging to her own sanity."[39]

Today's representative of Constance obviously faces not only the difficulties long recognized as inherent in the role but also some that did not disturb her predecessors. Her audience will be embarrassed rather than thrilled by a magnificent display of "the passions," however skillfully they are portrayed. As Eugene Waith has pointed out, the modern "suspicion . . . of emotional appeal" has made many people uncomfortable both with Constance's scenes and with Arthur's pathetic appeal to Hubert.[40] John Barton, in his production of *King John* (1974), was accused of frivolously undercutting Constance's effect in one of her scenes, as if this character were "the embarrassing product of over-writing."[41] The successful modern Constance has been described as "beautifully controlled" and one who contents herself with a "quiet force."[42] Constance's rhetorical virtuosity is a particular liability for the actress today, when the traditional suspicion of rhetoric's deceptiveness persists, without being balanced by the traditional admiration of its beauty and power. As Margaret Ranald notes, though Constance is "the sincere mouthpiece of conscience, the enemy of political necessity," she creates the effect of insincerity by the "intellectual artistry" of her speeches. Thus the best compliment that Irving Wardle could give Sheila Allen's Constance was that she was "believably intolerable" and that she "succeeded in making the tiresome wordplay expressive."[43] The modern Constance cannot even count on unequivocal sympathy for the mother's devotion to her son. Rather than feeling an automatic veneration of Motherhood, its tenderness and its pain, some members of the audience may pull back in dismay from this exemplar of maternal possessiveness or note with clinical detachment that Constance is the victim of a "fixation."[44] We do understand political oppression, however, and perhaps we can be made to sympathize with a woman who turns at bay against those that have betrayed her and her son.

When an actress must impersonate Constance for television, as Claire Bloom did in the BBC production of *King John* (released in England late in 1984 and in America early in 1985), the difficulties of the role are compounded. Acting that would not seem excessive even on the modern stage can be too large in this medium. Both the small screen of television and the domestic setting in which it is viewed are incongruous with anything "theatrical." As William B. Worthen observes, "the best effects are achieved in close-up, where the camera tends to magnify both gesture and facial expression. So television acting has come to demand the mastery of minimal effects." The actor faces a formidable challenge in trying to reconcile the demands of Shakespeare with the often-opposing demands of television. Most viewers have had experiences like those recalled by Stanley Wells—of feeling personally "harangued" during a strenuously declaimed soliloquy in one play but disappointed by the emotional inadequacy of the understated acting in another. The most difficult parts to transfer to television are, as Worthen notes, the big, "extroverted" ones "whose operatic rhetoric, and equally operatic 'thought processes' resist the camera's intimacy." Constance is undoubtedly one of those "public, expansive, 'hectoring' roles" that present the greatest challenge to the television actor.[45]

The idea of a woman caught in a complex political situation and necessarily dependent on men to fight her battles was conveyed very well by Claire Bloom in the BBC production. She was an unusually quiet Constance, even in her indignation and grief, and therefore she seemed a relatively passive one, even while standing her ground and unanswerably exposing the weaknesses of the other characters. The difference from Sarah Siddons and Helen Faucit in personality and manner was marked. In her emphasis on maternal devotion, however, not only did she resemble her predecessors but she kept Constance's love for Arthur and her emotional dependence on him more clearly and constantly evident than they seem to have done. The passages of "gorgeous affliction," the "withering" tirades, and the moments of regal grandeur, so admired in the great performances of the past, tended to offset, or at least qualify, the impression of Constance's tender and affectionate nature, even if they were conceived of as arising from that nature under pressure of desperation. Since such effects were largely absent from Miss Bloom's performance, there were few distractions from Constance's close relationship with her son and their growing isolation from the politically powerful people that surrounded them. (The television camera, which tends to focus separately on individuals or pairs, helped to stress this idea.)

Even the costume of this Constance, with its white dress and gold accessories, its silver crown delicately embellished with small pearls, and its white veil softly framing the face, enhanced the impression of madonna-like devotion. If her mantle had been blue rather than brown brocaded with silver, she would have seemed at first sight a mature but eternally innocent type of Virgin Mother.

Claire Bloom's Constance had a sweet, gravely smiling expression at the beginning of her first scene (2.1), and she fondled Arthur in an affectionate but not an unduly possessive manner. (This fondling became so frequent throughout her performance that the cumulative effect was to reveal the excessive absorption in her son that would find verbal expression in her final words.) When Elinor tried to refute Arthur's claim to the English throne by the charge of bastardy, Constance responded quietly but allowed her voice to become increasingly emotional in tone. When she spoke "His grandame's wrongs, and not his mother's shames, / Draws those heaven-moving pearls from his poor eyes" (168–69), one could hear some "tears" in her own voice. At "Call not me slanderer" (175), her voice deepened with anger, though it never became loud, and she concluded the speech by spitting at Elinor. This was the only moment in her performance when Miss Bloom's Constance suggested a mother animal at bay—and then it was not Mrs. Siddons's tigress but a household cat that came to mind.

In her next scene (3.1) Claire Bloom's "Gone to be married?" (1) was impassioned though quiet. When she accused Salisbury of lying in order to frighten her, Arthur went to his mother protectively and she clasped him to her as she asked in a dazed voice, "Lewis marry Blanch?" and then, in a higher tone, "O boy, then where art thou?" (34). When Arthur begged her to be "content," she held his face in her hands as she replied, "If thou that bid'st me be content wert grim . . ." (43), looking intently in his face and shaking her head a little in her emotion. In speaking of his beauty (51–54) she looked adoringly at him, and she stressed with pauses the words "to—make—thee—great." (Here I was reminded of Mrs. Jameson's idea of maternal love lifted by "poetical imagination" into a kind of idolatry.) The passage about Fortune's adulterating with John (54–61) was spoken as if in Arthur's ear—a strange, even false touch. Perhaps the naughty words should not be publicly uttered by a gentlewoman, but was her little son a fit recipient of them? To Salisbury's insistence that he could not go to the kings without her, the reply, beginning "Thou mayst, thou shalt" (67–74), was spoken quietly, almost with a smile, but with a direct look in his face which took the place of Helen Faucit's "withering scorn" here. She sank quickly to the ground, without the grandeur attributed to the action of her great predecessors. The famous passage, "Here is my throne, bid kings come bow to it" (74), in which Mrs. Siddons had created such a majestic effect and Helen Faucit such a hauntingly pathetic one, seemed almost commonplace, although it was accompanied with an imperious wave of the hand.

When the kings entered with their nobles and attendants, Constance was still seated on the ground, and (unlike former Constances) she remained so, propping herself up throughout the tirade beginning "A wicked day, and not a holy day!" (83–95). King Philip, in trying to comfort her, raised her to her feet—something the more aggressive Constances would not have allowed. Her following accusation, though quietly delivered, was impressive because she spoke it slowly and looked the king full in the face while doing so. When she came to "Arm, arm, you heavens!" (107) this normally restrained actress resorted to one of the large gestures that her predecessors had used: with her left arm around Arthur, she raised her right hand to heaven as she invoked divine aid. This was the one passage in her performance where she adopted a noticeably traditional piece of business, and it was an appropriate one. Her speech to Austria beginning "War, war, no peace!" (113) was louder than most of her others, though still not really loud. The scorn was evident, however. This Constance paced all around Austria, sizing him up with her eye as she spoke; she picked up the end of the lion's skin that hung off his shoulder and flung it back at him contemptuously as she said, "Thou wear a lion's hide! Doff it for shame . . ." (128). It was an effective treatment of the speech, contrasting as it did with Constance's natural sweetness, passiveness, and restraint. Her argument with Pandulph for her right to curse (185–90) gave the effect of logical reasoning, as Helen Faucit's "intellectual" treatment had evidently done. In the context of Pandulph's speciousness and the other characters' shifting loyalties, Constance's rhetoric seemed entirely sympathetic.

Constance's final scene (3.4), in which the grief-stricken mother loses the child that was "all the world," has often been called the "mad scene," though some critics have insisted that Constance's own argument for her sanity ought to be accepted. Claire Bloom entered with her brown hair loose on her shoulders; she no longer wore either her crown or her madonna-veil. One soon sensed, however, that giving up these symbols of royalty and motherhood was not a sign of madness but of a complete loss of hope. During most of this scene the lines that could have been spoken in frenzy were given with deadly calm. Only once or twice were there glimpses of feverish emotions imperfectly buried. When Philip tried to comfort her, she spoke, "No, I defy all counsel, all redress" (23) full in his face, and she continued to speak the invocation to Death in the same way, underlining the word *stench* and addressing "a carrion monster like thyself" (33) directly to the king. Turning the passage to an insulting identification of Philip with Death (a partial truth) was interesting but somehow it softened the effect of the grotesque imagery of Death as lover and reduced the impression of Constance's nightmarish state of mind. When Philip asked her to bind up her hair, she began feverishly plaiting bits of hair but soon abandoned the effort.

"And, father Cardinal, I have heard you say . . ." (76–89) was very different from Helen Faucit's "prayerful appeal."[46] It began with a sardonic tone of voice but became graver and sadder as the speech went on. There was nothing hysterical about "therefore never, never / Must I behold my pretty Arthur more." The second "never" was spoken with a flat certainty, as if to confirm the inevitability of the conclusion she had reached. As in her former speeches to Cardinal Pandulph, she had presented, step by step, a reasoned argument. One could almost imagine a "QED" at the end. Having spurned any comfort from Philip and Lewis except the comfort of death, she was now rejecting any possibility of comfort beyond death from the cardinal's religious doctrine. If she did see Arthur again in heaven, he would not be the same Arthur she had known. Everyone had failed her, and she must make it quite clear—to herself and to each of them—that she could hope for nothing now. When Pandulph charged that she was as fond of grief as of her child, she nodded several times in recognition of this truth before explaining very quietly, as if to make a backward person understand, "Grief fills the room up of my absent child . . ." (93–98). All of this led up effectively to her lines "Fare you well! Had you such a loss as I / I could give better comfort than you do" (99–100).

In delivering these lines with hopeless calm, Claire Bloom made the limitations of television and the "intellectual artistry" of Constance's rhetoric work *for* her interpretation in a remarkably successful way. At this point, however, a change of tone was needed. Shakespeare signals such a change with "I will not keep this form upon my head / When there is such disorder in my wit" (101–2). But there was little change in Miss Bloom's manner. Since she was wearing no crown, veil, or headdress, and since she had not obeyed Philip's injunction to bind up her hair, there was no "form" to tear down. She put her hands up to her head as if in pained recognition of the disorder within, but that was all. The passage leading to Constance's final exit, that outcry she can no longer hold back—"O Lord, my boy, my Arthur, my fair son!

. . ." (103–5)—was no outcry at all. If some Constances have screamed the words rather than making them intelligible (as James Boaden reported), perhaps they were attempting a female equivalent of Lear's "Howl, howl, howl." Claire Bloom did not have this choice, not wishing to blast her television viewers from their places, as they sat (to borrow Stanley Wells's phrase) "inoffensively on a sofa only a few feet away." She settled for a quiet but broken delivery, giving each group of words a separate emphasis and accompanying each with some physical movement. The rather mannered effect left me wishing, after all, for the scream.

Except for a few disappointing moments, when the limitations of television were painfully apparent, Claire Bloom's performance was successful in transferring a difficult and "stagey" character to the new medium. The quiet intensity of her passion, the subdued scorn in her speeches of sarcasm and derision, the cold logic of despair in a scene often given over to frenzy—all were generally effective. Just as impressive was the way Miss Bloom turned Constance's artful rhetoric to the advantage of her sympathetic interpretation, making it seem surprisingly natural to character and circumstances. Hers is not the Constance one imagines in reading the play, much less the Constance that would have appealed to Georgian or Victorian audiences, but it is a portrayal which, in its own way, vivifies and illuminates Shakespeare's character.

A few words remain to be said about the different degrees of prominence accorded Constance in the three portrayals I have been describing. Mrs. Siddons's biographer Thomas Campbell remarked that the brevity of Constance's part and its early disappearance from the play were a disadvantage for any actress but that with "repeated impressions" a fine portrayal might persuade the public to attend the play for the sake of Constance alone. According to his report, Mrs. Siddons did achieve such success, and spectators were known to leave the theater when her part was over.[47] There could be no clearer reminder of the emphasis on star performers at that time. Great as she was, however, Mrs. Siddons could not have stolen all the interest when she appeared in *King John* with her brothers John Philip Kemble (a successful King John) and Charles Kemble (a very popular Bastard). On such occasions, though she was the most brilliant of the luminaries, she was nevertheless a star among stars. Helen Faucit had little opportunity of making Constance a starring part in Macready's *King John,* for any center of attention in a Macready production would have to be the actor-manager himself. Besides, despite his egocentricity, Macready was unusually concerned with achieving unity and harmony. Emphasis upon the whole picture was at its greatest in a "grand revival" like his *King John*, in which a historical period was represented with as much accuracy as possible. Both tradition and rhetoric decreed, however, that Constance should stand out as one of the major roles, overshadowing such characters as Elinor and Blanch. In the BBC *King John*, Claire Bloom's restrained performance and the camera's sequential method of focusing now on one character, now on another, resulted in a Constance who seemed much on a par with the other women, particularly Elinor, with whom she was strikingly contrasted. The three of them—Constance, Elinor, and Blanch—formed a coherent but varied pattern within the larger pattern of the play.

Of the three portrayals discussed, Mrs. Siddons's Constance, by virtue of its grandeur and power, became the chief point of interest in the play and, because of its long life on the London stage, established a strongly influential tradition. Helen Faucit's Constance, coming between Mrs. Siddons's and Claire Bloom's chronologically, stood between them also in personality, manner, and position in the play. Miss Faucit introduced more moments of tenderness and pathos than Mrs. Siddons had done and created more effects of noble indignation and lofty sorrow than Miss Bloom would later do. Her Constance never came close to dominating the play, but she was unmistakably a heroine. This conception was much less influential than Mrs. Siddons's, but it was a clear reflection of the ideas and tastes of its time. Claire Bloom's portrayal was the most consistently gentle, sympathetic, and quietly rational of the three. This Constance kept her place among the other characters, contributing to a strong sense of the social and political world they all inhabited. Because there is a permanent record of the production, Miss Bloom's single performance will probably reach more spectators than did Mrs. Siddons's numerous performances over a period of three decades—and it will be seen by many who would not normally attend a theater. It will certainly be influential, though the kind and degree of its influence are unpredictable. Perhaps the next generation, accustomed to a quiet and reasonable Constance, will scratch their heads if they hear of Mrs. Siddons's Wagnerian heroine and will think, with A. B. Walkley, that the grand old actress must have been a "holy terror."[48]

Notes

1. Thomas Davies, *Dramatic Miscellanies*, 3 vols. (London, 1784), 1:35; William Hazlitt, "Mr. Kemble's King John," *Dramatic Essays by William Hazlitt*, ed. William Archer and Robert W. Lowe (London, 1895), 123; Westland Marston, *Our Recent Actors*, 2 vols. (London, 1888), 1:128.

2. Samuel Johnson, ed., *The Plays of William Shakespeare*, 8 vols. (London, 1765; rpt. New York: AMS Press, 1968), 3:440, 503. For comments on the she-

tragedies, their popularity, and Johnson's admiration of them, see Carol J. Carlisle, "The Critics Discover Shakespeare's Women," *Renaissance Papers 1979*, ed. A. Leigh DeNeef and M. Thomas Hester (Durham, N.C.: Southeastern Renaissance Conference, 1980), 62–65.

3. Davies, *Dramatic Miscellanies* 2:33. A useful summary of criticism by eighteenth-century writers is found in Tommy Glenn Moore's "Shakespeare's *King John*: The Critical History," 49–52.

4. See George W. Stone and George M. Kahrl, *David Garrick: A Critical Biography* (Carbondale: Southern Illinois University Press, 1979), chapters 2, 16; George Taylor, " 'The Just Delineation of the Passions': Theories of Acting in the Age of Garrick," *Essays on the Eighteenth-Century English Stage: The Proceedings of a Symposium Sponsored by the Manchester University Department of Drama*, ed. Kenneth Richards and Peter Thomson (London: Methuen, 1972), 51–72. (Taylor's interesting analysis may overemphasize the separateness of the passions in Garrick's acting.) See also Joseph Roach's comprehensive study, *The Player's Passion: Studies in the Science of Acting* (Newark: University of Delaware Press, 1985), chapters 2, 3.

5. *Macready's Reminiscences and Selections from His Diaries and Letters*, ed. Sir Frederick Pollock (New York, 1875), 40–41; Taylor, " 'The Just Delineation of the Passions,' " 62.

6. Quoted in *The Diary of Benjamin Robert Haydon*, ed. Willard Bissell Pope, 5 vols. (Cambridge, Mass.: Harvard University Press, 1960–63), 4:572.

7. Thomas Campbell, *Life of Mrs. Siddons* (New York, 1834), 88–89, 91.

8. Pollock, ed., *Macready's Reminiscences*, 42; Hazlitt, "Miss O'Neill's Juliet," *Dramatic Essays*, 19. The latter was first published in the *Champion*, 16 October 1814.

9. "[King John]" in *Leigh Hunt's Dramatic Criticism 1808–1831*, ed. Lawrence H. Houtchens and Carolyn W. Houtchens (New York: Columbia University Press, 1949), 39, first published in the *Examiner*, 5 July 1812.

10. James Boaden, *Memoirs of Mrs. Siddons* (Philadelphia, 1893), 265; Gilbert Austin, *Chironomia: or A Treatise on Rhetorical Delivery*, ed. Mary M. Robb and Lester Thonssen (Carbondale: Southern Illinois University Press, 1966), plate 11, figure 118. According to Austin, p. 495 (including note), the sketch of Mrs. Siddons as Constance was among several drawn by a young lady "from recollection . . . immediately after having seen her in her principal characters." The book was first published in 1806.

11. Hunt, "Miss Fanny Kemble as Constance" in *Dramatic Essays by Leigh Hunt*, ed. William Archer and Robert W. Lowe (London, 1894), 213, first published in *Tatler*, 28 March 1831.

12. Boaden, Memoirs, 264; Hunt, *Dramatic Essays*, 213. In the passage just discussed I have changed "sorrows" to "sorrow" since that is the way Mrs. Siddons spoke it (as did Helen Faucit). In my later discussion of Helen Faucit's Constance, the italicizing in the quoted passages duplicates the markings for emphasis in Miss Faucit's prompt-copy, now in the Furness Collection, Van Pelt Library, University of Pennsylvania.

13. Campbell, *Life*, 89–90; Austin, *Chironomia*, plate 11, figure 118.

14. Campbell, *Life*, 91; Boaden, *Memoirs*, 264.

15. Hunt, "[King John]," *Dramatic Criticism*, 39.

16. Campbell, *Life*, 87.

17. Boaden, *Memoirs*, 264–65.

18. Anna Brownell Jameson, *Characteristics of Women*, rev. ed. (rpt. Boston, 1887), 357–81; Charles Knight praised her conception of Constance in his 1842 edition of *The Comedies, Histories, Tragedies, and Poems of William Shakespeare*, 12 vols. (rpt. New York: AMS, 1968), 4:360.

19. Dates and number of performances are based on the Drury Lane playbills in

the Enthoven Collection, British Theatre Museum. Fletcher's reply to Mrs. Jameson is in "Female Characters in 'King John.' The Lady Constance," *Athenaeum*, 11 February 1843, 137–39; his critique of Helen Faucit's performance is in "Female Characters in 'King John.' Present Acting of The Lady Constance . . . ," *Athenaeum*, 18 February 1843, 161–63. For Helen Faucit's influence on Fletcher's Shakespearean criticism see his acknowledgment in the preface to *Studies of Shakespeare* (London: Longman, Brown, Green, and Longmans, 1847), xxiii–xxiv; also Sir Theodore Martin, *Helena Faucit (Lady Martin)* (Edinburgh: Blackwood, 1900), 92–93. (Note: Helen Faucit's real name was Helena, though she was always known as Helen on the stage.)

20. Charles H. Shattuck, ed., *William Charles Macready's "King John,"* 18; 21, figure 5.

21. For Macready's acting style see Alan S. Downer, *The Eminent Tragedian William Charles Macready* (Cambridge, Mass.: Harvard University Press, 1966), 69–80; for Helen Faucit's, see Carol J. Carlisle, "Helen Faucit's Acting Style," *Theatre Survey* 17 (1976): 38–56.

22. See Carol J. Carlisle, "Helen Faucit's Rosalind," *Shakespeare Studies* 12 (1979): 65–94; also Carlisle, "The Critics Discover Shakespeare's Women," 68–73.

23. For her illness, see *Britannia*, 29 October 1842, 719; for "constant effort" see *Times*, 25 October 1842; for "one Constance" see *Argus*, 29 October 1842, 11. I have read some twenty-one reviews of Helen Faucit's performances on the first few nights of the 1842-43 production. Seven are mostly complimentary, six are mostly or entirely derogatory, and the rest are mixed. I am grateful to Charles H. Shattuck for allowing me to use some of his copies of reviews of *King John*.

24. Extract, "In the Pit of a Theatre," from some unnamed book or journal, 282–87, pasted in a volume of reviews of Helena Faucit, Lady Martin's *On Some of Shakespeare's Female Characters*, MS. 16442, National Library of Scotland.

25 *Athenaeum*, 18 February 1843, 161, 162, reprinted in Fletcher, *Studies of Shakespeare*, 27–28, 31. For the sake of convenience further references to Fletcher will be to his book only.

26. Prompt-copy of Constance's part, with Helen Faucit's annotations, opp. 7. Helen Faucit's cryptic references in her promptbooks become clear when one reads the detailed analyses in her later essays on some of her Shakespearean heroines. She never wrote an essay on Constance, however.

27. Fletcher, *Studies*, 29–30; "In the Pit," 283.

28. The reference to the mantle is in Helen Faucit's prompt-copy, opp. 7; the rest of the description is from "In the Pit," 283–84.

29. Henry Turner, "Recollections of Ryder," *The Theatre*, 1 May 1885, 224.

30. Fletcher, *Studies*, 30.

31. Fletcher, *Studies*, 32–33 (references to pauses and to speech to Lewis); prompt-copy, 5; opp. 6 (direction for hysterical laughter).

32. Prompt-copy, opp. 7; 8.

33. "In the Pit," 284.

34. Fletcher, *Studies*, 34; prompt-copy, opp. 10.

35. "Too tame," from *The Age*, 30 October 1842; "Agonizing cry," from "In the Pit," 284.

36. James Orchard Halliwell [later known as Halliwell-Phillips], ed., *The Complete Works of Shakspere*, 3 vols. (London, 1850), vol. 2, introduction to *King John*, n.p.; G. G. Gervinus, *Shakespeare Commentaries*, trans. R. E. Bunnett, 2 vols. (London, 1863), 1:500–502, esp. 500; Frederick S. Boas, *Shakspere and His Predecessors* (1896; rpt. New York: Greenwood Press, 1969) 240; Stopford A. Brooke, *Ten More Plays of Shakespeare* (1913; reissued New York: Barnes and Noble, 1963) 245–51, esp. 247. These critics and others are discussed by Moore in "Shakespeare's *King John*," 58–67.

H. N. Hudson, whose criticism was published in *Shakespeare: His Life, Art, and Characters* (1872), is discussed, along with several later critics, in Arthur Colby Sprague's *Shakespeare's Histories: Plays for the Stage*, 22.

37. Mark Van Doren, *Shakespeare* (1939; rpt. Garden City, N.Y.: Doubleday/Anchor Book, n.d.), 91; Margaret Webster, *Shakespeare Without Tears* (Cleveland: World, 1955), 182–83.

38. Juliet Dusinberre, *Shakespeare and the Nature of Women*, 278–80.

39. Margaret Loftus Ranald, "Women and Political Power in Shakespeare's English Histories," 58–60; see also Phyllis Rackin's essay "Patriarchal History and Female Subversion in *King John*" in the present anthology.

40. Eugene M. Waith, "*King John* and the Drama of History," 200–201.

41. Peter Thomson, "The Smallest Season: The Royal Shakespeare Company at Stratford in 1974," *Shakespeare Survey* 28 (1975): 138–41.

42. Descriptions, respectively, of the Constance of Sheila Allen (1974–75) by J. C. Trewin and the Constance of Sybil Thorndike (1941) by Gordon Crosse. See Trewin, "One King after Another," *Illustrated London News*, June 1974, 77; Crosse, *Shakespearean Playgoing 1890–1952* (London: Mowbray, 1953), 106.

43. Ranald, "Women and Political Power," 59–60; Irving Wardle, "*King John*, Aldwych," *Times*, 10 January 1975, 11.

44. See, for example, E. A. J. Honigmann's comment in the New Arden *King John*, 84 n. 104.

45. William B. Worthen, "The Player's Eye: Shakespeare on Television," *Comparative Drama* 18 (Fall 1984): 196–97; Stanley Wells, "Television Shakespeare," *Shakespeare Quarterly* 33 (Fall 1982): 274.

46. "In the Pit," 284.

47. Campbell, *Life*, 86–87.

48. A. B. Walkley, *The Speaker*, 30 September 1899; quoted by Waith, "*King John* and the Drama of History," 200, from the New Variorum *King John*, ed. Horace H. Furness, 689. Walkley had been deploring Julia Neilson's exaggerated depiction of Constance's "hysterical grief."

11

Staging *King John*
A Director's Observations

EDWARD S. BRUBAKER

NINETEENTH-CENTURY PRODUCERS OF *KING JOHN*—FROM KEMBLE TO
Macready to Kean to Tree—used the play as the cue and excuse for
mounting lavish displays of medieval antiquities. Imitating history
painting in the grand manner, these actor-managers paraded barons
and clergy, lords and ladies, attended by as many servitors and soldiers
as the scene could allow, all furnished with period costumes and props,
through picturesque halls, battlefields, chapels, and chambers.[1]

How this grand tradition got attached to *King John* productions is
not easy to explain. Certainly the text hardly calls for such treatment.
Unlike *Henry VIII* where pageantry regularly illustrates the progress
of the story, or *Henry V* where epic aggrandizement of the king is the
main business of the chorus, *King John* is a play of little ceremony
where achievement is regularly undercut by duplicity and grandilo-
quence by plain speech.

Perhaps the tradition of lavish *King John* productions can be attributed to the habit of regarding history plays as being so loosely
organized as to need whatever embellishments the producer can think
of.[2] Medieval pageantry certainly enlivens the scene, and no matter
what the play says, added spectacle will make it seem respectable. The
antiquarian treatment made seeing the play as edifying as visiting a
museum. Then, too, the effect of pageantry is to sound a note of
celebration, and, in the case of a history play, of patriotism as well.

It is no wonder that Felix Schelling, the first scholar to survey
history plays as a genre, spoke of them in this way:

> It was in the very nature of things that the popularity of the Chronicle Play
> should find its origin in the burst of patriotism and the sense of national
> unity which reached its climax in the year 1588 and stirred England to
> meet and to repulse the Spanish Armada.[3]

If those words strike us as left over from the last century, we will not
do much better by accepting the more recent view that Shakespeare's
histories celebrate the political order imposed by the Tudor mon-
archs.[4] For in either case, when we come to stage the history plays,
they will seem to deserve and demand the large effects that troop with
majesty.

And, indeed, our own century has not exactly abandoned the
solemn aspect and heavy upholstery of the Victorian manner of staging *King John*. Photographs and costume designs of productions at the
Stratford festivals—in England (1948), Connecticut (1956), and Ontario (1960)—all show crowded scenes and bulky, richly ornamented
costumes. Bare, platform stages have replaced detailed, painted scenery, and obviously theatrical costumes have replaced antiquarian rep-
licas, but the effect of ceremonial pageantry remains and is made
stronger by a massive, stiff formality.[5]

In the case of *King John*, I would like to argue that such treatment,
however much theatrical tradition would seem to support it, is simply
wrongheaded. To do that I have to say, however briefly, what kind of a
play I think *King John* is.

In the first place, I think *John* is a play for thinking people and that
its mode is more comic than impassioned. It deals with serious matters, but like the plays of Brecht, it is designed to keep the audience
thinking rather than stirred up by the issues it raises. It is a world away
from official, celebratory history.

From the opening pomposity of "Our strong possession and our
right for us" (1.1.39), undercut by "Your strong possession much
more than your right" (1.1.40), the play proceeds to laugh the high-
falutin assertions of its characters out of court. The case of the Bastard
Faulconbridge brings into question any right based on paternity or
primogeniture. And the stalemate before Angiers reduces to absurdity
the rival claims of John backed by the English lords and of Arthur
supported by the sanctimonious France and Austria. Constance's
prayer:

> be husband to me, heavens!
> Let not the hours of this ungodly day
> Wear out the [day] in peace; but ere sunset,
> Set armed discord 'twixt these perjur'd kings!
>
> (3.1.108–11)

may be answered by Cardinal Pandulph's sudden entrance, but it is
hard to see heaven's hand in the upshot. If we find ourselves touched

by Constance's long laments, their very length may make us impatient enough to remember that she stirred up this storm in the first place.

Again, if we want to applaud John's success, the cardinal asks us to consider the matter from another angle:

> 'Tis strange to think how much King John hath lost
> In this which he accounts so clearly won.
>
> (3.4.121–22)

And if John stirs our blood by defying the pope:

> Thou canst not, Cardinal, devise a name
> So slight, unworthy, and ridiculous,
> To charge me to an answer, as the Pope.
>
> (3.1.149–51)

we later witness his handing over his crown to the legate.

All this may seem a bit too satiric for the sweet Master Shakespeare we have been told about, inconsistent with his supposed conservatism, and with theatrical pleasure. But let us not overlook the fact that although John and the Dolphin win when they have the big battalions, they lose those battalions when they stoop to treachery. Nor should we overlook the point that Hubert does not succumb after all to the temptations of the devil, Commodity.

That is enough to indicate what kind of play I think *King John* is and why I believe the grand treatment will not do. Idol ceremony and the tide of pomp will swamp its complex intelligence.

Turning now to my own experience in staging *John* at the Oregon Shakespearean Festival, I would like to discuss some of the ways this view of the play affected the production.

At the Oregon Festival the play has been part of the repertory four times. The second time round in 1959, I stage-managed the production directed by Richard Risso. Ten years later, I directed the production, stage-managed by Pat Patton, who directed the fourth production sixteen years later in 1985. Although this chain of events would suggest that a particular *King John* tradition might have developed, such was not the case. Stage managers are likely to develop reservations about a director's work as they guide it through the set number of performances, noticing things they want to avoid as much as things worth trying to recapture. And with the passage of time, working with different actors and designers, a director looks for new possibilities.

If the Oregon Festival has a tradition, it has been shaped largely by the use of its large outdoor "Elizabethan" stage where the attempt is made to mount practically uncut versions of the plays, marked by a flow of action from one scene to another. The festival's founder, Angus Bowmer, was trained by B. Iden Payne whose approach to Shakespearean production came directly from his working with William Poel, the guiding spirit of the Elizabethan Stage Society in the early twentieth century.[6] Until recent years, the festival budget would not allow much by way of spectacle. Even if a director visualized *King John* as richly costumed with impressive numbers of extras crowding the corners, or with an elaborate decor to transform the stage facade, he had to be satisfied with staging that was direct and simple. Such were the traditions and constraints that prevailed when I staged *King John* in 1969.

If memory serves, I thought of the play pretty much as I have outlined it above. I suggested in a program note that *John* combined melodrama and historical romance, but I do not think that is quite what I meant. I was trying to tell the audience to expect a lighter tone and a play of dash, resilience, and excitement, rather than of portentous movement as the very word "history" suggests. I wanted to alert them to rapid turns and switchbacks. Remembering how ponderous and impressive the production I stage-managed earlier seemed to be, I thought the audience should be prepared for the lighter moments that had been missed.

In the first scene when John switches to talking frankly like a farmer—"This calf, bred from his cow" (1.1.124)—the mood and style of the sequence needs to establish a noticeable contrast to the opening sequence with the French ambassador. When Elinor, Constance, Blanch, the Bastard, and Austria fall into wrangling banter before the gates of Angiers, their manner should justify King Philip's rebuke, "Women and fools, break off your conference" (2.1.150). And if the audience hesitates to find fun in the matching set of victory proclamations by the two heralds, the sequence will certainly seem inept. Near the end of act 3, after Constance's affecting lament in which she unbinds her hair in grief for the loss of her son, the Dolphin's sense of the vanity of this world is undercut by Pandulph's line, "Your mind is all as youthful as your blood" (3.4.125); by its tone of condescension, the line should modulate the mood of the scene in preparation for the exciting proposal that the Dolphin make a claim to the English crown.

If one thing is true about Shakespeare it is that he keeps switching keys and tempos and we have to be able to match his agility so as not to ride roughshod over them. This is, of course, a problem for the cast, as much as for the audience, but an audience will not go along with the actors unless they sense early in the game that this sort of thing is to be expected.

How well did I succeed in developing a production that reflected my interpretation of the play? With mixed success. Partly because I wasn't all that sure I was right and found myself accepting compromises. And partly because theater is a collaborative art requiring that a director bring everyone's creative abilities into play.

Actors are trained to develop characterizations that are consistent from start to finish, and they feel insecure when they discover the sort of inconsistencies Shakespearean characters so often have. John is at first a successful and, I think, an ebullient person, then a man sorely afflicted by his conscience. The Bastard is an adventurer on the make, then a patriot of unswerving loyalty. The Dolphin is fresh and green in this old world, then as treacherous a worldling as can be found. Hubert is a man eager to sell his services, then a man incapable of treachery. It seems to me that the changeable nature of the characters is an important point to get across, for the play exhibits so many examples of that human quality. Actors are not often convincing in presenting such transformations and inevitably project one characteristic of their role better than another. We were not very successful in solving this problem. My Bastard turned out to be the patriot; my Dolphin was fresh and green in this old world. The audience, however, was probably unaware of the difficulty for an audience is likely to assume that characters are meant to be consistent.

Another problem arises in dealing with the long stretches of public oratory that run throughout the play. As neither actors nor audiences are very familiar with the fine points of oratory, it is tempting to pare the speeches down to their main points by cutting the amplifications and elaborations. We did not take that easy way out because I believe saucy and audacious eloquence can be entertaining. Unfortunately, particularly in a history play, the usual way these blocks of material are handled is for the actor to take a stride, lock into a stance and stare, and let go in a loud voice. For some reason we tend to imagine great moments in history as confrontations between great persons who stand for two sides in some epochal conflict. We imagine such individuals as very earnest and very sincere, but not as very bright, or subtle, or as simply out for themselves.

I think we came pretty close to solving this problem. At least we got rid of the stance and stare, and it seemed to me that the actors were enjoying the challenge. But I should report that the late Bertram Joseph, the authority on such matters, found the speeches before Angiers inept and left his seat. (You can do that in the outdoor

Ashland theater without disturbing others too much.) At the rear of the seating area, I asked him if something was wrong. "They don't know how to handle blank verse," he said, or words to that effect. I was about to introduce myself, but thought better of it.

To emphasize the idea that John's initial success in defeating the French depended on the backing of the English lords and that he lost power when they went over to the Dolphin, I decided to have each peer accompanied by a banner bearer, a sort of borrowing from the Chinese theater where a banner equals a battalion. When the lords were with John the stage seemed crowded, and when they left, the stage was emphatically bare. To mark the offstage excursions, it was decided the banner bearers could do a sort of choreographed drill, brief and punctuated by live drums and trumpets. I particularly wanted live sound because of a fear that sound on tape might jolt the play into the modern era. As it turned out, the sound did not seem very impressive in the outdoor theater and there was no way to turn up the volume. Then the sound man came up with the bright idea that we should get orchestral brasses on stereophonic tape. Although I felt this idea might shift the play into Wagnerian solemnities, I decided to give in to his persuasion. Better get with it than be an Elizabethan fuddy-duddy.

It's hard to tell what the audience made of all this. The play was the least well attended, which may be why the festival waited sixteen years before scheduling *John* again.[7] The comment I heard most often was that the choreography of waving banners in the excursions backed by brasses in stereophonic sound was the best thing in the show. Newspaper reviews were mixed, ranging from:

> Thanks to the direction . . . "King John" again strongly confirms that Shakespeare wrote no bad plays. It is a play about a bad king, in an ancient mold, but it is a good play . . .[8]

through:

> This production of "King John" seems to be made up of a series of outstanding scenes which do not quite add up to an effective and cohesive whole . . .[9]

to the discouraging, "A not-very-good production of a not-very-good play."[10]

And so my conclusion is that audiences are not as malleable as I was counting on. Their preconceptions about Shakespeare's histories cannot easily be set aside. They may accept history in the modern fashion of Brecht's *Mother Courage*, Osborne's *Luther*, or Arden's *Left-Handed*

Liberty. But with Shakespeare's *King John*, they still look for what they have been conditioned to expect, the pageantry of celebratory history. Nevertheless, if I were given the chance to do *John* again, aside from paying more attention to the women's roles, I would push for the same interpretation and be more stubborn about it. I'm not sure I could keep the ghost of Beerbohm Tree out of the production, but I would do my best to present a *King John* that would speak more penetratingly to the "ordering of this present time."

Notes

1. Charles H. Shattuck, *William Charles Macready's "King John"*; and Arthur Colby Sprague, *Shakespeare's Histories: Plays for the Stage*, chapter 2. See also Susan M. Williams's " 'To Paint the Lily': Sir Herbert Beerbohm Tree's Production of *King John*," a paper presented at the second session of the *King John* seminar of the Shakespeare Association on 29 March 1986. Williams argues that just "as Charles Kean had o'er-topped Charles Kemble and Macready, so Tree sought to o'er-top Kean, at least in terms of pictorial splendor and lofty aspirations (2). She goes on to single out two tableaux added by Tree to emphasize his favoring of pageantry: "The Fight Near Angiers," which followed act 3, scene 2, and "The Granting of Magna Charta," which preceded act 5, scene 1 and formed the opening of Tree's act 3" (4).

2. Sprague, *Shakespeare's Histories*, chapter 1.

3. Felix Schelling, *The English Chronicle Play*, 39.

4. Nearly twenty years ago, Herbert Howarth moved for "a moratorium on the teaching of the order-theory as the decisive background of Shakespeare." (See "Put Away the World Picture" in *The Tiger's Heart: Eight Essays on Shakespeare* [London: Chatto and Windus, 1970], 187.) As we all know the motion has yet to be passed.

5. For the Stratford-upon-Avon production, see J. C. Trewin, *Shakespeare on the English Stage, 1900–1964*, plate 28, and *Shakespeare Survey* 2 (1949): plate 8B. For the Stratford, Connecticut, production, see John Houseman and Jack Landau, *The American Shakespeare Festival* (New York: Simon and Schuster, 1959), 12–13, and 51–53. For the Stratford, Ontario, production, see *Made Glorious: Stage Design at Stratford, 25 Years* (Stratford, Ontario: The Gallery Stratford, 1977), 13, plates 6A, 6B; see also Arnold Edinborough, "Artistic Success in Canada," *Shakespeare Quarterly* 11 (1960): 456. The Royal Shakespeare Company production of *King John* (1974) cannot be used as an example because the text was adapted from Shakespeare with additions from *The Troublesome Raigne of Iohn King of England* and from Bishop Bale's *King Johan*, along with some rewriting by John Barton, the director. See Peter Thompson, "The Smallest Season: The Royal Shakespeare Company at Stratford in 1974," *Shakespeare Survey* 28 (1975): 137–41.

6. Ben Iden Payne, *A Life in a Wooden O* (New Haven: Yale University Press, 1977), 62; Angus L. Bowmer, *As I remember, Adam* (Ashland: Oregon Shakespearean Festival Association, 1975), chapter 2.

7. Of the 1985 Ashland production Charles Frey has written: "This was millinery Shakespeare. This was big-crowd, tableaux stuff, leaning perilously backward toward the spectacularism of Beerbohm Tree"—see Frey's *"King John* at the Oregon Shakespearean Festival 1985," a paper presented at the second session of the *King John* seminar of the Shakespeare Association on 29 March 1986 (13). Perhaps that overstates the case, but I suspect that with its huge genealogical chart visibly present from

beginning to end, the Ashland production would have been more to the liking of Beerbohm Tree than to that of William Poel. Somehow the grand old tradition keeps sneaking in as fast as the budget allows.

8. Robert D. Horn, " 'King John' Regarded as Good Play," *Ashland Tidings*, 23 July 1969, 1 and 14.

9. Anonymous, " 'King John' Production Made Up of Outstanding Scenes," *Medford Mail Tribune*, 23 July 1969, A 9.

10. Don Bishoff, " 'King John'—So So All the Way," *Eugene Register-Guard*, 24 July 1969, A 15.

12

The "Un-end" of *King John*
Shakespeare's Demystification of Closure

LARRY S. CHAMPION

WHETHER IN THE THEATER OR THE STUDY, *KING JOHN* HAS ALWAYS evoked a baffling variety of responses. Spectators frequently do not know quite what to make of an English king who bravely defies the pope in one scene only to capitulate abjectly in the next and who dies in slow agony on stage without a touch of retrospection—or of an ambitious young bastard of Richard I whose proclamations of self-serving commodity convert to a somewhat brassy display of patriotism—or of a dauphin who, moments after adamantly refusing the Church's order to cease aggression against John, peremptorily withdraws his forces from English soil at the point of highest military advantage. In a general sense and in various ways critics have long suggested that something significant is at work in Shakespeare's developing concept of drama. The present essay argues that the closure of *King John* is a key to Shakespeare's larger pattern, a design by which, in effect, he shapes from the chronicle play a form that—free from Tudor ideology—reveals historical process as human process determined innately by fundamental self-interest, a concept vital to the nature of his subsequent histories and tragedies.

In this play of "profound moral complexities,"[1] one of the most curious lines occurs in act 4 in John's order to the Bastard to seek out his rebellious lords and request that they return to him: "I have a way to win their loves again. / Bring them before me" (4.2.168–69). Pembroke, Salisbury, Bigot, and other English lords, believing young Arthur to be a victim of John's foul play, have threatened disobedience to the tyrant: "This must not be thus borne. This will break out / To all our sorrows, and ere long I doubt" (101–2). A scene later they will secretly agree to meet with Cardinal Pandulph in order to work out the details of their defection to France; Salisbury even notes that he has a private message from Lewis, the Dolphin, imputing much love and honor to the English nobles. Moments later, their discovery of Arthur's broken body seems to provide a convenient justification for the direct and flagrant rebellion they, in fact, have already privately determined:

> The King hath dispossess'd himself of us.
> We will not line his thin bestained cloak
> With our pure honors, nor attend the foot
> That leaves the print of blood where e'er it walks.
>
> (4.3.23–26)

Their response to the Bastard's message that John commands their return is to repudiate their loyalty to the king and, kneeling before Arthur's body, to pledge themselves to "the worship of revenge" (72).

John knows his situation is critical, and his using the Bastard as an emissary to the lords is clearly an act by which he hopes to contain their insurrection. The question, quite simply, concerns what John plans to tell them; what is the "way" he hopes "to win their love again"? Perhaps he has already decided to capitulate to Pandulph (something he does with no forewarning in act 5, scene 1), and he assumes such a peacemaking effort and his implicit repentance will regain their support. Perhaps, as H. H. Furness, Jr., suggests, he has decided to blame Arthur's death entirely on Hubert,[2] something he does indeed attempt to do a few lines later with feigned indignation clothed in hypocritical piety. Perhaps he assumes that the presence of a foreign invader will fire his lords with a patriotism that will mitigate their rebellious fury; this is a possibility since a messenger only moments earlier has brought him news of his mother's death in France and of the landing of a mighty French force on English soil, and since immediately after his command he speaks of wanting "no subject enemies / When adverse foreigners affright [his] towns" (4.2.171–72).[3] Perhaps, since Faulconbridge has just reported a general discontent among the commoners who are "strangely fantasied, / Possess'd with rumors, full of idle dreams" (144–45), John assumes that aristocratic self-interest will dictate their renewed support in order to prevent a general rebellion among the masses.[4] Perhaps C. Porter is correct in assuming that John has decided to make concessions inherent to Magna Charta,[5] an issue that Shakespeare does not otherwise mention in the play. Certainly the one thing he cannot intend is to claim that Arthur is still alive since at that particular moment he believes the young prince to have been murdered by Hubert on royal command.

While one assumption may be more plausible than others, the drama finally does not admit a definitive answer. Admittedly, a spectator without benefit of retrospective contemplation would experience nothing of such a variety of responses, but by the same token any one or two explanations might well occur to any given spectator. The salient point is that, whatever John might have in mind by the comment, it does not work. If he plans to announce his capitulation to Pandulph, for instance, we know that intention wins him only the disdain of the Bastard:

> O inglorious league!
> Shall we, upon the footing of our land,
> Send fair-play orders and make compromise,
> Insinuation, parley, and base truce
> To arms invasive?
>
> (5.1.65–69)

and the defiance of the Dolphin and his English defectors:

> I will not return
> Till my attempt so much be glorified
> As to my ample hope was promised.
>
> (5.2.110–12)

If John's plan is to blame Arthur's death on Hubert, we see that intention exploded into a series of almost pathetically comic contradictions. Hubert responds to John's accusation with an admission that Arthur still lives, in turn becomes another emissary to the lords with that news, ironically arrives when Arthur lies dead before them, and—even though we know him to be the only individual in the stage world to have acted on grounds of selfless mercy in sparing Arthur's eyesight—is blamed for the murder and threatened with death.

Any presumption that John harbors of rallying his lords to patriotic fervor at the report of a French invasion is again dashed with high irony. Whereas in *The Troublesome Raigne of Iohn King of England* the English lords defect only after actually seeing Arthur's body and in Holinshed's *Chronicles* only—thirteen years following Arthur's death—when they are demanding that John consent to the liberties granted in Magna Charta and the Charta de Foresta, Shakespeare depicts their defection as occurring before the Bastard even reaches them, well before they know Arthur in fact to be dead. Their concern, clearly, is not a sense of patriotism or a lack of it but their "safety" and "the Dolphin's love" which they have been promised (4.3.12, 16).

Whatever John means by the line, the larger question is what Shakespeare means by it. Obviously the choice of using it is his own; it is in neither *The Troublesome Raigne* nor Holinshed. Possibly the

command is purely a dramaturgic device by which to heighten the
tension of the scene. After all, John has no more than sent the Bastard
on his way to the nobles when Hubert arrives and, with his news that
Arthur lives, is dispatched as yet another messenger. With the lords'
discovering Arthur's body between the arrival of the two, what is
admittedly a flurry of events is rendered coherent and dramatically
effective. Also, as William Matchett has noted, this particular sequence provides a crucial test for the Bastard, who must choose
between the lords' and Hubert's conflicting claims concerning responsibility for Arthur's death and between loyalty to John or to the rebels
with their emotional pledge of vengeance.[6] Yet another possibility,
Shakespeare may have intended John's assertion that he has a way to
regain his subjects' loyalty as nothing more than an act of rattled
desperation, a signal of the king's loss of political control and of his
need to buy time by whatever means comes to mind.

Most likely, Shakespeare's real reason is—whatever the individual
spectator's assumption—to raise an anticipation only to dash it; in the
failure of each of these possibilities lies the convolution of ironies and
ambiguities with which the play concludes.[7] John's comment, in a
word, seems to set in motion a series of actions that methodically
cancel out any presumed moral or political virtues in the historical
process, reducing government and society to the chaos of individual
machination at worst and an unstable nexus of conflicting self-interests
at best; the deity "is spoken for by voices which not only contradict
each other but repeatedly belie themselves."[8] Lewis, leader of the
French forces, for example, warmly welcomes the English nobles,
receiving them in a highly ritualistic manner as he draws up a con-
tractual agreement, and then takes the sacrament in pledge of keeping
his faith "firm and inviolable" (5.2.7). No doubt without realizing the
irony, he mocks any high principle that might have motivated their
joining him by assuring them they shall "thrust [their] hand as deep /
Into the purse of rich prosperity / As Lewis himself" (60–62). Similarly, any assumption that he is fighting as champion of the Holy
Church against the heretical English king collapses when he refuses
Pandulph's command to "wind up" the "threat'ning colors" of war
now that John is reconciled with Rome (73):

> What is that peace to me?
> I . . . claim this land for mine,
> And now it is half conquer'd, must I back
> Because that John hath made his peace with Rome?
> Am I Rome's slave?
>
> (92–93, 94–97)

Lewis's final act of treachery is prevented only by the dying Count Melun's revelation to the English lords that they "are bought and sold! . . . He means to recompense the pains you take / By cutting off your heads" (5.4.10, 15–16).

The defecting lords hardly fare better. Their display of patriotic affection—lamenting that "we, the sons and children of this isle" must take such action to cure "the infection of the time" (5.2.25, 20)—brings tears to Lewis's eyes. As we have noted, however, their patriotism seems little more than self-interest when Lewis promises them material compensation. And when the Dolphin, in their presence and with not a single protest, defies Pandulph, they suddenly find themselves fighting against both their country and their religion. It is surely difficult for the spectator to suppress at least a degree of repulsion in their sudden desire, purely in order to save their lives, to "untread" their "damned flight," to "Stoop low," to "run on in obedience / Even to our ocean, to our great King John" (5.4.52, 55, 56–57). When—"their lilies thrice-gilded"[9]—they drag in young Henry as their advocate, it is not, considering the full context, a particularly auspicious entrance for England's future king. As Virginia Mason Vaughan has recently observed, the "English nobles return to the fold not because they are true but because they discover that Lewis is untrue."[10]

Certainly the final phase of John's reign is so pathetic as to derail any tendency to side with the king on grounds of fundamental nationalism. Admittedly, throughout the play Shakespeare has forced us to view John from a variety of perspectives provoking both sympathy and disdain;[11] as Michael Manheim has observed, in comparison with his role in *The Troublesome Raigne,* John "seems more genuinely heroic in facing down the Cardinal and blacker than ever in his relations with Prince Arthur."[12] But, in any case, his capitulation to Rome, in the face of his earlier vaunted assertions of English independence, strikes the spectator as nothing less than treason, a desperate effort to save his life and his kingship. That these are his final moments of physical health might well also be symbolically ironic. The Bastard in his subsequent confrontation with the Dolphin describes John as "well prepar'd," as smiling at his "pigmy" opponents (5.2.134, 135); the "gallant monarch is in arms" and hovers "like an eagle" (148, 149); in "warlike" John's "forehead sits / A bare-ribb'd death" (176–77). In actuality we see John six lines later sick at heart and wasted by fever (5.3.3–4), and our next view (scene 7) finds him in agonized death throes. Moreover, these last moments evince from John not a hint of remorse or spiritual sensitivity. There is simply no evidence to support

Ribner's claim that John is sincerely repentant for his sins, and only slightly more credible is Adrien Bonjour's observation that the final words of Prince Henry and the Bastard are "like a pardon giving lasting rest to a tormented soul."[13] Whatever the degree of sympathy from the spectator, it is provoked entirely by the spectacle of the suffering man.

Then, too, the Roman Church offers no haven for the spectator who in his search for some abiding principle or value becomes increasingly dislocated during the play's closure. John's poisoning by a monk is but the final treacherous deed of a church that throughout has consistently acted not on spiritual but temporal principle. One has only to consider the behavior of Cardinal Pandulph to find specific examples. Whether in his excommunicating John for failure to recognize the Roman candidate for Archbishop of Canterbury followed by his subsequent abolition of the papal curse when the king agrees to become a vassal of the Church, in his inciting the French to war on the infidel John so as to bring him to heel followed by the later command that Lewis peremptorily cease his aggression and retire from England, or in his counseling Lewis to invade England even though he knows that event will surely cost young Arthur his life, the cardinal is a major source of England's problems, his function "nothing less than the conjuring of chaos in the achieving of Rome's goals."[14] Shakespeare has indeed toned down the violent anti-Catholic sentiment of *The Troublesome Raigne,* but what remains is an all-the-more insidious pattern of religion pandering to power politics. It is thematically appropriate that an arm of the Church is surreptitiously present in the events leading to John's unnatural death.

Many critics seize upon Faulconbridge as the positive force, whether humanistic or political, in the play's final scenes. Presumably borrowed from *The Troublesome Raigne,* the Bastard becomes in Shakespeare's hands in the early acts a more cynical observer of a commodity-driven world; then according to prevailing views he experiences a kind of maturation through which he is prepared to speak for the body politic in the face of foreign invaders and of only recently quelled outbreaks of civil dissension. Matchett, for example, sees him as changing from a "naïve enthusiast [who] follow[s] chance to a man of mature insight and ability,"[15] and James L. Calderwood sees a full maturation in his withstanding the temptation to usurp Henry's right in the final moments.[16] We should be permitted to wonder, though, if we have not chosen a hero by default. He may indeed appear to be more worthy of sympathy than any of the surrounding figures, but, as Blanpied notes, "What we hear beneath the highly polished rhetoric . . . is a persistent grating lust for violence and blood."[17] When, following his denunciation of John's deference to Rome, he is given control of the English forces, he leads John's army to at best a standoff with Lewis. Hubert reports to John in act 5, scene 3 that things go "badly" for the English forces, and the king in scene 7 dies on the Bastard's own report that successful defense against the approaching Lewis is virtually impossible. Lewis himself in scene 5 boasts that the French are lords of the battlefield and that the English have "measure[d] backward their own ground / In faint retire" (3–4); he eagerly awaits the "fair adventure" (22) of the next day's battle. The Bastard's patriotic oratory, in other words, does not translate into deeds, and clearly he is the most surprised figure on stage to learn in the final scene of the Dolphin's decision to return to France, leaving to Pandulph the arrangement of a negotiated peace. In a word, Pandulph— not he—is responsible for whatever peace comes to England. He obviously can claim no responsibility for the storm that destroys a large part of Lewis's reinforcements; and he, having suffered a similar loss of troops, must watch the struggle wind down with a sense of futility on both sides.

The Bastard puts the best face on this turn of events, to be sure; and the play ends on his rousing assertion that England shall never fall so long as Englishmen are true to one another, words almost universally praised as effecting a closure that points toward the resurgence of a powerful and unified kingdom. Such a reading is undercut, however, by what A. R. Braunmuller in his recent Oxford edition of the play claims to be the proverbial nature of these final words, as having a quality of cliché that at least some spectators would perceive as ironically appropriate to Shakespeare's shaping (or unshaping) of this history play. Eugene Waith may well speak of the Bastard's "unexpectedly total commitment to the cause of his country" as a *"coup de théâtre"*;[18] but, as David Kastan correctly observes, Faulconbridge's "vision of England 'true' to itself is no less a fiction than his vision of England's dauntless king" even as John lies dying.[19] Moreover, when one considers that Shakespeare's history of Henry IV is soon to depict the ravages of civil war at a later point in time, the words become as ominously prophetic as those final lines of *Henry V* in which the Chorus points to Henry VI and his bleeding England. In both cases the cold chill of reality tempers the fire of political patriotism.

Strikingly different is the more traditional closure of *The Troublesome Raigne*. There the focus throughout is more directly on the title figure, and the treatment far more sympathetic. The prologue announces the story of a "warlike Christian" Englishman who endured peril and pain "For Christs true faith" (5–6),[20] and true to character John describes his ultimate submission to Pandulph as only an act of dissembling (*2 TR* 283). Praised even by Arthur for his stamina and mettle (*1 TR* 451), he nonetheless possesses a modesty and sensitivity not present in Shakespeare, a quality evident in his initial comments that he is unworthy of so high a place as the kingship (*1 TR* 10). He is also a man capable of a moral introspection bordering on anagnorisis in his dying moments:

> The world hath wearied me, and I have wearied it.
>
> . . . .
>
> Me thinks I see a cattalogue of sinne,
> Wrote by a friend in Marble characters,
> The least enough to loose my part in heaven.
>
> . . . .
>
> Dishonor did attaynt me in my life,
> And shame attendeth *John* unto his death.
>
> > (*2 TR* 798, 1046–48, 1066–67)

In *The Troublesome Raigne*, more specifically, additional emphasis on the villainy of the Roman Church, on John's penitence in the final lines, on Henry's firm assumption of kingship, and on the impact of the reunited English state once Lewis has decided to abort his invasion and return to France—all serve to provoke a sense of coherence, unity, and patriotism common to the English history play. It is interesting to note as well that the major points comprising the closure of *The Troublesome Raigne* are also found in Holinshed. There, too, collusion described at some length between two members of the abbey or between a convert and John's servants brings about the king's death. In both there is reference to John's concern with religion, Holinshed noting that the deeds of this "noble & righteous prince"[21] reflect a zeal to religion, and *The Troublesome Raigne* depicting his conviction that his agony is inflicted on him for his "grievous sins" and his fear that God is not sufficiently merciful to forgive his evil deeds. In both young Henry assumes the kingship in a demonstrably impressive manner. Holinshed records that the defecting nobles were prompted to return by the great potential they saw in Henry and that they, "with one consent, proclaimed the yoong gentleman king of England" (48); and in *The Troublesome Raigne* Henry confidently and successfully challenges Lewis and a continued French presence in England.

Shakespeare's *King John*, to the contrary, lacks such generically comforting touches. His aim is to present the character in starker and more ambiguous detail, with equally persuasive views of the usurper, the would-be murderer, the terror-stricken capitulator, the sufferer, the patriot, and the kingly defender of his nation against the avarice of

France and the superstition of Rome. For the same reason Shakespeare apparently rejects those scenes in which anti-Catholic sentiment is so flagrantly exploited that sympathy would automatically accrue to John—for instance the scene of venery between Friar Lawrence and Nun Alice and the scene in which a monk proclaims without remorse that he has committed a righteous murder against a king who dared to challenge the True Church. John's poisoning is the act of a single fanatical monk described in only five lines of the text. Similarly, Shakespeare depicts Arthur as simple and innocent, deleting all traces of an impetuosity which helps to explain and to meliorate, if not to justify, John's villainy (*1 TR* 1095–98).22 Neither is there a single word of remorse on John's lips through the entire ordeal. Absent, too, is any significant degree of confidence in the young Henry, either of word or of deed. The nobles swear their loyalty, and Salisbury even observes that Henry will "set a form upon [their] indigest" (5.7.26). But the new king utters not one word concerning the advancing Lewis; the tenderhearted nature reflected in his tears of thanks to his nobles is touching, but it emphasizes his innocent youthfulness rather than his potential leadership. And the spectator is unlikely to have forgotten so quickly the fate of Arthur's innocent youthfulness earlier in the play.23

From the point of John's assertion that he has a way to win back the nobles, Shakespeare seems consciously and methodically to deconstruct the chronicle play, raising expectations only to leave them unfulfilled as the governmental process grinds to a virtual halt. It is not difficult to infer, from the extant histories and historical pageants prior to the mid-1590s—including Shakespeare's first tetralogy—that the chronicle play had assumed at least a loose kind of identity and that the spectators would have come to anticipate particular patterns or themes. Whether the earlier playwrights were directly influenced by the humanist historian's perception of himself as, not a collector of facts, but "an artist who organized the facts into a coherent and attractive form"24 (an assumption supported by Bullough's contention that *The Troublesome Raigne* does just that in using the chosen facts to illustrate predetermined political and moral themes centering on "the shameful invasion of England"),25 they most certainly were exploiting the conscious patriotism in the years immediately after the Armada, addressing what J. P. Brockbank has called the "audience's heroic sense of community."26

With *King John* those inferences no longer obtain. No character on the stage possesses a significant level of awareness; that is, no one figure is in a position to have an overview of the various political forces at work in the stage world. Consequently, the play itself offers no guidance or shaping of events in such a manner as to give a particular meaning or significance to history, and the spectator individually is forced to come to terms with the welter of contradictions and conflicting ironies. As Eamon Grennan has recently noted, "No longer permitted the luxury of being spectators at a pageant played before them, the audience must, because of how the playwright puzzles their response, become active participants."[27] Precisely how the spectator does so either in Shakespeare's day or our own is as ambiguous as the issues of the play itself. He may leave the theater assuming that Shakespeare has depicted the canker at the very heart of monarchical government and hierarchical society, convinced that the play encodes an attack upon the Tudor establishment to which the general public would be attuned. He may, on the other hand, be convinced that the play is not an attack upon monarchism itself but on its visions of limitless power, that the struggle between the king and his nobles effectively delimits the powers of both ruler and aristocracy. He may with the Bastard (and with Holinshed) believe that the play above all exhibits the grave dangers of political division and civil dissension, that England's potential national greatness will be limited only by the degree to which all subjects fail to share a monolithic political vision. He may, of course, leave the theater in a muddle, confused at his inability to bring consistent moral values to bear on a political situation in which "the right, and truth . . . / Is fled to heaven" (4.3.144– 45). The genuinely perceptive spectator might well leave the theater with precisely that conviction, but without the confusion, viewing the play dispassionately as an artistic attack upon the very form itself and the tendency to provide closure where it is impossible in a corrupt political process.

What is clear, in any case, is that there has been nothing before in English drama quite like Shakespeare's *King John*. If the complex political vision of the later Henriad bridges the gap between the stage and Renaissance academic political theory, so does *King John* bridge the gap between the two tetralogies—like a "dramatic broom with which Shakespeare sweeps away many of the no longer convincing or functional props of the historico-dramatic world of his Yorkist plays."[28] The conclusions of the future Henry plays bear witness to the development of this vision—with martial valor counterpointed by the pragmatics of survival in one, political efficiency counterpointed by a gradual but inevitable process of dehumanization in another, and the heroics of national ambition counterpointed by occasional glimpses of the price of that dehumanization and the grim reminder of the brevity of both life and empire in yet another. Again the spectator, the director, or the critic can convincingly argue any one of several points of view in these plays, but Shakespeare's vision refuses to be bound by a particular design or ideology; it is as rich and ultimately as contradictory as the motivations that generate human action. If the second Henriad is more powerful than *John,* it is simply because the dramatic realization of that vision is less fragmented; the contrarieties represented in *King John* by the individual characters become in the later plays internalized in the figure of Prince Hal/Henry V. An open-ended chronicle play with historical process transformed into human process, stripped bare of Tudor providentialism and reduced to an individual self-interest that only in its best moments might be communally enlightened, *King John* is nothing less than a proclamation for the popular stage of a new historiography. The play, to borrow a phrase from Calderwood's recent description of the "un-end" of *Lear,* gives the impression that it "has not ended but merely stopped."[29]

Notes

1. J. L. Simmons, "Shakespeare's *King John* and Its Source," 61.
2. Horace H. Furness, ed., *The Life and Death of King John,* 319.
3. As Wolfgang Clemen notes, Shakespeare masses the reports of Constance's death, Elinor's death, the nobles' rebellion, and the French invasion to achieve an overwhelming effect (*Shakespeare's Dramatic Art,* 105).
4. Paul Siegel has recently argued that the struggle inherent in the evolution of the classes is a central conflict in all of Shakespeare's histories ("Monarchy, Aristocracy and Bourgeoisie in Shakespeare's History Plays," *Science and Society,* 42 [1978–79]: 478).
5. C. Porter, as cited in Furness, *The Life and Death of King John,* 319.
6. William Matchett, ed., *King John,* the Signet Classic Shakespeare, xxxi–xxxii.
7. Two distinct concepts of King John coalesced in the mind of the Elizabethan spectator: the medieval image of the tyrant and the Reformation image of the Protestant martyr (John R. Elliott, "Shakespeare and the Double Image of King John," 65–66; Jonathan Reeve Price, "*King John* and Problematic Art," 26). "[R]ight and wrong . . . are question-begging words" (M. M. Reese, *The Cease of Majesty,* 284); the "ambivalence of response . . . constitutes the central political and theatrical interest" (H. M. Richmond, *Shakespeare's Political Plays,* 100).
8. Sigurd Burckhardt, *Shakespearean Meanings,* 138. The play, according to John Masefield, is "an intellectual form in which a number of people with obsessions illustrate the idea of treachery" (*William Shakespeare,* 76); a "struggle of kingly greed and priestly pride" (Edward Dowden, *Shakespeare* [London: Macmillan, 1877], 168), it reflects a "mixture of philosophical materialism and Machiavellian politics" (Ronald Berman, "Anarchy and Order in 'Richard III' and 'King John,'" 54). Right can only be asserted, not legitimized (David Scott Kastan, "'To Set a Form Upon That Indigest,'" 9).
9. John W. Blanpied, *Time and the Artist in Shakespeare's English Histories,* 118.
10. Virginia Mason Vaughan, "Between Tetralogies," 419.
11. Larry S. Champion, *Perspective in Shakespeare's English Histories* (Athens: University of Georgia Press, 1980), 97–98.
12. Michael Manheim, *The Weak King Dilemma in the Shakespearean History Play,*

131. If to call John a tragic figure is an exaggeration (Charles Stubblefield, "Some Thoughts About *King John*," 27), it is also misleading to claim that as a usurper he forfeits all sympathy" (J. Dover Wilson, ed., Cambridge *King John*, xliv).

13. Irving Ribner, *The English History Play in the Age of Shakespeare*, 122; Adrien Bonjour, "The Road to Swinstead Abbey," 265.

14. Sidney C. Burgoyne, "Cardinal Pandulph and the Curse of Rome," 238. Topical critics are especially attracted to this scene as a parallel to jesuitical equivocation (Reese, *Cease of Majesty*, 272; E. A. J. Honigmann, ed., the New Arden *King John*, 69n) or to the advice to Philip of Spain to await Mary's death before expecting papal support for his cause (Lily Bess Campbell, *Shakespeare's Histories*, 147).

15. Matchett, ed., *King John*, xxxvi.

16. James L. Calderwood, "Commodity and Honour in *King John*" in *Shakespeare: The Histories*, ed. Eugene M. Waith, 100. Emrys Jones finds a structural parallel in *Mundus et Infans*, in which the moral innocent must encounter the world of experience (*The Origins of Shakespeare*, 235). Julia C. Van de Water sees Faulconbridge as two separate characters, a vice in the first three acts and a patriot in the last two ("The Bastard in *King John*," 143), and to F. P. Wilson he is a split Shakespearean personality leading to both Falstaff and Hal ("The English History Play" in *Shakespearian and Other Studies*, ed. Helen Gardner, 38). Jacqueline Trace, who suggests a sixteenth-century source for the figure, speaks of his "becoming an able statesman and a man of compassion and faith through the course of the play" ("Shakespeare's Bastard Faulconbridge," 61).

17. Blanpied, *Time and the Artist*, 105. Ronald Stroud claims that Faulconbridge "must either embrace the erring obsessions of his world or remain a moral 'bastard'" ("The Bastard to the Time in *King John*," 155). He sets his character for us when he "frankly admits to cynical role-playing" in his commodity speech (Douglas C. Wixson, "'Calm Words Folded Up in Smoke,'" 111).

18. Eugene M. Waith, "*King John* and the Drama of History," 211.

19. Kastan, "'To Set a Form,'" 14.

20. Citations from *The Troublesome Raigne of Iohn King of England* are from the edition of Geoffrey Bullough, *Narrative and Dramatic Sources of Shakespeare* 4:72–151.

21. Citations from Raphael Holinshed's *Chronicles of England, Scotland, and Ireland* are from Bullough, *Sources* 4:25–49.

22. Champion, *Perspective*, 109–10.

23. That each of these narrative elements is present in both Holinshed and *The Troublesome Raigne* but absent in Shakespeare strongly supports the assumption that *The Troublesome Raigne* is a source of Shakespeare's play, not the reverse. Similar events include the intention of the defecting English nobles to crown Lewis as king of England (in Shakespeare the lords merely join the invading force) and Pandulph's arrival with news of John's subjection to the Church before Lewis and his forces have sailed from France (in Shakespeare the invasion is well underway).

24. Leonard Dean, "Tudor Theories of History Writing," *University of Michigan Contributions in Modern Philology* 1 (1947): 4.

25. Bullough, *Sources* 4:8.

26. J. P. Brockbank, "The Frame of Disorder—*Henry VI*," in *Early Shakespeare*, ed. J. R. Brown and B. Harris (London: Arnold, 1961), 75.

27. Eamon Grennan, "Shakespeare's Satirical History," 33–34. Grennan's argument is that Shakespeare, by so obviously and blatantly transforming the Bastard from the role of satirist and parodist to that of the official mouthpiece of patriotism, forces us to question the very essence of teleological history. On the active role of the

spectator in *King John*, see also Wixson, "'Calm Words,'" 112–21, and Blanpied, *Time and the Artist*, 119.

28. Grennan, "Shakespeare's Satirical History," 21. The play is "a bridge, a transition" (Sidney Shanker, *Shakespeare and the Uses of Ideology*, 56), an "experimental play between two tetralogies" (Robert B. Pierce, *Shakespeare's History Plays*, 125). S. C. Sen Gupta describes it as "a new type of historical drama, in which the dramatist projects an idea through the interaction of plot and character" (*Shakespeare's Historical Plays*, 98). See also Champion, *Perspective*, 110.

29. Calderwood, "Creative Uncreation in *King Lear*" in *Shakespeare Quarterly* 37 (1986): 17.

King John
Select Performance History

(Editor's note: While this listing does not include every performance of the play, an effort has been made to cite as many major productions as possible and to include the names of the leading players if available. This listing, then, reflects the frequency of the performances of *King John* from the early eighteenth century to the present day. The information has been compiled from many sources, including H. Howard Furness's New Variorum edition of *The Life and Death of King John*, David Hirvela's "*King John:* An Interpretation Using Its Stage History," Tice Miller's "*King John*" in *Shakespeare Around the Globe*, edited by Samuel Leiter, and actual performance records.)

Stage

1737	Covent Garden. John, Delane; the Bastard, Tom Walker; Constance, Mrs. Hallam.
1741	Covent Garden. John, Delane; the Bastard, Hale; Constance, Mrs. Mullart.
1745	Drury Lane. John, David Garrick; the Bastard, Delane; Constance, Mrs. Cibber.
1747	Drury Lane. John, Delane; the Bastard, Sparks; Constance, Mrs. Gifford.
1751	Covent Garden. John, Quin; the Bastard, Barry; Constance, Mrs. Cibber.
1754	Drury Lane. John, Mossop; the Bastard, Garrick; Constance, Mrs. Cibber.
1758	Covent Garden. John, Sparks; the Bastard, Barry; Constance, Mrs. Bellamy.
1760	Covent Garden. John, Sparks or Ross; the Bastard, Smith; Constance, Mrs. Ward.
	Drury Lane. T. Sheridan and Garrick alternated the parts of John and the Bastard; Constance, Mrs. Yates.
1766	Drury Lane. John, Powell; the Bastard, Holland; Constance, Mrs. Yates.

Covent Garden. John, Ross; the Bastard, Smith; Constance, Mrs. Bellamy.

1768   Philadelphia, Southwark Theatre. John, Douglass; the Bastard, Lewis Hallam; Constance, Miss Cheer.

1770   Haymarket. John, Sheridan; the Bastard, Fleetwood; Constance, Mrs. Burton.

1774   Drury Lane. John, Reddish; the Bastard, Palmer; Constance, Mrs. Barry.

1775   Covent Garden. John, Sheridan; the Bastard, Lewis; Constance, Mrs. Barry.

1783   Drury Lane. John, J. P. Kemble; the Bastard, Smith; Constance, Sarah Siddons.

1792   Drury Lane. John, J. P. Kemble; the Bastard, Palmer; Constance, Mrs. Siddons.

1801   Drury Lane. John, J. P. Kemble; the Bastard, Charles Kemble; Constance, Mrs. Siddons.

1804   Covent Garden. John, J. P. Kemble; the Bastard, Charles Kemble; Constance, Mrs. Siddons.

1816   Covent Garden. John, J. P. Kemble; the Bastard, Charles Kemble; Constance, Miss O'Neill.

1818   Drury Lane. John, Edmund Kean; the Bastard, Wallack; Constance, Miss Macauley.

1822   Covent Garden. John, Young; the Bastard, Charles Kemble; Constance, Mrs. Faucit (Harriet Diddear); Hubert, Macready.

1823   Covent Garden. John, Macready; the Bastard, Charles Kemble; Constance, Mrs. Faucit. Scenery and costumes by J. R. Planché. In vol. 2 of his *Shakespeare From Betterton to Irving*, George Odell refers to this revival as "an epoch-making event" (159).

1832   New York City, Park Theatre. John, Barry; the Bastard, Charles Kemble; Constance, Fanny Kemble.

1834   New York City, Bowery Theatre. John, J. B. Booth; the Bastard, Hamblin; Constance, Mrs. McClure.

1836   Covent Garden. John, Macready; the Bastard, Charles Kemble; Constance, Helen Faucit.

1842   Drury Lane. John, Macready; the Bastard, J. Anderson; Constance, Helen Faucit; Hubert, Samuel Phelps. Costumes by Charles Hamilton Smith; scenery designed by William Telbin.

1846   New York, Park Theatre. John, Charles Kean; the Bastard, George Vandenhoff; Constance, Ellen Tree Kean.

1852   London, Princess Theatre. John, Charles Kean; the

Bastard, A. Wigan; Constance, Mrs. Kean; Arthur, Kate Terry.

1858   Princess Theatre. John, Charles Kean; the Bastard, Walter Lacy; Constance, Mrs. Kean; Blanch, Kate Terry; Arthur, Ellen Terry.

1865   Drury Lane (under Chatterton's management). John, Samuel Phelps; the Bastard, J. Anderson; Constance, Miss Atkinson.

1866   Drury Lane. John, Phelps; the Bastard, B. Sullivan; Constance, Mrs. Vezin.

1874   New York, Booth's Theatre. John, J. B. Booth; the Bastard, J. McCullough; Constance, Agnes Booth.

1889   London, Crystal Palace. John, Beerbohm Tree; the Bastard, Macklin; Constance, Miss Roselle.

1890   Stratford-upon-Avon Festival, Shakespeare Memorial Theatre. Osmund Tearle, director. John, Osmund Tearle; the Bastard, Edwin Lever; Constance, Marianne Conway.

1899   Haymarket. John, Beerbohm Tree; the Bastard, Lewis Waller; Constance, Julia Neilson; Elinor, Mrs. Crowe (Kate Bateman).

1901   Stratford-upon-Avon, Shakespeare Memorial Theatre. F. R. Benson, director. John, E. Lyall Swete; the Bastard, Frank Rodney; Constance, Elsie Chester.

1907   Chicago, Grand Opera House. John, R. B. Mantell; Constance, Marie Russell.

1908   New York, New Amsterdam Theatre. John, R. B. Mantell; Constance, Marie Russell.

1909   Stratford-upon-Avon Festival, Shakespeare Memorial Theatre. F. R. Benson, director. John, F. R. Benson; Constance, Constance Benson.

1911   Birmingham Repertory Theatre Company.

1913   Stratford-upon-Avon Festival, Shakespeare Memorial Theatre. F. R. Benson, director. John, F. R. Benson; the Bastard, Randle Ayrton; Constance, Ethel McDowall.

Birmingham Repertory Theatre Company. The Bastard, Barry Jackson.

1916   Stratford-upon-Avon Festival, Shakespeare Memorial Theatre. F. R. Benson, director. John, F. R. Benson; the Bastard, Edward Thane; Constance, Constance Benson.

1917   London, Old Vic. John, Russell Thorndike; Constance, Sybil Thorndike.

1921   London, Old Vic. Robert Atkins, director. John, Ernest Milton; the Bastard, Rupert Harvey; Constance, Florence Saunders.

1924   Strand. Fellowship of Players. John, Ernest Milton. (9 November)

1925   Stratford-upon-Avon Festival, Shakespeare Memorial Theatre. W. Bridges-Adams, director. John, Randle Ayrton; the Bastard, James Dale; Constance, Florence Saunders.

1926   Old Vic. Andrew Leigh, director. John, Duncan Yarrow; the Bastard, Baliol Holloway; Constance, Dorothy Massingham.

1931   Old Vic. Harcourt Williams, director. John, Robert Speaight; the Bastard, Ralph Richardson; Constance, Phyllis Thomas.

1938   New York, "Thursday Night Club" of the Church of the Transfiguration. John, James Bell. (4 March)

1940   Stratford-upon-Avon Festival, Shakespeare Memorial Theatre. Iden Payne and Andrew Leigh, directors. John, George Skillan; the Bastard, Baliol Holloway; Constance, Joan Sanderson.

1941   Old Vic Company, New Theatre. Tyrone Guthrie and Lewis Casson, directors. John, Ernest Milton; the Bastard, George Hagan; Constance, Sybil Thorndike; Pandulph, Lewis Casson; Hubert, Ernest Hare; Arthur, Ann Casson.

1945   Birmingham Repertory Theatre. Peter Brook, director. John, David Read; the Bastard, Paul Scofield; Constance, Eileen Beldon; Hubert, John Harrison.

1948   Stratford-upon-Avon Festival, Shakespeare Memorial Theatre. Michael Benthall, director. John, Robert Helpmann; the Bastard, Anthony Quayle; Philip of France, Paul Scofield; Constance, Ena Burrill; Blanch, Claire Bloom.

Open Air, Regent's Park. Robert Atkins, director. John, David Read. (6 July)

Ashland, Oregon Shakespeare Festival. Allen Fletcher, director. John, John Hume; the Bastard, Richard Graham; Constance, Kathryn Hume.

1952   Angers, France. Marcel Herrand, director.
1953   Old Vic. George Devine, director. John, Michael Hor-
            dern; the Bastard, Richard Burton; Constance, Fay
            Compton; Pandulph, Paul Daneman.
1956   Stratford, Connecticut, American Shakespeare Festival.
            John Houseman and Jack Landau, directors. John,
            John Emery; the Bastard, Fritz Weaver; Constance,
            Mildred Dunnock.
1957   Stratford-upon-Avon. Shakespeare Memorial Theatre.
            Douglas Seale, director. John, Robert Harris; the Bas-
            tard, Alec Clunes; Constance, Joan Miller.
1959   Ashland, Oregon Shakespeare Festival. Richard Risso,
            director. John, Philip Hanson; the Bastard, William
            Oyler; Constance, Mary Jo Randall.
1960   Stratford, Ontario, Stratford Shakespeare Festival.
            Douglas Seale, director. John, Douglas Rain; the Bas-
            tard, Christopher Plummer; Constance, Ann Casson.
1961   Old Vic. Peter Potter, director. John, Maurice Denham;
            the Bastard, Paul Daneman; Constance, Maxine
            Audley.

            Stockholm, Sweden, Royal Dramatic Theatre. Alf
            Sjöberg, director. John, Georg Rydeberg; the Bastard,
            Max von Sydow; Constance, Gertrud Fridh.

            Berlin, Berliner Festwochen. Hans Schalla, director.
            John, Manfred Heidmann; the Bastard, Hubert
            Suschka.
1963   Paris, Théâtre de l'Est Parisien. Guy Rétoré, director.
1964   Boulder, Colorado, Colorado Shakespeare Festival.
            James Sandoe, director. John, Edgar Reynolds; the Bas-
            tard, Barry Grugan Kraft; Constance, Ricky Weiser.
1967   New York, Delacorte Theatre, New York Shakespeare
            Festival. Joseph Papp, director. John, Harris Yulin; the
            Bastard, Robert Burr; Constance, Marian Winters.
1969   Ashland, Oregon Shakespeare Festival. Edward S. Bru-
            baker, director. John, George Taylor; the Bastard, Tom
            Donaldson; Constance, Carol Condon.
1970   Stratford-upon-Avon, Royal Shakespeare Theatre and
            Theatregoround. Buzz Goodbody, director. John, Pat-
            rick Stewart; the Bastard, Norman Rodway; Constance,
            Sheila Burrell.

1973	Turin, Italy, Edizioni Teatro Stabile. Aldo Trionfo, director.
1974	Stratford, Ontario, Stratford Shakespeare Festival. Peter Dews, director. John, Edward Atienza; the Bastard, Douglas Rain; Constance, Martha Henry.

Stratford-upon-Avon and London, the Royal Shakespeare Company. Adapted and directed by John Barton; incorporated material from Bale's *King Johan* and *The Troublesome Raigne*. John, Emrys James; the Bastard, Richard Pasco; Constance, Sheila Allen; Elinor, Hilda Braid; Hubert, David Suchet. (In 1975 Ian McKellen played the role of the Bastard when the production moved to the Aldwych Theatre in London.)

1978	Rijeka, Yugoslavia. Petar Šarčević, director. John, Nenad Šegvić; the Bastard, Ratko Vojnović.
1979	Louisville, Kentucky, C. Douglas Ramey Amphitheater. Albert J. Harris, Jr., director. John, Jim Logsdon; the Bastard, Morris Shaw; Constance, Diane Houghton.
1980	Weimar, Deutsches Nationaltheater. Fritz Bennewitz, director.

Sydney, Australia, Australian National Institute of Dramatic Art. Aubrey Mellor, director. John, Matthew Crosby; the Bastard, Hugo Weaving; Constance, Helen Jones.

1981	Spring Green, Wisconsin, the Outdoor Theatre. American Players Theatre. Anne Occhiogrosso and Mik Derks, directors. John, Randall Duk Kim; the Bastard, Jeffrey Lowell Jackson; Constance, Rita Litton.
1982	High Point, North Carolina, High Point Theatre. North Carolina Shakespeare Festival. Malcolm Morrison, director. John, Eric Zwemer; the Bastard, Lucius Houghton; Constance, Barbara Tirrell.
1983	New York, Bouwerie Lane Theatre. Jean Cocteau Repertory Company. Eve Adamson, director. John, Harris Berlinsky; the Bastard, Craig Smith; Constance, Margaret Dulany.
1985	Ashland, Oregon Shakespeare Festival. Pat Patton, director. John, James Edmondson; the Bastard, John David Castellanos; Constance, Joan Stuart-Morris.

Berlin, Theater im Palast. Vera Oelschlegel, director. John, Ekkehard Schall; the Bastard, Eberhard Esche; Constance, Barbara Dittus.

Film
  1899   Excerpts from Beerbohm Tree's Haymarket production were the first Shakespearean scenes preserved on film— no longer extant.

Television
  1952   BBC, London. John, Donald Wolfit; the Bastard, John Southworth; Constance, Sonia Dresdel.
  1984   BBC, London. John, Leonard Rossiter; the Bastard, George Costigan; Constance, Claire Bloom.

Recordings

Caedmon LC R67–572. *King John.* Sir Donald Wolfit reads John, Kenneth Haigh reads the Bastard, and Rosemary Harris reads Constance.

Argo ZRG 5168–71. *King John.* Michael Hordern reads John, Anthony Jacobs reads the Bastard, and Margaretta Scott reads Constance.

King John
Select Bibliography

Only those articles, books, and parts of books dealing exclusively or at some length with *King John* that have also been cited by the contributors are included in this bibliography.

Axton, Marie. *The Queen's Two Bodies: Drama and the Elizabethan Succession. Royal Historical Society Studies in History,* 5. London: Royal Historical Society, 1977.

Berman, Ronald. "Anarchy and Order in 'Richard III' and 'King John.'" *Shakespeare Survey* 20 (1967): 51–59.

Berry, Edward I. *Patterns of Decay: Shakespeare's Early Histories.* Charlottesville: University Press of Virginia, 1975.

Berry, Ralph. *The Shakespearean Metaphor.* Totowa, N.J.: Rowan and Littlefield, 1978.

Blanpied, John W. *Time and the Artist in Shakespeare's English Histories.* Newark: University of Delaware Press, 1983.

Boklund, Gunnar. "The Troublesome Ending of *King John.*" *Studia Neophilologica* 40 (1968): 175–84.

Bonjour, Adrien. "The Road to Swinstead Abbey: A Study of the Sense and Structure of *King John.*" *Journal of English Literary History* 18 (1951): 253–74.

Braunmuller, A. R., ed. *The Oxford Shakespeare King John.* Oxford: Oxford University Press, 1988.

Bullough, Geoffrey, ed. *Narrative and Dramatic Sources of Shakespeare.* Vol. 4. London: Routledge, 1962.

Burckhardt, Sigurd. *Shakespearean Meanings.* Princeton: Princeton University Press, 1968.

Burgoyne, Sidney C. "Cardinal Pandulph and the Curse of Rome." *College Literature* 4 (1977): 232–40.

Calderwood, James L. "Commodity and Honour in *King John.*" *University of Toronto Quarterly* 29 (1960): 341–56. Reprinted in *Shakespeare: The Histories,* edited by Eugene M. Waith, 85–101. Englewood Cliffs, N.J.: Prentice-Hall, 1965.

Campbell, Lily Bess. *Shakespeare's Histories: Mirrors of Elizabethan Policy.* 1947. Reprint. San Marino, Cal.: Huntington Library, 1968.

Carr, Virginia M. *The Drama As Propaganda: A Study of The Troublesome Raigne of King John.* Salzburg: Institut für Englische Sprache und Literatur, 1974.

Champion, Larry S. " 'Confound Their Skill in Covetousness': The Ambivalent Perspective of Shakespeare's *King John*." *Tennessee Studies in Literature* 24 (1979): 36–55.

———. *Perspective in Shakespeare's English Histories*. Athens: University of Georgia Press, 1980.

Charlton, H. B. *Shakespeare, Politics, and Politicians*. London: The English Association, 1929.

Clemen, Wolfgang. *Shakespeare's Dramatic Art*. London: Methuen, 1972.

Danby, John F. *Shakespeare's Doctrine of Nature*. London: Faber and Faber, 1968.

Dusinberre, Juliet. *Shakespeare and the Nature of Women*. New York: Barnes and Noble, 1976.

Edwards, Philip. *Threshold of a Nation: A Study in English and Irish Drama*. Cambridge: Cambridge University Press, 1979.

Elliott, John R. "Shakespeare and the Double Image of King John." *Shakespeare Studies* 1 (1965): 64–84.

Ellis-Fermor, Una M. *The Frontiers of Drama*. London: Methuen, 1964.

Elson, John. "Studies in the King John Plays." In *Joseph Quincy Adams Memorial Studies*, edited by G. E. Dawson and E. E. Willoughby, 183–97. Washington, D.C.: The Folger Library, 1948.

Furness, Horace H., ed. *The Life and Death of King John*. A New Variorum Edition of Shakespeare. Philadelphia: Lippincott, 1919.

Grennan, Eamon. "Shakespeare's Satirical History: A Reading of *King John*." *Shakespeare Studies* 11 (1978): 21–37.

Hirvela, David. "*King John*: An Interpretation Using Its Stage History." Ph.D. diss., University of Wisconsin, 1971.

Honigmann, E. A. J. Introduction to the New Arden Edition of *King John*. London: Methuen, 1954.

———. "*King John, The Troublesome Reigne*, and 'documentary links': A Rejoinder." *Shakespeare Quarterly* 38 (1987): 124–26.

Jones, Emrys. *The Origins of Shakespeare*. Oxford: Clarendon Press, 1977.

———. *Scenic Form in Shakespeare*. Oxford: Clarendon Press, 1971.

Jones, Robert C. "Truth in *King John*." *Studies in English Literature* 25 (1985): 397–417.

Kastan, David Scott. *Shakespeare and the Shapes of Time*. Hanover, N.H.: University Press of New England, 1982.

———. " 'To Set a Form Upon That Indigest': Shakespeare's Fictions of History." *Comparative Drama* 17 (1983): 1–16.

Knights, L. C. *Some Shakespearean Themes*. London: Chatto and Windus, 1959.

Leggatt, Alexander. "Dramatic Perspective in *King John*." *English Studies in Canada* 3 (1977): 1–17.

Levin, Richard. "*King John's* Bastard." *The Upstart Crow* 3 (1980): 29–41.

Manheim, Michael. *The Weak King Dilemma in the Shakespearean History Play*. Syracuse, N.Y.: Syracuse University Press, 1973.

Masefield, John. *William Shakespeare*. New York: Holt, 1911.

Matchett, William. Introduction to the Signet Classic *King John*. New York: New American Library, 1966.

———. "Richard's Divided Heritage in *King John*." *Essays in Criticism* 12 (1962): 231–53. Reprinted in *Essays in Shakespearean Criticism*, edited by J. L. Calderwood and H. E. Toliver, 152–70. New York: Prentice-Hall, 1970.

Mattsson, May. *Five Plays About King John*. Uppsala: Borgatroms Tryckeri AB, 1977.

Miller, Tice. "*King John*." In *Shakespeare Around the Globe: A Guide to Notable Postwar Revivals*, edited by Samuel Leiter, 283–95. New York: Greenwood Press, 1986.

Moore, Tommy Glenn. "Shakespeare's *King John:* The Critical History." Master's thesis, University of South Carolina, 1974.

Odell, George C. D. *Shakespeare From Betterton to Irving*. 2 vols. 1920. Reprint. New York: Benjamin Blom, 1963.

Ornstein, Robert. *A Kingdom for a Stage: The Achievement of Shakespeare's History Plays*. Cambridge: Harvard University Press, 1972.

Palmer, John. *Political Characters of Shakespeare*. 1945. Reprint. London: Macmillan, 1961.

Pierce, Robert B. *Shakespeare's History Plays: The Family and the State*. Columbus: Ohio State University Press, 1971.

Price, Jonathan Reeve. "*King John* and Problematic Art." *Shakespeare Quarterly* 21 (1970): 25–28.

Rackin, Phyllis. "Anti-Historians: Women's Roles in Shakespeare's Histories." *Theatre Journal* 37 (1985): 329–44.

Ranald, Margaret Loftus. "Women and Political Power in Shakespeare's English Histories." *Topic* 36 (1982): 54–65.

Reese, M. M. *The Cease of Majesty: A Study of Shakespeare's History Plays*. London: Arnold, 1961.

Ribner, Irving. *The English History Play in the Age of Shakespeare*. Rev. ed. London: Methuen, 1965.

Richmond, H. M. *Shakespeare's Political Plays*. New York: Random House, 1967.

Rose, Edward. "Shakespeare as an Adaptor." Reprinted in the Facsimile Edition of *The Troublesome Raigne of Iohn King of England*, v–xvii. London: Charles Praetorius, 1888.

Schelling, Felix. *The English Chronicle Play*. 1902. Reprint. New York: AMS Press, 1971.

Sen Gupta, S. C. *Shakespeare's Historical Plays*. London: Oxford University Press, 1964.

Shanker, Sidney. *Shakespeare and the Uses of Ideology*. The Hague: Mouton, 1975.

Shattuck, Charles H. *William Charles Macready's "King John."* Urbana: University of Illinois Press, 1962.

Shirley, Frances A., ed. *King John and Henry VIII: Critical Essays*. New York: Garland, 1988.

Simmons, J. L. "Shakespeare's *King John* and Its Source: Coherence, Pattern, and Vision." *Tulane Studies in English* 17 (1969): 53–72.

Smallwood, Robert. Introduction to the New Penguin Edition of *King John*. London: Penguin Books, 1974.

Smidt, Kristian. *Unconformities in Shakespeare's History Plays*. Atlantic Highlands, N.J.: Humanities Press, 1982.

Sprague, Arthur Colby. *Shakespeare's Histories: Plays for the Stage*. London: The Society for Theatre Research, 1964.

Stroud, Ronald. "The Bastard to the Time in *King John*." *Comparative Drama* 6 (1972): 154–66.

Stubblefield, Charles. "Some Thoughts About *King John*." *CEA Critic* 35:3 (1973): 25–28.

Thomas, Sidney. "'Enter a Sheriffe': Shakespeare's *King John* and *The Troublesome Raigne*." *Shakespeare Quarterly* 37 (1986): 98–100.

———. "'Enter a Sheriffe': A Shakespearean Ghost." *Shakespeare Quarterly* 38 (1987): 130.

Tillyard, E. M. W. *Shakespeare's History Plays*. 1944. Reprint. New York: Collier, 1962.

Trace, Jacqueline. "Shakespeare's Bastard Faulconbridge: An Early Tudor Hero." *Shakespeare Studies* 13 (1980): 59–69.

Traversi, Derek A. *An Approach to Shakespeare*. Rev. 3d ed. Vol. 1. Garden City, N.Y.: Doubleday, 1969.

Trewin, J. C. *Shakespeare on the English Stage, 1900–1964: A Survey of Productions*. London: Barrie and Rockliff, 1964.

Van de Water, Julia C. "The Bastard in *King John*." *Shakespeare Quarterly* 11 (1960): 137–46.

Vaughan, Virginia Mason. "Between Tetralogies: *King John* as Transition." *Shakespeare Quarterly* 35 (1984): 407–20.

Waith, Eugene M. "*King John* and the Drama of History." *Shakespeare Quarterly* 29 (1978): 192–211.

Werstine, Paul. "'Enter a Sheriff' and the Conjuring up of Ghosts." *Shakespeare Quarterly* 38 (1987): 126–30.

Wilson, J. Dover. Introduction to the Cambridge Edition of *King John*. Cambridge: Cambridge University Press, 1936.

Wilson, F. P. "The English History Play." In *Shakespearian and Other Studies*, edited by Helen Gardner, 1–53. Oxford: Clarendon Press, 1969.

Wixson, Douglas C. "'Calm Words Folded Up in Smoke': Propaganda and Spectator Response in Shakespeare's *King John*." *Shakespeare Studies* 14 (1981): 111–27.

Contributors

EDWARD S. BRUBAKER, Alumni Professor of English Literature and Belles Lettres at Franklin and Marshall College and Director of the Festival Institute, a program of the Education Office of the Oregon Shakespearean Festival, is the author of *Shakespeare Aloud: A Guide to His Verse on Stage* (1976) and *Golden Fire* (1985), a fiftieth anniversary book published by the Ashland Festival. His association with *King John* includes his having stage-managed (1959) and directed (1969) the play at the Oregon Shakespearean Festival.

JOSEPH CANDIDO, associate professor of English at the University of Arkansas, Fayetteville, has had articles on the history plays published in *Shakespeare Quarterly, Shakespeare Studies, English Studies*, and *Texas Studies in Literature and Language*. He is the cocompiler of *Henry V: An Annotated Bibliography* (1983) and is currently coediting the Variorum *King John*.

CAROL J. CARLISLE, professor emerita of English at the University of South Carolina, Columbia, is the author of *Shakespeare from the Greenroom* (1969). Her articles have appeared in *Studies in Philology, Shakespeare Quarterly, Shakespeare Studies, Renaissance Papers, Theatre Survey, Theatre Notebook, Nineteenth Century Theatre*, and *Shakespeare and the Victorian Stage*. She is currently coediting the Variorum *The Two Gentlemen of Verona*. Her essay "Passion Framed by Art: Helen Faucit's Juliet" was named Outstanding Article of 1985 by the Association for Theatre in Higher Education.

LARRY S. CHAMPION, professor of English at North Carolina State University and former chairman of the department, is the author of several books on Shakespeare including *Perspective in Shakespeare's English Histories* (1980), *King Lear: An Annotated Bibliography* (1980), and *The Essential Shakespeare* (1986). He has written on Thomas Dekker, and his current attention is on political ideology in the English chronicle plays.

Deborah T. Curren-Aquino, former associate professor of English at The Catholic University of America, has published articles in *Hamlet Studies, The Shakespeare Film Newsletter, Journal of the Rocky Mountain Medieval and Renaissance Association, The Literary Review,* and *Names.* She is currently compiling the Garland bibliography on *King John.*

Guy Hamel, associate professor of English at the University of Toronto, has published articles in *University of Toronto Quarterly* and *Shakespeare Survey.*

Dorothea Kehler, associate professor of English at San Diego State University, has written on the history plays for *Rocky Mountain Review,* the *Citadel Conference Proceedings,* and *Upstart Crow.* She is presently working on a book-length study of widows in Shakespeare and is coediting an anthology of feminist criticism of Renaissance drama.

Michael Manheim, professor of English at The University of Toledo and past president of the Midwest Modern Language Association, is the author of *The Weak King Dilemma in the Shakespeare History Play* (1973), *Eugene O'Neill's New Language of Kinship* (1982), and numerous articles and reviews on Elizabethan and modern drama.

Joseph A. Porter, assistant professor of English at Duke University, is the author of *The Drama of Speech Acts: Shakespeare's Lancastrian Tetralogy* (1979) and articles in *South Atlantic Review* and *Poetics.* He is currently working on a book about Mercutio.

Phyllis Rackin, associate professor of English in General Honors at the University of Pennsylvania, Philadelphia, is the author of *Shakespeare's Tragedies* (1978) and of articles in *Shakespeare Quarterly, Theatre Journal, Modern Language Studies,* and *PMLA.* She is presently writing a book-length study of Shakespeare's English histories examined in the context of Renaissance theories and practice of historiography.

Marsha Robinson, former teaching fellow at the University of Pennsylvania, Philadelphia, and the recipient of a Mellon Dissertation Fellowship, has recently completed her dissertation entitled "Shakespeare and the Rhetoric of History."

BARBARA H. TRAISTER, professor of English at Lehigh University, is the author of *Heavenly Necromancers: The Magician in English Renaissance Drama* (1984). She is currently writing a biography of the Renaissance physician and astrologer Simon Forman with the support of a Rockefeller Fellowship at the Francis C. Wood Institute, College of Physicians of Philadelphia.

VIRGINIA M. VAUGHAN, associate professor of English and department chair at Clark University, is the author of *The Drama As Propaganda: A Study of The Troublesome Raigne of King John* (1974) and several articles on Shakespeare's histories including "Between Tetralogies: *King John* as Transition" in *Shakespeare Quarterly.* She is currently cocompiling the Garland bibliography on *Othello* and is editor of the Variorum *Othello.*

Index

Alexander, Peter, 25 n.12, 59 n.4
Ambiguity: in Shakespeare, 123–24. See also *King John:* ambiguity in
Ambivalence. See *King John:* ambivalence in
Anti-Catholic sentiment. See *King John:* anti-Catholic sentiment in, suppression of; Religious issues; *The Troublesome Raigne:* anti-Catholic sentiment in, prominence of
Arden, John: *Left-Handed Liberty*, 16, 170
Arthur (character), 33, 45–46, 70, 71, 72, 86–87, 95–96, 101, 105–6, 107, 109, 112 nn. 19 and 24, 116, 174, 175, 176, 181

Bale, John: *King Johan*, 54, 63–64, 171 n.5, 191
Barton, John: 1974 RSC production of *King John*, 16, 26 n.26, 155, 171 n.5, 191
Bastard, the (character), 13, 14, 67, 134 n.7, 139, 174, 178; antecedents of, in history, 59 n.9, 90 n.13, 184 n.16; "Commodity" soliloquy, 13, 69, 130, 184 n.17; development of, through different voices, 20, 126–34; as fictional character, 23, 39 n.5, 55, 85; final speech of, 20, 38, 40 n.16, 55–57, 73–74, 127, 135 n.12, 179, 184 n.27; genesis of, in romance and folklore, 43, 55; and Hal/Henry V, 132–33; and Hamlet, 114–15, 124–25; historiographic perspective of, 32, 35, 36–38, 56; "I am amaz'd" speech, 13, 110–11, 113 n.34, 122–23, 131; iconoclastic idiom of, 85; inconsistency of and tensions in, 55–56, 125 n.6, 126, 169, 184 nn. 16 and 17; and John, 21, 120, 136, 140–41, 143 nn. 8 and 9; and legitimacy, issue

of, 31, 42–43, 66–67, 85, 119–20; as a Machiavel, 21, 23, 36, 127, 129–34; as "moral-oxymoron," 119–23; as "non-idealized," less than heroic figure, 22–23, 38, 178–79, 184 n.17; in the Oregon Shakespeare Festival 1969 production, 169; political realism of, 30, 32, 36–37, 124–25; religious conversion of, 101–2, 106–7; as Renaissance individualist, 67; speech acts of, 139–41; and the subversive voice of women, 85; as transitional figure between the two tetralogies, 134; in *The Troublesome Raigne*, 42–43, 55–56
BBC production of *King John* (1984), 12–13. *See also* Constance: Claire Bloom as; Television Shakespeare
Beckett, Samuel: *Waiting for Godot*, 16, 24
Bilson, Bishop Thomas: *The True Difference Betweene Christian Subjection and Unchristian Rebellion*, 71
Blanch (character), 17, 67–68, 69, 72, 80, 81, 82–83, 95, 102–3, 161
Blanpied, John W., 178
Bloom, Claire. *See* Constance: Claire Bloom as
Bodin, Jean: and historiography, 35–36, 38. *See also* Bastard: historiographic perspective of
Bonjour, Adrien, 13, 134 n.7, 178
Braunmuller, A. R., 12, 179
Brecht, Bertold, 22, 24, 62, 166; *Mother Courage*, 170
Burckhardt, Sigurd, 13, 22, 56, 59 n.14, 67, 74, 75 n.14, 88 n.3, 100, 112 n.20, 123, 176, 183 n.8
Burton, Richard, 26 n.39

Calderwood, James L., 12, 58 n.1, 99, 134 n.7, 178, 183

201

DATE DUE			